The Military Operations at Cabul—
The Kabul Insurrection of 1841-42
And
Rough Notes During Imprisonment in Affghanistan, 1843

The Military Operations at Cabul—
The Kabul Insurrection of 1841-42
And
Rough Notes During Imprisonment in Affghanistan, 1843

Vincent Eyre

*The Military Operations at Cabul—
The Kabul Insurrection of 1841-42
And
Rough Notes During Imprisonment in Affghanistan, 1843*
by Vincent Eyre

First published under the titles
*The Military Operations at Cabul,
With a Journal of Imprisonment in Affghanistan*
and
The Kabul Insurrection of 1841-42

Leonaur is an imprint of Oakpast Ltd

Copyright in this form © 2011 Oakpast Ltd

ISBN: 978-0-85706-589-6 (hardcover)
ISBN: 978-0-85706-590-2 (softcover)

http://www.leonaur.com

Publisher's Notes

The opinions of the authors represent a view of events in which he was a participant related from his own perspective, as such the text is relevant as an historical document.

The views expressed in this book are not necessarily those of the publisher.

Contents

The Miltary Operations at Cabul—The Kabul Insurrection
of 1841-42   7

Rough Notes During Imprisonment in Affghanistan, 1843   213

The Military Operations at Cabul—
The Kabul Insurrection of 1841-42

Contents

Preface	11
Brief Account of Afghanistan and its Inhabitants	15
A Retrospect of the First Afghan War	32
First Symptoms of Disturbance	51
Popular Outbreak in Kabul	59
Engagements With Afghan Horse and Foot	69
Further Engagements With the Enemy	79
Treachery of the Nijrao Chiefs	89
Unprofitable Operations at the Village of Bemaru	100
Our Force Driven Back With Severe Loss	106
Conferences and Negotiations With the Insurgent Chiefs	117
Preparations for Evacuating	129
Suspense in Cantonment	152
The Retreat of the Army, and its Annihilation	160
Captivity of the Hostages	183
Appendix A	197
Appendix B	205
Appendix C	209

Preface

This narrative, originally written to utilize the otherwise vacant hours of an Afghán captivity, has been long out of print, having been withdrawn from publication by the author, with a view to subsequent revision and republication, should opportunity offer. But amid the vicissitudes of an Indian career, new duties and more attractive subjects gradually withdrew his thoughts from the saddening reminiscences of the Kábul catastrophe. Meanwhile the public mind seemed to have grown weary of the matter, and the cotemporary journal of the author's distinguished fellow-captive. Lady Sale,[1] seemed amply sufficient to supply whatever popular appetite might still survive for so plentiful a "supper of horror."

But now that history seems to be to some extent repeating itself, and with a new Afghán war actually on our hands, there has been naturally a general rush to the bookshelves in search of the dusty records of past transactions and adventures beyond the Indus, and thus the quondam captive of Akbar Khán finds himself, not without some reluctance, yielding to the newly awakened popular impulse and to the pressure of the times, and figuring, perhaps superfluously, as a 'Veteran on the stage" in the evening of life.

The narrative was originally published simultaneously with Lady Sale's volume, and passed rapidly through several editions before the writer himself had an opportunity of reading it in print. His supply of stationery being scanty, the manuscript was cramped into the smallest possible space, and thus admitted of being conveyed by stealth to General Pollock's camp at Jallálábád. On one occasion a considerable portion was lost in transit and had to be entirely re-written, no copy having been kept. After perusal by General Pollock it was transmitted by him to Lord Ellenborough's private secretary, the late Sir Henry

---

1. *Lady Sale's Afghanistan* by Florentia Sale also published by Leonaur.

Durand, and was then, at his Lordship's suggestion, transmitted to the writer's family in England with a view to immediate publication.

It may, in fact, be said to have supplied the British public with the first regularly detailed accounts of the British military and political operations at Kábul from the outbreak of the insurrection on the 2nd November, 1841, to the final catastrophe in January, 1842. It was written under circumstances more than usually favourable to ensure strict historic fidelity; for, besides having been personally an eye-witness throughout, the author found himself in daily close proximity with many of the chief survivors, among whom were the unfortunate General himself and his second in command, besides several members of the military and political staff. He was thus in a position to hear and to record much that would otherwise have been beyond his reach; and, by a diligent and careful comparison of their various statements and experiences, as well as by access to the public documents in their possession, to combine the whole into a faithful and, he hopes, impartial narrative, which has so satisfactorily stood the crucial test of time as to be deemed worthy to be interwoven with the standard histories of that memorable period.

It has been considered advisable, for the benefit of readers of the present day, to prefix two preliminary chapters, the first containing a brief description of the geography and the inhabitants of Afghánistán, derived partly from his own notes, but chiefly from the best published sources available to him while wintering in Italy.

The second chapter gives a retrospective summary of the first Afghán war, and contains the substance of a lecture delivered by the author at the Royal United Service Institution in 1869. It is to be hoped the reader will thus be aided to a more complete understanding of the main narrative.

As a plain relation of facts, he has found but little requiring suppression or alteration, but inasmuch as, in the fervid ardour of youth, some of his own commentaries on the acts of officers far his superiors in rank, though made in fearless honesty of purpose, do not altogether meet the approval of his maturer judgement, and are, moreover, no longer needed to instigate public inquiry, they have, in the present edition, been either modified or altogether omitted. It is hoped that the occasional omission of those "youthful indiscretions" may not be found to detract from the vital interest of the main narrative, and that this revival of an "over-true tale" may be not without its public use, even in the midst of present triumphs, on account of the solemn warnings it conveys. The valuable aid so generously afforded by the author's friend Colonel Malleson in superintending this volume through the press, in the midst of his own pressing literary avocations, demands an expression of more than ordinary gratitude.

Vincent Eyre,
Major-General, late Royal Artillery (Bengal).

Rome, 1st January 1879.

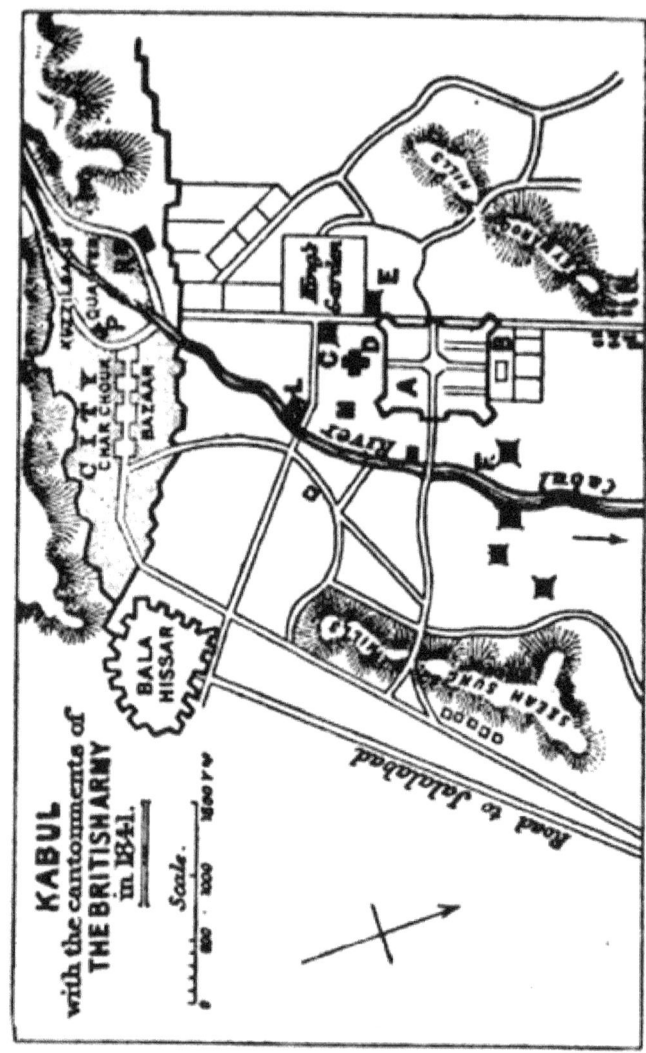

A. Cantonment.
B. Mission Residence.
C. Commissariat Fort.
D. Magazine.
E. Mahomed Shereef's Fort.
F. Bihnabashee Fort.
H. Zulficar's Fort.
L. Mahmood Khan's Fort.
M. Spot where the Envoy was murdered.
N. Village of Beymaroo.
P. Sir A. Burne's House.
B. Anquetil's Fort.

CHAPTER 1

Brief Account of Afghanistan and its Inhabitants

Geographical Position.—The country now inhabited by the numerous tribes known by the common name of Afgháns may be briefly said to be bounded on the north and north-west by the stupendous mountain range of Hindú-Khush, or Indian Caucasus, on the south by Bilúchistán and part of Sindh, on the east by the great River Indus, and on the west by the extensive desert tracts that border the Persian empire.

The difficulties of access that Afghánistán opposes on all sides to an invading army, surrounded as it is by vast tracts of mountain and desert, the former only to be traversed by surmounting steep ridges and threading narrow defiles where a few hundreds of well armed and resolute men could effectually oppose the passage of as many thousands, entitle it to be considered, in a military sense, as one of the strongest countries in the whole worlds whilst the manly independence of its hardy inhabitants, their sturdy valour, and their skill in the use of weapons of war, to which they are trained from early boyhood, combine to render them far from despicable opponents, especially on their own ground, for even the disciplined warriors of Europe.

Cities.—The chief cities of Afghánistán are Kábul, Ghazní, Kandahár, Hirát, Jallálábád, and Pesháwar, each situated in a fertile and well-watered valley, enclosed more or less by lofty hills, and fortified in the usual oriental style with high walls, either of mud, stone, or brick, with round or polygonal flanking towers. Pesháwar became a Sikh possession in 1828, and has formed part of the British Indian dominions since 1849.

Mountains.—The three principal mountain ranges, from which innumerable branches diverge in all directions, are those of Hindú-

Khush, Safaid Koh, and Sulaimán. The first, under which I include the great Paropamisan chain which forms the northern barrier extending from east to west, is a continuation of the great Himálayan range of northern India, the last of whose long line of giant snow-clad peaks, the *Koh-i-Baba*, rears its hoary head about seventy miles to the north-west of Kábul. Its height is eighteen thousand feet above the sea. Thence to its termination in the vicinity of Hirát this prodigious rampart of mountains loses much of its sublimity. The race of people called Hazáras are dispersed among its valleys, where they have been settled from time immemorial.

The *Sufaid Koh*, or great "White Mountain" range, whose culminating snow-clad peak attains an elevation of fifteen thousand six hundred and twenty-two feet, stretches from east to west, between the Khaibar hills and Ghazní, like a stupendous impassable barrier, whose minimum height is said to be twelve thousand five hundred feet, and from whose long uniform ridge are thrown off an infinity of spurs on. either flank to north and south. At intervals along its course it sends forth long mountainous ramifications in a southerly direction towards Bilúchistán, and gives rise to several rivers, including the *Arghandáb* (a feeder of the Helmand), flowing west towards Kandahár; the *Kábul* River, flowing north towards the capital and thence turning eastward to Pesháwar; the *Kuram* and *Gomál* Rivers, flowing south and east through the famous valleys and passes so named, to mingle their respective waters with those of the great river Indus in the vicinity of Isakbel and Derá Ismáíl Khán.

The *Sulaimán* range runs in a direction nearly parallel with the Indus and perpendicular to that of Sufaid Koh. Its highest peak, the *Takht-i-Sulaimán*, or "Throne of Solomon," is eleven thousand five hundred feet above the sea, and the average height of the whole range is about equal to that of the Pyrenees.

The valleys enclosed within these vast mountain ranges, and their numerous ramifications, are peopled by almost as many distinct tribes, each governed in a great measure by its own simple laws and customs: of these a brief account will be given from the best sources available.

Passes.—There are four principal routes available for military purposes and general traffic between India and Afghánistán from along the line of our Indus frontier, between Pesháwar in the north and Rorí in the south. These are known as the Khaibar, the Kuram, the Gomál, and the Bolán passes.

The direct route from Pesháwar to Kábul lies through the Khaibar pass, over a total distance of one hundred and ninety miles. The pass itself is thirty-three miles long, and is defended, at a distance of eight miles from its eastern entrance, by the fort of Alí Masjid. Sixty-seven miles beyond that is the walled town and fertile valley of Jallálábád, about one thousand nine hundred and sixty-four feet above the sea. Thence to Kábul the route presents a continuous series of ascents and of tedious and difficult passes; those chiefly worthy of mention being *Gandámak, Jagdallak, Tizín, Haft Kotul*, and *Khurd Kábul*, the latter only ten miles from Kábul itself, and all have been the scenes of deadly struggles with British forces during the first Afghán campaign, with its series of successes, disasters, and final retributive triumphs.

The *Kuram* valley is entered at Thal, sixty-six miles from the British fortress of Kohát. A march of fifty miles along the bank of the river leads to Kuram fort, and sixty miles beyond that is the Paiwar pass, at a height of eight thousand feet above the sea. Thence to the summit of the Shatar Gardan pass, on the ridge of the Sufaid Koh, the route lies between precipitous peaks and over rugged spurs of a most formidable character, if defended by a skilful and resolute enemy. The descent to the valley of the Logar on the northern side is of a similar character, and leads eventually through a comparatively easy route to Kábul.

The *Gomál* pass penetrates the Sulaimán range about sixteen miles west of Tánk, through a narrow defile, with a continuous ascent to Kotal-i-Sarmand, seven thousand five hundred feet above the sea, one hundred and forty-five miles by road. Thence following the course of the river another easy pass leads to the final ascent of the crest of a steep mountain range, beyond which the city of Ghazní is readied.

This route has been followed during many centuries by the mercantile clan known as *Povindahs*, in their annual journeys to and from India with merchandise, and who boldly encounter considerable peril from the robber tribes that persistently beset their path through the passes, obliging them to fight their way with loss of life and property, and yet still adhere to their favourite time-honoured route.

The *Bolán* pass has its entrance near the town of Dádar, seven hundred and forty-two miles above the sea, and five hundred miles south of the *Khaibar* pass. There is a continuous ascent through the Hálá mountains for sixty miles to the crest of the pass, which is five thousand eight hundred feet above the sea, and thence to Qetta, which has an elevation of five thousand five hundred and forty feet. The Bolán River flows through the greater portion of the pass. The last three miles are very contracted, between towering precipitous cliffs.

Qetta has lately become an advanced British frontier post, and is distant one hundred and fifty miles from Kandahár; to reach which it is necessary to traverse the Pishín valley and the lofty Khojak pass, which reaches an elevation of seven thousand four hundred and fifty feet; whence to the plain of Kandahár there is a long descent of four thousand feet.

Climate.—The superior coolness and salubrity of the climate in most parts of Afghánistán would appear to be due less to the differences of latitude than of elevation. The following table exhibits the comparative heights of the principal places on the two grand routes lately travelled by our armies, and, as a general rule, the climate may be said to improve in proportion to the increase of altitude. (I derive the heights here given from Major Hough's valuable narrative of the march and operations of the army of the Indus.)

	Above the sea.		Above the sea.
Route from Pesháwar to Kábul { Pesháwar	1,068 feet	Route from Shikárpur to Kandahár & Ghazní { Shikárpur	250 feet
Jallálábád	1,964 „	Dádar	743 „
Sultánpur	2,300 „	Sir-i-bolán	4,494 „
Fathábád	3,098 „	Qettah (in the valley of Shawl)	5,637 „
Gandámak	4,616 „	Kojak pass	7,457 „
Jagdallak	5,375 „	Kandahár	3,484 „
Tizín	6,488 „	Qalát-i-Ghalzí	5,773 „
Haft Kotal	8,173 „	Ghazní	7,726 „
Khurd-Kábul	7,466 „		
Kábul	6,247 „		

At Pesháwar and Jallálábád the summer heat, though less intense than in India, is still dreadfully oppressive and unfavourable in its effects on the European constitution. On the Kábul route the temperate climate begins at Gandámak, beyond which snow usually covers the ground during the middle of winter, when few travellers expose themselves voluntarily to the risks and inconveniences of the road. On the route from Shikárpur to Kandahár the Bolán pass forms a similar boundary between the hot and cold climates; Dádar, which lies on the south side, being insufferably hot, whilst the splendid valley of Shawl, at the northern extremity, enjoys a delightfully cool and healthy temperature. The Khojak pass, through which lies the direct line of communication between Qettah and Kandahár, being blocked up by snow during winter, all traffic along that route is suspended.

Nevertheless, the rigorous winters for which Kábul and Ghazní are so notorious are unknown at Kandahár, where snow seldom falls, and where an army can with ease keep the field throughout the year. Snow begins to cover the hills around Kábul about the beginning of

October, but seldom visits the plain before December, when it accumulates fast upon the ground until the end of January or middle of February, from which period to the end of April rain falls in great abundance. The remainder of the year is dry. *Tribes.*—The principal Afghán tribes, of whom it is desirable to give some, account in this work, are comprised in four great divisions, *viz.*:—

1. The Abdális, or Dúránís.
2. The Ghalzís.
3. The Bírdúránís.
4. The Kaukars.

The two first are distributed over that portion of Afghánistán which lies west of the Sulaimán range, whilst the two last occupy the less civilized tracts on the opposite side of it.

Dúránís.—The Abdális, or Dúránís, as they are more commonly designated, are divided into nine great clans, of which the four principal are the *Popalzís, Alakhzís, Baurikzís,* and *Achikzís.* These again are subdivided into *Khails,* or families, of which by far the most eminent is that of the Sadúzís, a branch of the Popalzís, which, from a very remote period, has been regarded as the head of all the Dúránís,

From this distinguished stock sprang the celebrated Ahmad Sháh, the founder of the Dúrání monarchy, by whose talents, energy, and prudence, the Afghán nation was for the first time united under a native king, and whose grandson, Sháh Shujá-ul-Mulk, was destined, a century later, to become a tool in the hands of European politicians, and to experience some of the most extraordinary reverses of fortune that are recorded in the annals of the world.

The whole Dúrání population is conjectured to fall little short of one million souls.

The *kháns,* or chiefs, hold their lands by military tenure, originally granted by their Persian conqueror, Nádir Sháh, on the express stipulation that they should furnish a horseman for every plough, the performance of which engagement has been exacted as rigidly as circumstances would admit by every subsequent occupant of the throne. Under the Sadúzí dynasty all the great offices of state were monopolized by chiefs of the Dúrání tribe, who having been mainly instrumental in the original constitution of the empire, and being bound by the ties of clanship to their monarch, were naturally considered to have a primary claim to honorary rewards and courtly distinctions.

Each of the great Dúrání clans has, or had, its own *Sirdár*, or commander chosen by the king out of the head family, the *Sirdár* in his turn appointing some of the leading *kháns* to the chief civil and military control of each *ulús*, or subdivision of a clan.

The administration of justice in criminal and civil cases is not, however, except in large towns and cities, entrusted to any one individual, but has, from time immemorial, been vested in a *jirga*, or council, composed, in the more important cases, of the *kháns*, elders, and *mullás* of the neighbourhood; but minor offences and disputes are settled by village *jirgas*, elected by the people themselves.

This primitive system of judicature is not peculiar to the Dúránís, but is common to all the Afghán tribes.

The title of *Khán* was held, under the monarchy, by a patent from the king, but is bestowed by general courtesy on the petty chiefs of each small community. Every such titular *khán* invariably resides in his own little fort, or castle, commonly built in a square form, with high mud walls about twelve feet thick at the base and tapering to the same number of inches at the top, having numerous loopholes for musketry, and flanked at each angle by substantial towers or bastions. These forts, scattered far and wide over the face of the whole country, each having its little orchard attached, and surrounded by verdant fields of cultivation, with perchance a gushing rivulet shaded by the willow, poplar, and oleaster, in graceful groups, form one of the most pleasing characteristics of Afghán scenery.

The Dúránís, like the majority of Afghán tribes, are divided into agricultural and pastoral classes, the former having their fixed places of residence, and the latter dwelling altogether in tents, with which they form large camps and move about with their flocks and herds to find pasture. The *Achikzís* are almost wholly pastoral, and possess a large portion of the mountain range of Khojá Amrám as well as of the neighbouring plains. They are greatly addicted to plunder, and are the least civilized of all the Dúránís; yet as soldiers they rank high, and their *Sirdárs* have generally exercised a more .than ordinary share of influence in the country.

Each Dúrání village has its *mullá*, or Muhammadan teacher, by whom the offices of religion are performed. Considerable attention and regularity is evinced by the commonalty in offering up their daily stated prayers. Hospitality is one of the most pleasing traits in the popular character, every stranger being secure of a ready welcome to such entertainment as they can provide. To these remarks the Achikzís form a solitary exception, being alike careless of the rites of hospitality and of religion.

The personal appearance of the Dúránís is manly and prepossessing, their features are generally well formed and strongly defined, and their manners are seldom otherwise than frank, social, and friendly in the extreme. The conversation of the upper orders is often remarkably animated, intelligent, and free from prejudice and bigotry, a freedom which constitutes them, on the whole, very agreeable companions.

These excellent traits are somewhat counterbalanced by the vices common, in a greater or less degree, to all Asiatics, among the most prominent of which may be enumerated avarice, duplicity, sensuality, meanness, and revenge, but in these, as in most other respects, they exhibit a manifest superiority to all other Afghán tribes, by whom they are in consequence regarded with a proportionate degree of respect.

Ghalzís.—The Ghalzís next claim our attention. They were formerly the most powerful, and are still the most numerous, of all the Afghán tribes. Their name is supposed to indicate a Turkish origin, but their settlement in Afghánistán is referred to a very remote period, and their military power and prowess are recorded by some of the earliest Muhammadan writers. In the early invasions of India by the Afgháns they took a prominent part, but their fame reached its climax by their conquest of Persia early in the last century, over which country, after having defeated in succession the armies of the Ottoman empire, they established their dominion under three consecutive kings.

The last of these Ghalzí monarchs was driven from his throne by Nádir Sháh, then in the morning of his fame, though not without a prolonged and desperate resistance on the part of the former.

With him the power of the Ghalzís expired, but they nevertheless maintained a fierce and obstinate struggle for their liberties in Afghánistán on the invasion of that country by the same ambitious warrior. Their defence of Kandahár lasted for eighteen months, and was only terminated by a desperate but unsuccessful sortie, in which great numbers were slain. Their ascendancy received its final blow by the rise of the rival tribe of Dúránís, to supreme power under Ahmad Sháh.

The remembrance of their supersession still embitters the minds of the Ghalzí nobles, who regard their successful rivals with undisguised jealousy and dislike, although in some of the leading families of the present day these inimical feelings have been much abated by judicious intermarriages. The Ghalzí chiefs exercise but little influence or authority in their own tribes beyond the circle of their own immediate dependants. In this respect their position differs from that of the Dúrání nobles, who derived additional powers from the crown, the stability of which must however in a great measure depend on the maintenance of a settled government in the country. Under the monarchy a Dúrání governor was appointed by the king over the whole Ghalzí tribe, in whom authority was vested for the management of the revenue, the maintenance of troops, and the administration of justice in all cases requiring his interference.

Under such a system the influence of the Ghalzí *kháns* gradually declined, the people becoming accustomed to act independently of them, and referring almost every dispute to the village *jirga*.

The absence of any minor local controlling authorities renders blood feuds of common occurrence, both between private individuals and whole communities. The Ghalzís to the west of Ghalzí conform more nearly to the Dúránís in their general habits than those to the east of that city. They are, taken as a whole, a brave, hardy, warlike, and handsome race, simple and frugal in their fare, possessing great bodily strength, stern, violent, vindictive, impatient of control, intelligent, energetic, and ever ready to unite under their own chiefs against a common foe or in a popular cause.

Though all are either husbandmen or shepherds, yet every man can, on emergency, at once transform himself into a soldier. They are more ignorant and barbarous than the Dúránís, and possess a large share of their virtues and vices in common.

Under the restraining and improving influence of a strong and civilized government they might probably be transformed into valuable subjects, but there seems little likelihood of any such desirable metamorphosis at present. The table on the following page exhibits the distribution, numbers, and occupations of the different divisions of the tribe.

Birduranis.—The Bírdúrání tribes are next to be considered. They are strictly an agricultural people, and inhabit the hills and plains east and north of the Suleiman range, extending from the foot of the Indian Caucasus to the latitude of Dera Ismaíl Khán, and including every imaginable variety of climate from the bleak, wintry, and scarcely habitable regions of perennial snow, to the equally uncomfortable extreme of excessive heat.

The only clans requiring particular mention here are the *Yúsufzís* and the *Khaibarís*, the former inhabiting the mountains and valleys

DISTRIBUTION OF THE GHALZI TRIBES.

Family.	Clan.	No. of Families.	Locality.	General observations.
Túrán, the elder branch.	Hotakí	6,000	South of Mukúr range.	Chiefly follow agriculture and commerce, but live much in tents and feed flocks.
	Tokhí	12,000	Qalát-i-Ghalzí, valley of Tarnák, and hill country on edge of Paropamisan mountains.	
Búrán, the younger branch.	Sulaimán Khail.	35,000	East and north of Ghazní.	viz.:—Ahmadzís, in Altámúr and Spaiza, and are pastoral. Stánízís, north of Ghazní; agricultural. Qaisar Khail and Ismaílzís, south and east of Ghazní, and part of Zurmat; agricultural and pastoral.
	Alikhail	8,000	Plain of Zurmat	Agricultural.
	Sahák	6,000	Pughmán and Kharwár.	Agricultural and pastoral.
	Andar	12,000	Shilghar . . .	Agricultural.
	Tarakí	12,000	Mukúr and neighbourhood.	Agricultural and pastoral.
	Khárotí	6,000	Hills between Gomál river and Sulaimán range.	Agricultural and pastoral.
	Shírán.	6,000	Part of Koh-Dámán and along bank of Kábul river.	Agricultural and pastoral.

INDEPENDENT PATHAN TRIBES ON THE PANJAB FRONTIER.

Tribes.	Frontier Districts adjoining.
Hussainzís	Hazára.
Jadans, Bonairwais, Swátís, Ránízís, Usmánkhailís, Upper Momands	Pesháwar.
Afrídís	Pesháwar and Kohát.
Bazotís, Sípáhs, Urakzís, Zímasht Afgháns, Túrís	Kohát.
Wazírís	Kohát and Dera Ismaíl Khán.
Sheoránís, Ushtiránís	Dera Ismaíl Khán.
Khitráns	Dera Ghází Khán.

north of Peshāwar, and the latter the hilly regions on the right bank of the Kābul River between Jallālābād and the Indus. South of these are the *Khattaks, Bangashís, Túrís,* and *Wazírís,* together with the numerous clans of *Dámám,* which latter are considered altogether distinct from the Bírdúránís, To the left of the Kābul River are the *Momands* and *Tarkúlánís,* the latter possessing the country called *Bájúr.*

Yusufzis.—Elphinstone estimates the *Yúsufzí* population at seven hundred thousand souls. They are the most vicious and barbarous of all the Afgháns, and being perpetually engaged in intestine strife are in a state but little removed from anarchy, blood feuds being so numerous that there are few villages whence the husbandman dares to venture forth to plough and sow unarmed with his sword and rifle. The collection of revenue has generally been found impracticable. Yet, sunk as they are in the very depths of depravity, in no part of Afghánistán are the outward observances of the Muhammadan religion so strictly observed and intolerance so unhappily prevalent.

The *Sikhs,* during their rule in the Panjáb, found the Yúsufzís to be brave and formidable opponents, rendering the continued presence of a large force at and around Peshāwar necessary to inspire dread and enforce submission. I may add that the Yúsufzí soldiers who were enlisted in the British service during our first campaign in Afghánistán, performed excellent and faithful service on various occasions under Captain Ferris and other English officers.

Khaibaris.—The *Khaibarí* tribes are so called from inhabiting the Khaibar mountains, separating the valley of Peshāwar from that of Jallálábád.

This range, in fact, forms the north-eastern barrier of Afghánistán, through whose stupendous defiles the tide of invasion was wont to pour its predatory hordes of hardy warriors from the north-west into the rich and fertile plains of Hindústán. The Khaibarís, firmly established as the acknowledged guardians of this important thoroughfare, have not failed to reap every possible advantage from their position by levying a heavy toll on every traveller, from the invading conqueror at the head of his armed hosts down to the solitary and peaceful wayfarer venturing with his little stock of merchandize to a distant market.

Besides the toll levied on travellers, the Khaibarís have for many generations past received an annual stipend from the ruler of Kábul for the benefits derived from an open road for commerce.

The three principal clans are the *Afrídís,* the *Shainwarís,* and the *Urakzís,* numbering altogether about twelve thousand souls.

They are esteemed excellent marksmen with the Afghán *jazail*, or rifle, which has an iron or wooden projection at the end of the barrel, which they rest on the ground, and thus take steady and effectual aim at a distance of eight hundred yards. They are proverbially faithless in their engagements, being constantly tempted by the hope of plunder, to attack parties whose safety they have previously guaranteed.

These people are barbarians of a rude patriarchal type—without any government beyond the *jirgas*, or Councils of Elders, and without any religion beyond the worst form of Muhammadanism. Blood for bloody and fire and sword against all *infidels*, are their ruling ideas. They are priest-ridden, sensual, avaricious, and predatory; faithless, also, and bloodthirsty. Each tribe and section of a tribe has its internecine wars, each family its hereditary blood feuds, and each individual his personal foes. Consequently they are always armed, even while grazing cattle, driving beasts of burden, or tilling the soil. They will undertake military service, but are impatient of discipline, and are true to their salt unless led away by fanaticism.

The task of establishing friendly relations with tribes so fickle and treacherous is one of extreme difficulty—friendship with one tribe is apt to be enmity with another; and treaties ratified one day are repudiated the next. Nothing unites them but a common danger, and a common jealousy of the intrusion of strangers.

These tribes always resisted Sikh rule, under which such heavy duties were levied as to reduce trade to the lowest ebb, and heavy revenue was demanded from those tribes within the Sikh border.

Conciliatory measures have been adopted under British rule, transit duties have been abolished, taxation reduced, and friendly relations cultivated.

The border Patháns are freely admitted into the public service, military, police, or civil. Charitable dispensaries have been established all along the border, open, free of charge, to all nationalities and creeds, and patients are often fed at the public expense. Land and water communications have been improved, new roads constructed, *serais* and resting-places set up where required, and weekly steamers established on the Indus.

Satisfactory results have followed. The former hatred against the ruling power is passing away; raids, once chronic, are now exceptional; cultivation is rapidly extending; and many frontier clans pray for protection and permission to settle in British territory. The trade through the Pesháwar passes is rapidly increasing. The tolls on the Indus ferries have risen from four thousand *rupees* in 1857 to twenty-five thousand in 1867. The tonnage on the Upper Indus has increased from eight hundred boats with cargoes aggregating two hundred and sixty-five thousand *maunds* in 1855, to more than three thousand boats with nearly one million and a quarter *maunds* in 1865-66.

Mercantile fairs are about to be established at Pesháwar and Dera Ismaíl Khán. The study of Pushtú is encouraged by rewards, and Pushtú schools in the interior of frontier districts are aiding in the work of civilization.

Kákars.—The Kákar tribes occupy a large tract of country to the south of the *Khoja Amrán* mountains and to the north-west of Bilúchistán. They are chiefly a pastoral people, yet possessing many small highly-cultivated valleys. Though more rude and ignorant, they are far less turbulent than other Afgháns, but owing to their remote position they are also less known and appreciated; nor are they of sufficient importance, in a political or military view, to require a more lengthened notice in this work.

To the four great tribes already described the common name of *Afghán* strictly appertains, but besides these Afghánistán has other inhabitants, of an origin altogether distinct, of whom it is expedient to give a separate account. The most important of these are the *Tájiks* and the *Hazáras,*

Tájiks,—The Tájiks, though now forming a part and parcel of the Afghán nation, were formerly a distinct people, and are supposed by Mr. Elphinstone to be descended from those Arabian soldiers of the Prophet who, in the first century of Muhammadanism, after overrunning the whole of Persia and Túrkistán, and propagating their faith by force of arms in those countries, carried the war into Afghánistán, where they obtained possession of the plains, but the inhabitants subsequently, collecting their forces in the mountains and descending upon their invaders, partially reduced them to a state of dependence from which they have never since emerged.

These are now mixed up with the Afghán population, to whom they have become in most respects assimilated, and with whom they frequently intermarry.

They possess but little landed property, and reside principally in the neighbourhood of the large towns, where they employ themselves in manufactures or trade, or as servants to Afghán masters. They are usually denominated *Pársíwáns.*

Kohistánís.—Of those Tájiks who retained their independence and landed possessions, the people now called Kohistánís are the modern representatives. These differ widely from their subjugated brethren, and possess the strong, fertile, and extensive province of *Kohistán*, to the north of Kábul, comprising the valleys of *Panjshír, Ghurband,* and *Nijráo*. The Kohistání population has been estimated at forty thousand. The principal town is *Istálif*, situated at the base of the Ghurband mountains, and unsurpassed in picturesque beauty.

The houses being built on the slope of a hill, and rising in a succession of irregular terraces, one above another, form an imposing spectacle, the beauty and grandeur of which is greatly augmented by the innumerable orchards and vineyards that enliven the surrounding landscape, and the magnificent snow-clad peaks of Hindú-Khush, with its mountainous progeny spreading their mazy branches far and wide, towering in the rear and perfecting a picture that has but few parallels in nature. Istálif is celebrated for the superior excellence of its fruit, but more especially of its, grapes, which are grown in prodigious abundance, and in size, flavour, and variety are perhaps equal to any in the world.

Apples, pears, peaches, apricots, plums, cherries, and other European fruits, grow in the greatest profusion, but the mulberry tree is. more extensively planted than any other, the dried fruit' being ground into flour and converted into bread, which forms a cheap and wholesome article of food for the common people. The Kohistánís are rude, violent, and contentious, their chief delight being war. They are very efficient as infantry, especially in mountain warfare, and can take the field in large bodies, at the shortest notice, subsisting for weeks together on dried mulberries alone, of which each soldier carries a bagful. The people are more completely under the control of their *kháns* than is the case with any of the tribes before noticed.

They are regarded by their neighbours with mingled feelings of dread, distrust, and aversion. They have generally resisted every attempt to render them tributary to the Kábul rulers, and have always enjoyed a considerable degree of independence.

Hazáras.—The *Hazáras* inhabit the Paropamisan mountains between Hirát and Kábul, and though formerly composing but one people have long been derided by religious schism into two sects or branches, the *Suní* and the *Shíahs*, the former occupying the western, and the latter the eastern, half of their wild and rugged country. The *Suní* Hazáras are usually called *Aimáks*, whilst the *Shíah* branch alone retains the name of *Hazáras*.

Their square *Tátar* features sufficiently distinguish them from the Afgháns, independent of their many essential differences in other respects. The *Aimáks* dwell almost wholly in tents, feeding flocks and cultivating the few arable strips of land that nature has allotted them. Their chiefs possess many strongholds in the most inaccessible parts of the mountains, and exercise an almost despotic sway over their own tribes.

The *Hazáras* dwell in open villages defended by high towers, and the chiefs in small forts. Their country is more rugged and barren, and its climate more inclement, than that of the Aimáks. They are simple, good humoured, and sociable, but hot tempered, and, when their enmity is aroused, at once stubborn, fierce, and revengeful. They are constantly engaged in strife, either amongst themselves or against the Aimáks, Uzbegs, and Afgháns, sturdily resisting the payment of tribute to the Kábul government whenever opportunity offers. In religion they are zealously attached to their own sect, and uncompromising in their hatred of all Sunís. Their chiefs are, with a few exceptions, equally despotic as those of their Aimák brethren.

Kazilbáshís.—I next proceed to notice the principal foreign settlers whose numbers, wealth, and influence, entitle them to distinct consideration. Foremost among these are the *Kazilbáshís*, or Persian colonists, who emigrated from their own country in the time of Nádir Sháh, and of whom not less than twelve thousand dwell in the city of Kábul alone, where they occupy a fortified quarter called the *Chandaul.* They have smaller settlements in the towns of Kandahár and Hirát, and have obtained several small grants of land in various other parts of the country.

Many of the chiefs held situations of trust and importance under the Dúrání monarchs.

Amid the frequent struggles for the empire that have distracted the land after the death of Ahmad Sháh, their usual policy has been to maintain an armed neutrality, cautiously abstaining from joining either party until the issue of the struggle seemed no longer doubtful, when they of course declared in favour of the strongest. But although politically timid, they are personally brave, and, being able to muster a strong force in the field, they are always certain of being welcomed as acceptable auxiliaries to whichever party they attach themselves.

The sectarian differences in religion between them and the Afgháns must ever prevent anything like real cordiality on either side, the Kazilbáshís being Shíahs, like the Persians, whilst all the Afgháns are Sunís in faith. The Kazilbáshís are vain and fond of display. They usually dress well, and attend more to domestic comfort and personal cleanliness than the Afghans, who are very careless of such matters. They also surpass the latter in general refinement and civilization, but are inferior to them in manly virtues and in religious toleration.

Arabs.—The Arabs are the only other foreign settlers of any importance. They are computed at two thousand families, and a large portion of their number were employed under the Dúrání monarchs to garrison the Bálá Hisár, or royal citadel, of Kábul.

Sháh Shujá, on his restoration to the throne in 1839, enlisted several hundreds in his service, who remained faithful to him amid his subsequent disasters.

Description of Kábul.—The city of Kábul has been so often described that its principal features must be already pretty familiar to the majority of English readers. The traveller who for the first time approaches it from the direction of Jallálábád, after having passed through the savage defiles and toiled, over the barren steeps that intervene, feels both relieved and delighted, on entering the plain of Kábul, by the cheerful and picturesque aspect of the distant city, descried afar off in a gorge between two lofty hills, up and along whose steep and rocky ridges is discernible a long line of massive wall, with numerous half-ruined towers, once forming an imposing barrier of defence against the sudden and devastating inroads of the western tribes.

On the left, or eastern extremity, occupying a low spur of hill and commanding the entire town, the Bálá Hisár, or citadel, with its lofty stone walls, bulky bastions, and enclosed crowd of high-storied dwellings, forms a striking object. The mountains of *Pughmán* and *Koh Dámán*, covered with snow during two-thirds of the year, form a magnificent background to the scene. Green fields of various kinds of grain and clover, blossoming orchards, and small square forts, are thickly interspersed over the adjacent plains, which, however, are intersected on the eastern side by low barren hills that somewhat injure the otherwise rich and extensive prospect. On the western side of the city, and separated from it by the gorge through which the Kábul River flows, is a most beautiful valley, varying in width from eight to twelve miles, encircled by a succession of mountain ranges whose most distant summits reflect a dazzling glare from their white mantles of perennial snow. On the gentle slopes at the base are well-stocked orchards, cultivated terraces, and villages embosomed in wood, whilst the plain below presents to view one vast garden of lavish plenty through which the river of Kábul and its tributary streams pursue their winding courses, distributing their crystal waters, *en route*, among innumerable artificial canals that diverge in all directions to irrigate the upland fields.

Castles, villages, orchards, and plantations of poplar, willow, and other trees, are thickly scattered over the diversified landscape, the view of which from an eminence near Bábar's tomb deservedly constitutes one of the chief boasts of Kábul. The city is very irregularly laid out, and, with exception of the celebrated covered *bazar* and the tomb of Taimúr Sháh, contained no public buildings at all striking.[1] The streets are narrow, and the houses lofty with flat roofs. To many of the better sort of private dwellings a garden is attached. The largest portion of the city stands on the right bank of the river, the opposite side being principally lined with walled gardens and private forts of the upper classes.

The covered *bazar* consisted of five open squares connected by four arcades, down the centre of which a marble aqueduct conveyed a small running stream. The sides were lined with shops exhibiting a wealthy display of home and foreign produce.

That which most excited a stranger's admiration was the number of fruiterers' shops, where every variety of tempting and delicious fruit was piled up in matchless profusion.

Crowds of busy merchants and lounging idlers, in the various costumes of Asia, thronged this favourite mart during the greater part of the day and night, excepting on Fridays, when the shops of all true believers were shut and business suspended, whilst the inhabitants attended to their religious duties, or enjoyed their diversions in the gardens and fields of the suburbs. The garden that contains the tomb of the Emperor Bábar was their usual place of resort on these occasions, and they could not possibly have selected a more suitable spot. One of the strangest sights in Kábul is that of the ladies gliding about the crowded streets enveloped from head to feet in white sheets, having a very small network in front of the eyes to peep through. This ghostly costume affords the most perfect concealment to both face and figure, and has a tendency to excite a feeling of curiosity in all foreign beholders. That is, under the circumstances, very excusable, their reputation for beauty being amply sustained by the handsome

---

1. The former no longer exists, having been destroyed by General Pollock in October, 1842, as an act of retributive vengeance for the insult there offered to the body of a British envoy on the 23rd of December, 1841.

features and rosy complexions of their offspring. So impenetrable is the disguise of this outdoor dress, the fashion of which is never varied, that it is impossible for a man to distinguish his own wife when he meets her abroad.

The facility thus afforded for intrigue may be easily conceived, although it is probable that even the most fertile imagination of an Englishman would fall short of the reality.

The plains to the north and east of Kábul are low and swampy in many places, being subject, during the rainy months, to inundation from the river.

Much more might be written illustrative of a country and people that recent events have rendered so interesting to Englishmen, but I believe there is scarcely anything of importance on these subjects that may not he found most ably and adequately described in the admirable work of the Hon. Mountstuart Elphinstone, the correctness of whose information has now been fully tested, and in hardly a single instance impugned.

CHAPTER 2

A Retrospect of the First Afghan War

Perhaps no Governor-General of India ever assumed the reins of office with more benevolent inclinations and more peaceable intentions than Lord Auckland in 1836; yet, within less than two years, he plunged headlong into a war to which, there is reason to believe, he was all along secretly averse, and which has been since stamped by universal public opinion as the most unjust, ill-advised, and unnecessary that had ever engaged the energies of a British army, or risked the honourable reputation of the British name throughout the East.

It is now a well-established fact that the initiative in the Afghán war was taken in opposition to the opinion, and even in defiance of the protests, of the Court of Directors, who were at that time the nominal trustees of India; and that a large share of the responsibility belongs to Her Majesty's Ministers in England, who, in common with Lord Auckland's official advisers, believed that the stability of our Indian empire was being so seriously threatened by the warlike operations of Persia, secretly influenced by Russian diplomacy in Central Asia, as to render it absolutely necessary for the rulers of India to arouse themselves to ward off the impending danger by some outward demonstration of power in that quarter.

A new monarch had recently succeeded to the throne of Persia, whose partialities had betrayed themselves in favour of a Russian alliance, in opposition to the interests of Great Britain, whose influence had heretofore prevailed over all rivals at the Court of Tehrán; and among the earliest results of this change, was the determination to hurl a Persian army against the fortress of Hirát, which had long been in possession of the Afgháns, but to which an old claim on the part of Persia was now conveniently revived.

A general belief prevailed among European and Asiatic diplomatists of that period that the possession of Hirát by Persia must necessarily threaten not only the safety of Afghánistán, but of the rich plains of the Panjáb (at that time in possession of the great Sikh ruler Ranjít Singh) and of British India lying beyond. Therefore it was but natural that Afgháns, Sikhs, and English should be anxious for some sort of alliance for purposes of mutual defence against a common enemy.

But, when it is considered what large disciplined forces might have been easily concentrated on any threatened point of our Indian frontier, how powerful an army of friendly Sikhs at that time occupied the Panjáb, and what formidable physical obstacles the intervening country presents at all times to the march of a large invading force, hampered with artillery, commissariat, and other necessary *impedimenta*, it is difficult to account for the panic that so generally prevailed, on any other rational ground than a consciousness of some weak and combustible points in the heterogeneous fabric of our Indian empire, which might cause it to collapse or explode suddenly and disastrously on the application of any sufficiently exciting forces from without.

It is to be hoped that the interval of forty years which has since elapsed has gradually placed our moral and material hold of India upon a much sounder basis than then existed.

At that time the chief power in Afghánistán was in the able hands of Dost Muhammad Khán, whose capital was Kábul and three of whose brothers governed at Kandahár. Hirát itself was held as an independent principality by Sháh Kámrán, a Sadúzí prince, whose father and uncles once reigned over Afghánistán, betraying and supplanting each other by turns, until themselves betrayed and supplanted by the great Bárakzí chiefs, whose power now predominated, and whose elder brother, Fath Khán, had long acted the part of minister and king-maker, until at length treacherously put to a cruel death by Sháh Kámrán, against whom Dost Muhammad and the other surviving brothers of Fath Khán accordingly cherished the bitterest feelings of hatred and revenge.

To gratify this dire hostility, the Kandahár brothers were now willing to lend themselves to the designs of Persia, not without hope of some benefit resulting to themselves. But their great chieftain at Kábul, more far-sighted and patriotic than they, had solemnly cautioned them against the danger of incurring the enmity of the British, to the superior value of whose alliance he was fully alive, although Russia was at that very time bidding high for his adherence.

Matters were in this unsatisfactory state when, in September, 1837,

Sir Alexander Burnes presented himself before Dost Muhammad at Kábul, as the accredited agent of the Indian Government, on a so-styled "commercial" mission, the real object of which was, however, sufficiently transparent.

The two men were already personally known to each other; Burnes having, about five years previously, been most hospitably entertained by the Kábul chief when passing through that city as a private traveller *en route* to Europe; hence his reappearance at the present momentous crisis could not but be hailed as a favourable omen of the friendly intentions of the British Government, whose representative he now was. His reception was, accordingly, of the most cordial and flattering description, and to all appearance he had an easy game to play; and it is probable that had he been allowed to arrange matters in his own way, all difficulties would have been smoothed over, and all motive for hostilities removed.

The obvious policy of the British Government at that period was to conciliate the goodwill of the Afghán nation (of whom Dost Muhammad was the acknowledged and popular *de facto* ruler), as the most effective barrier we could raise against present and future innovations of the Western powers; and this we had now a glorious opportunity of effecting through the timely instrumentality of Burnes, than whom no agent could have been found so appositely qualified for such a task, or more zealous to consummate so desirable a result.

But it was not so to be! Lord Auckland and his official advisers had, from the very first, conceived an inveterate distrust of Dost Muhammad for the difficulties of whose position they failed to make due allowance, and whose many sterling qualities as a ruler they equally failed to understand and appreciate. In point of fact, they had meanwhile conceived a favourite policy of their own, entirely opposed to that so earnestly recommended by Burnes, and the result was his summary recall from Kábul early in 1838, and the temporary triumph of Russian and Persian interests in the councils of Kábul and Kandahár.

A Persian army, with some Russian officers in its train, had meanwhile already laid siege to Hirát, and all India looked on in wonder and alarm at the eventful drama enacting at her distant portal in the north-east.

Fortunately, few Asiatic powers understand how to conduct siege operations; and Persia, even with the aid of Russian officers, and with its own monarch in person at the head of a sufficiently powerful army and battering train, formed no exception to the rule. The siege lingered on from November, 1837, until September, 1838, affording ample time for intermediate action on the part of the British.

The credit of this prolonged defence was due, in an eminent degree, to the accidental presence within the walls of Hirát of a young British officer of the Bombay Artillery, Eldred Pottinger by name. His professional skill and personal energy were of the utmost use in directing the defensive operations, and keeping alive the martial spirit of the garrison. On more than one occasion the Afghán commander, Yár Muhammad (who was also Sháh Kámrán's prime minister), was on the point of yielding to his assailants, but was shamed into a show, at least, of fresh courage by the entreaties, reproaches, and even friendly violence of Pottinger, who would not suffer him to retreat from the breach when retreat on his part must have been the signal for general flight; but literally dragged him forcibly again and again to the fronts until the enemy, in despair at the pertinacity of resistance encountered, retired discomfited and crestfallen to their trenches.

According to the authority of Russian officers engaged in the siege, the *Sháh* of Persians army amounted to forty thousand men, with sixty guns; and among the former was a Russian battalion, which I understand to have been composed of Russian refugees settled in Persia. Not content with eighteen-pounder and twenty-four-pounder siege guns, the fire from which, if properly concentrated and sustained, must have speedily effected a practicable breach, the Persian engineer entrusted with the siege operations established a foundry in the midst of the camp, wherein four monster seventy-pounder guns were cast, from whose fire vast and immediate results were expected. Two of these burst on trial, killing several bystanders; the other two stood the test better, and several days were then occupied in hewing stone balls of the required calibre from the marble supplied by the monuments of a neighbouring burial-place; and it may have been the periodical advent of these unfriendly, though fortunately harmless visitors, which Pottinger likens in his journal to the "three shots a-day which the Spanish army before Gibraltar fired for some time, and which the garrison called after 'The Trinity.'"

The garrison of Hirát possessed very few pieces of ordnance wherewith to return these boisterous compliments; but, happily for them, it was not until five months had elapsed that Persian self-conceit could bring itself to take council from the Russian officers by erecting regular breaching batteries against particular points of the fortifications. The situation of the defenders then became more critical, and

Pottinger's professional abilities were called into constant request.

The walls of Hirát, as then existing, formed a large quadrangle, enclosing a space of nearly one square mile, being about one thousand six hundred yards long by one thousand four hundred broad, each face having about thirty round bastions; those at the four angles surpassing the rest in height and bulk; a deep wet ditch, having a *fausse-braye*, surrounding the whole. The walls, which were from twenty-five to thirty feet high, stood on an elevated mound of earth, varying from forty to sixty feet above the level of the ground, and were of unburnt brick. There were five gates, each defended by a small outwork. On the north side stood the citadel, overlooking the city and enclosed by lofty defences of a similar character, but in a very dilapidated condition. The defenders of Hirát justly felt more faith in their double *fausse-braye* than in their walls, which now began to crumble rapidly under the concentrated fire of the enemy's round shot.

At length, on the 24th of June, the long-threatened assault took place, which was confidently expected to carry all before it. The Persian astrologers, after closely consulting the stars, had predicted a signal triumph for their monarch on that day. The assaulting force was to advance in five divisions, each under its own independent commander. The Russian battalion formed the forlorn hope of one of them; but its leader (General Borowski) was shot down at the very first onsets and, by some accident, the men composing it contrived to get under the fire of the Persian batteries, in addition to the bullets and missiles of the Afgháns, and were obliged to beat a retreat, with a loss of four officers and two hundred and fifty men killed and wounded. Better success for some time seemed in store for another of the storming columns, which actually penetrated the defences, carrying all before it, but being feebly supported from behind, was again and again driven back, though more than once on the very verge of victory, but was as often baffled by the indomitable pluck of Eldred Pottinger, who, when all seemed lost, drove the faint-hearted Yáh Muhammad before him to the rescue, as already related. Russian accounts do not hesitate to give the young English officer full credit for the result, so triumphant to the Afgháns, so humiliating to their opponents; and one of them adds:

> The *Sháh* was in a violent rage at the failure, and gave orders to encompass the place with a high wall of mud, armed with towers, in order to starve the garrison out.

This desperate struggle was succeeded by a prolonged lull, during which famine and discord seemed but too likely to effect that wherein ordinary appliances of war had failed; when at a most critical juncture, the *Sháh* took alarm at some open hostilities of the British on the Persian coast, and suddenly withdrew his forces, being careful, however, before his departure, to saw asunder the seventy-pounder guns which were to have accomplished such wonders, each weighing five tons, and which he was unwilling to leave behind as an additional trophy for the now exulting Hirátís.

As Eldred Pottinger, whom history will always celebrate as the "Hero of Hirát," was subsequently my honoured friend and associate in the eventful episode of my own early experiences during the Kábul troubles, I have been unable to resist the temptation, at the risk of repeating what some may deem a threadbare tale, of entering into the above details (partly obtained from original sources) relating to the first great drama wherein he so conspicuously and so honourably figured, and whereupon, in fact, the chief interest of the war was so long concentrated. Should any similar crisis occur, whether in India or elsewhere, let us hope that another such British hero as Eldred Pottinger may as opportunely start forth into the full blaze of fame, fired by his example, animated by his spirit, and as competent to uphold the glory of his country, and to disconcert the ambitious schemes of its enemies.

It is time I should now return to Lord Auckland and his new project, whereby the future safety of our north-west frontier was to be secured against the designs of Russian and Persian ambition. This consisted originally of a tri-partite treaty, wherein the British Indian Government, Ranjít Singh, the ruler of the Panjáb, and Sháh Shujá, the long-dethroned monarch of Afghánistán, were the principal parties concerned. Thirty years had elapsed since the last-named personage had been driven from his throne to find, after some years of perilous adventure in Kashmir and the Panjáb, a hospitable asylum in British territory; from which he twice issued forth at long intervals to engage in ineffectual efforts to regain his lost dominions. Meanwhile, Dost Muhammad, a younger brother of the murdered Fath Khan, had risen to supreme power through his military ability and irrepressible force of character.

Since 1826, he had contrived to hold his own against all antagonists, and had, by his frank urbanity of demeanour, his aptitude for business, manliness, and uniform success in the attainment of his aims, acquired a strong hold on the hearts and minds of the great mass of the Afghán people. Sháh Shujá, on the contrary, was remembered chiefly for the absence of all those high qualities as a man and a ruler which shone so conspicuously in his rival; nor was his return to power a subject of desire to any save a few self-interested partisans and needy relatives. In spite of these drawbacks, however, it had been determined by the British Indian Government to suit their own policy by dispossessing the one and reinstating the other, without any real deference to the wishes and aspirations of the people most interested in the matter.

Accordingly, in a manifesto dated the 1st October, 1838, this new policy was publicly set forth, whereby our Sikh ally, Ranjít Singh, being "guaranteed in his present possessions, bound himself to co-operate with the British for the restoration of Sháh Shujá to the throne of his ancestors." On the 8th of November following, the news of the retirement of the Persians from Hirát was published by Government, but was not allowed to alter the political programme which had been already determined, further than by causing a diminution of the numerical strength of the British force to be employed, which afforded the Commander-in-Chief, Sir Henry Pane, a pretext for withdrawing from the personal command of the expedition, the policy of which he had never approved, his place being filled by Sir John Keane.

On the 10th December the Bengal force, under Sir Willoughby Cotton, marched from Farozpur, proceeding by the left bank of the River Satlaj to Rohrí, where that river joins the Indus. Sháh Shujá had already started in advance to Shikápur, escorted by Hindústání levies numbering six thousand men, raised and disciplined by British officers for his special service. He was accompanied by Sir William Mac-Naghten, who had been appointed envoy and minister at his courts and who had been one of the chief promoters of the expedition. Another force, five thousand six hundred strong, moved from Bombay through Sindh to the same point, where an admirable bridge of boats had been prepared by officers of the Bengal Engineers for the passage of the whole over the great River Indus. The entire invading force, when combined, amounted to twenty-one thousand, together with about four times that number of camp followers and upwards of thirty thousand camels. This long miscellaneous array, consisting of cavalry, infantry, artillery, with their attendant *impedimenta* of wheeled carriages and laden animals of every description, filed over the bridge in perfect order, presenting a picturesque and memorable spectacle.

Owing to the undisguised dislike manifested by the *Amirs* of Sindh to the passage of so many British troops through their country, there seemed every probability of hostilities breaking out in that quarter at the very commencement of the campaign, which must necessarily have delayed the onward progress of the army towards Afghánistán; but yielding to the force of circumstances, backed by the undeniable arguments of strong battalions eager for the plunder of the rich capital of Haidarábád, they had the good sense to succumb before compromising themselves too far, although they thereby obtained but a brief respite from the hard and inevitable fate in store, and which overtook them about four years later.

It is needless that I should dwell minutely on the military events of a campaign so well known as that which replaced Sháh Shujá on his throne; but it may, nevertheless, be useful to glance, *en passant*, at some of the physical difficulties which the country opposed to the passage of our army. Having safely crossed the Indus, the vast invading host dragged its seemingly interminable length over one hundred and forty-six miles of dreary desert, bordering Biluchistán on the east; and there many hundreds of poor horses, camels, and bullocks perished from weariness and thirsty leaving their skeletons to mark unmistakably to future travellers the track of the invaders.

Then came the formidable Bolán Pass, sixty miles in length, where fortunately, no enemy occupied the heights, although stragglers ran considerable risk from stray Bilúchí robbers, ever on the watch behind the rocks for passing prey. Here the animals suffered severely, and perished by hundreds. Emerging from this dismal gorge into the lovely and inviting valley of Shawl, seemed like passing from purgatory to paradise; but here, owing partly to a scanty harvest and partly to the wanton devastation caused by some of the troops themselves, provisions fell alarmingly short for so great a multitude, and famine prices prevailed. The neighbouring Khán of Kalát was suspected of aggravating these difficulties, and was marked for future punishment

Pushing on, therefore, with the least possible delay, the Khujak Pass was reached, presenting a long succession of steep and difficult ascents and descents, with some exceedingly narrow gorges where no draught cattle could work with effect. The artillery, including a heavy battering-train, was therefore dragged up and lowered down by the persevering manual labour of the English soldiers, occupying five days. The summit of the pass is seven thousand four hundred and forty-nine feet above the sea. Here, too, much loss was sustained in commissariat baggage-animals, and much valuable property sacrificed in consequence. Fortunately, the Afgháns were too disunited among themselves to offer any organized resistance, and the army reached Kandahár on the 25th April, 1839, without any show of opposition. The Kandahár chiefs had fled for refuge to Persia without striking a blow, and the inhabitants tendered their reluctant homage to the old monarch, who was thus unceremoniously thrust upon them by foreign bayonets.

On the 27th June died Ranjít Singh, the famous old "Lion of the Panjáb," and our ally in the present expedition. On the self-same day Sir John Keane, leaving behind him a strong garrison at Kandahár, and even the siege-train which had been brought so far with such heavy cost and labour, pursued his march to Ghazní, where he encountered his first openly defiant foe in the person of Prince Haidar, a son of Dost Muhammad, who, with a garrison of three thousand five hundred Afgháns, defended the fortress and citadel, which were of formidable strength and susceptible of a prolonged defence. Now was discovered the extraordinary blunder that had been committed in leaving behind the battering-train, without the aid of which the risk of utter failure seemed imminent.

At this crisis Major George Thomson, of the Bengal Engineers, came to the rescue with the happy proposal to blow open the only accessible gate with gunpowder. This was successfully accomplished in the partial obscurity of early dawn by a party of sappers, headed by Lieutenant Durand, of the Bengal Engineers, who volunteered for the duty, and who survived the dangerous hazard to attain high rank and distinction among those illustrious soldier-statesmen who have contributed so largely to the maintenance of our national honour in India.[1]

The governor, Haidar Khán, was taken prisoner, and such was the panic produced among the troops of Dost Muhammad, who had taken up a position at Arghandí to dispute the British advance to Kábul, that, abandoning for the time all hope of maintaining his sovereignty, he fled with about two thousand faithful adherents towards Bámíán. A select party of British officers, headed by the since illustrious Outram, and escorted by two thousand Afghán horse under command of Hájí Khán Kákar, a notorious turncoat, volunteered to start in pursuit, and, pushing their way by forced marches over stupendous mountain

---

1. He became widely known to fame as Sir Henry Durand, and was Governor of the Panjáb, when an accidental death overtook him, in the midst of an useful career that promised to culminate in a still loftier sphere of action.

passes, must have overtaken the fugitive *Amir*, encumbered as he was with his family and baggage, before he could reach the frontier, had not the aforesaid "Hají" proved himself a traitor, whose real object was to throw every obstacle in the way of their progress and success. Thus Dost Muhammad escaped to Bukhárá, not without the sympathies of many British hearts, until the wheel of fortune should once more give a revolution in his favour.

On the 6th of August, Sháh Shujá, attended by Sir William Mac-Naghten, and escorted by the British troops, made his triumphal entry into Kábul, and took up his abode in the Bálá Hisár, or Royal Citadel. There, on the 8th of September, he was joined by his eldest son, Prince Timúr, who had meanwhile penetrated through the Khaibar Pass from Pesháwar, under the escort of a Sikh contingent furnished by Ranjit Singh, and under the political control of Colonel, afterwards Sir Claude, Wade, encountering but little opposition. And thus was the first act of this wondrous drama of real life brought to a successful termination.

Sir Henry Fane, the experienced general to whom the conduct of the Afghán expedition had been originally offered, had been also among the first to caution Lord Auckland of the dangers and difficulties that would inevitably beset the British troops in that country after the first successful result should have been achieved. Sir William Mac-Naghten, the British envoy, upon whom the chief political management of affairs was thenceforth to fall, was not long in experiencing the prophetic nature of that counsel. It soon became evident that Shah Shujá could only be maintained on his throne by the continued presence of a British force. This was, however, reduced to a moiety by the return of nearly the whole Bombay and a portion of the Bengal divisions to India. With the latter went Sir John Keane, soon to be made a peer for the conquest of Ghazní, leaving Sir Willoughby Cotton in chief command of the remaining troops across the Indus, amounting to about ten thousand men, distributed over a wide extent of country, to garrison the chief cities and such other places as required their protecting presence.

Advantage was taken of the return of the Bombay column to punish Mihráb Khán, the unlucky *Khán* of Kalát, for his so-called refractory conduct, to which allusion has already been made. He now offered an obstinate but ineffectual resistance to the attack on his stronghold, which was taken by assault by General Wiltshire on the 15th October, wherein the brave chief himself was killed. His death must have occasioned some pangs of remorse to Sháh Shujá, whom he had formerly befriended in distress.

The two years which followed the establishment of Shah Shujá at Kábul were chiefly remarkable for the activity of our political officers, great and small, who were scattered far and wide over the land to assist in carrying out, as far as in them lay, the policy of our Government, which seems to have mainly consisted in consolidating the power of the *Sháh*, and in extending, as Lord Auckland himself expressed it, "the salutary influence of the British name." The most prominent of these political agents, both in ability and influence, were D'Arcy Todd at Hirát; Rawlinson (now Sir Henry) and Leech at Kandahár; Eldred Pottinger in Kohistán; Macgregor (now Sir George) at Jallálábád; Arthur Conolly, on a special mission at Khukand; and Sir Alexander Burnes at Kábul. But besides these was a host of minor stars, each of whom added his quota to the grand work of "consolidation," which was not always synonymous with "pacification," and very generally ended in carving out some active work for the military in his immediate vicinity.

Foremost of those worthy of honourable mention was D'Arcy Todd, who had succeeded Pottinger as British representative at Hirát, on the departure of the latter to recruit his health after the siege. Of Todd's long series of political encounters with the arch-intriguer Yár Muhammad, whose sole object seemed to be to extort money by working on our political fears and jealousies, I refrain from entering into the unedifying particulars; but that which really formed the distinguishing feature of his mission to Hirát was his successful effort to induce the *Khán* of Khaiva to set at liberty some four hundred and sixteen unfortunate Russian captives whose detention as slaves in Khaiva had been made a convenient and, it must be admitted, a perfectly just, pretext by Russia for invading that country. This noble triumph of humanity and of sound policy he accomplished by twice deputing a British officer, entirely on his own responsibility, to work on the fears and hopes of the Khaivan chief.

The negotiations auspiciously begun by James Abbott were judiciously followed up and brought to a successful issue by Richmond Shakespear, both being at that time subalterns of the Bengal Artillery; and to the latter fell the enviable lot of escorting the whole party of emancipated captives to the Russian frontier at Oranburgh, where they were safely delivered over to the commandant for restoration to their friends. The Russians, not to be outdone in acts that grace humanity, restored to the Khaivans merchandise valued at two millions sterling, and, more precious than all beside, forty prisoners, among whom were representatives of the wealthiest families in Khaiva. Seldom, if ever, has a negotiation been effected in the East so creditable to all parties concerned; nor since the brightest days of chivalry have the honours of knighthood which rewarded Shakespear been more worthily won. Sir Richmond Shakespear amply fulfilled the promise of his youth, and rose to high political position in India; dying in 1861. But James Abbott is still to the fore, with the rank of general in the army, and during our subsequent struggles with the Sikhs in the Panjáb rendered eminently good service at a critical period and in a manner well deserving of honourable remembrance.

Thus the Afghán campaign, with all its faults and drawbacks, bore some really good fruit, and evidenced in a remarkable manner what a store of excellent raw *matériel* for the manufacture of heroes and statesmen had been previously lying dormant in the Indian army. In this respect, indeed, it may be said to have awakened to new life the latent but laudable ambition of our officers, young and old, and to have transmitted a forward impulse even to the present generation—an impulse which I earnestly hope may never cease to operate for their own and the public good. Many remarkable episodes, accompanied by gallant deeds and victorious issues, imparted an interest to the first year of our occupation of Afghánistán, and the temporary success of our policy may be said to have reached its culminating point on the defeat of Dost Muhammad at Bámián, and his subsequent unconditional surrender on the 3rd November, 1840.

As an old Bengal artilleryman, I cannot pass by in silence the successful passage of Major Garbett's troop of horse artillery over the stupendous passes of Hindú Khush, at an altitude little below that of Mont Blanc, although the feat (of which we were then so proud) has very recently been creditably rivalled by some British batteries in Lord Napier's glorious Abyssinian expedition.

The year 1841 opened with a smiling prospect of peace and tranquillity, to be soon rudely disturbed by rebellious risings in various directions. The faults of our policy and the real weakness of our position began to grow more and more manifest to friends and foes. Had but Shah Shujá, our puppet king, proved himself a proper man for the position into which we had thrust him, all might have gone on swimmingly until such time as we could, with a good grace, have left him to the loyal care of his own subjects, with all the *éclat* due to our own success and moderation. But his unpopularity naturally extended to us as his supporters, although our political leaders were wilfully blind to the fact; and, in the fullness of time, just as a winter of Siberian severity was setting in, the popular volcano Suddenly burst forth, and found us unprepared. The result is too well known and too bitterly remembered to need repetition here.

It was my own youthful fate to be the first to narrate the dismal tragedy to my countrymen in all its miserable details. I have been since informed, by competent authority, that my humble volume had the unprecedented and perhaps unpardonable effect of depriving the great Duke of Wellington of a whole night's slumber; and severe might have been the penalty for the author (then only a youthful subaltern of artillery) had not his statements, wherein many unwelcome truths were faithfully though perhaps indiscreetly blurted out, been so abundantly confirmed by the concurrent testimony of trustworthy witnesses as to have held their ground in the pages of history down to the present day.

I have often since thought that perhaps too much importance has been attached to the Kábul disaster, viewed in its military aspects. Politically and morally its awful lessons can never be over-rated, and certainly should never be forgotten; but regarded simply as a military discomfiture, it was in fact the result of a *surprise*, somewhat like that whereby the celebrated Gulliver found himself tied and bound during sleep, and at the mercy of the Lilliputians. We English went on slumbering contentedly, as though the Afgháns, whose country we had so coolly occupied, were our very best friends in the world, and quite content to be our obedient servants to boot, until one cold morning in November we woke up to the unpleasant sounds of bullets in the air, and an infuriated people's voices in revolt, like the great ocean's distant, angry roar, in a rising tempest. The best troops and the ablest generals in the world must ever find themselves placed at a great disadvantage under such circumstances.

It should always be remembered that our winter supplies of food, and firewood, and forage, had not yet been laid in; that the few days' supply in store was indifferently guarded, and fell an easy prey to the enemy before we had quite recovered our senses from the first scare of our rude awakening; that thenceforward we had to turn out and fight daily against greatly superior numbers, backed by the strong forts wherewith the Kábul valley was studded, and which latter we had to batter and carry by storm one after the other, in order thereby to obtain the needful supplies for our daily wants; so that, while our position was in a general sense defensive, we were obliged, in point of fact, to act continually on the offensive, which we nevertheless contrived to do with success until such time as we had exhausted the supplies laid up in the forts within our reach. Then, indeed, our position became, for the first time, hopeless; for even soldiers cannot sustain life on cannon balls and leaden bullets; and so it came to pass that our destiny became eventually dependent on the persuasive powers of our political officers in their attempts to treat with wily and embittered Afghán chiefs.

And this induces me to say that my own historical recollections and experiences have not impressed me with a profound confidence in the efficacy of mere diplomacy, conducted by even the most talented and sagacious of political agents, with Oriental potentates. These latter are far greater proficients than ourselves in that peculiar use of language which consists in successfully "concealing the thoughts;" and I entirely coincide with the view taken of such matters by the honest artillery gunner who was overheard, during one of our Indian campaigns, to say to a comrade, while pointing exultingly to a field battery of big guns drawn by elephants, "I say. Bill! *Them's the Politicals!*" At all events, matters fared very badly with us at Kábul when the arguments of big guns ceased to prevail: and we were soon made to experience the truth long ago enunciated by the old Roman poet:—

Donec eris feliz multos numerabis amicos,
Tempora si fuerint nubila, solus eriis!

While, therefore, I freely concede all due honour to the illustrious garrisons of Kandahár and Jallálábád, which, under Nott and Sale, so gallantly held those important posts against all opponents during the revolt, I claim for the defenders of Kábul that fair allowance should be made for the serious disadvantages under which they struggled from the very first, and beneath which they eventually succumbed, so far at least as to become the unconsenting victims of a hollow treaty formed with the assassin of our envoy—a treaty whose sole object on his part was to lure our garrison outside of its defences into those savage and formidable passes which form the highway from Kábul to Pesháwar, and where treachery, cold, and famine would, they well knew, effectually combine for its destruction.

Still, their triumph was but of brief duration:—a few short months sufficed to place Kábul again in our possession. Sir George Pollock, with his noble army of retribution, amply retrieved past disasters, and happily effected the liberation of those British captives (myself included) who had meanwhile been the unwilling recipients of rough Afghán hospitality—sometimes confined closely to lofty forts, sometimes hurried about from spot to spot on the backs of horses and camels in narrow valleys, as nomadic wanderers amid precipitous mountain-passes; lodging the while in such rude huts as they could construct for themselves from the branches of juniper bushes, or in the mud hovels of the primitive inhabitants; sometimes treated with friendly deference, at others with systematic rudeness; and finally, when General Pollock approached Kábul, forced to fly, escorted by a strong guard? of soldiers, over those self-same lofty mountain-passes leading to Kullum, in Uzbeg Tartary, across which Major Garbett had in happier times, as previously related, dragged his horse-artillery guns.

Had we once got into the clutches of the Uzbegs, I opine this chapter would never have been written, but, in a happy moment of inspiration, my old hero Pottinger (for he was of the party) betook to mesmerising our keeper with the prospect of a sufficiency of gold to keep him in comfort for the remainder of his life; and one fine morning, in the valley of Bámíán, within sight of those gigantic images cut in the perpendicular rock which excite the wonder of travellers, we found ourselves all at once in the position of free agents. General Pollock, learning how affairs stood, despatched Sir Richmond Shakespear to our aid with six hundred Kazzilbásh horsemen from Kábul; and thus the latter officer enjoyed once more the triumph and *éclat* of taking a conspicuous part in proclaiming "liberty to the captives;" his own countrymen and countrywomen being this time the favoured objects of his zeal.

Kábul reconquered, we might possibly have maintained our military hold upon Afghánistán even to the present day; but our game there had been played out. Sháh Shujá was dead, having been basely murdered by one of his own trusted followers about two months after the British retreat from his capital. There was no longer any object to gain by remaining against the wishes of the people, whilst the drain upon our Indian finances caused by this war had already swelled the public debt by fifteen millions, and every month's delay threatened but to accelerate our financial ruin. Lord Ellenborough, therefore, wisely determined to evacuate the country, and to restore the exiled Amír Dost Muhammad Khán; an act of retributive justice which we have never had cause to repent; for he proved himself a most able and politic ruler till his deaths which took place so late as June 1863.

No one now doubts that our position in Afghánistán was a false one—and fraught with danger in more ways than one. Apprehensive of Russian aggression and intrigue, and counting on the fears and forbearance of our powerful neighbours and rivals, the Sikhs, we had the temerity to march an army past their country into the wild and unknown regions of Afghánistán, and thus to risk our force being cut off from its base of operations, and from its nearest available supports; and although no such catastrophe actually occurred, and temporary success attended the hap-hazard invasion of a friendly country, still we eventually were taught a lesson in the school of adversity which ought assuredly to suffice as a salutary caution in the future.

But matters have meanwhile become very much altered for the better on our north-western frontier. The great Sikh army no longer exists; and British rule extends throughout the Panjáb, even up to the very borders of Afghánistán.

Our north-western frontier is by name one of the strongest in the worlds being protected along its whole length by the great and rapid River Indus, which would, of course, in case of necessity, be strongly guarded at its few assailable points; whilst immediately beyond its banks lie the rugged mountains of Afghánistán, only to be penetrated by a few formidable defiles, which we could occupy on very short notice, and safely bid defiance to all comers. The Sulaimáin range runs nearly parallel with the Indus, and its average height is about the same as that of the Pyrenees, the lofty peaks attaining from six thousand to eleven thousand five hundred feet.

To these natural defences may be added those vast desert tracts that border our possessions in Sindh crossed by our army in 1838, and of which I have already given some account; and when, in addition to all these obstacles to the progress of an invading army, we take into consideration the immense facilities at our disposal for concentrating troops and munitions of war by river, road, and railway, at any particular point of attach, of which we must necessarily have ample means of ascertaining sufficiently beforehand to afford ample time for preparation, and the strong, British reserves which could so readily be poured in by sea from our various colonies, I cannot bring myself to believe that any Russian general would risk his own and his country's reputation in any such Quixotic adventure.

But it may be urged that Russia might possibly count on the near approach of her army being the signal for a general revolt and rising among our own native soldiers and subjects. If so, I firmly believe she would reckon without her host. The character of Russian rule, as popularly described, has not failed to reach the ears of the inhabitants of India, who are generally very shrewd judges of their own worldly interests; and when the question merely turned on a change of European masters, I believe their answer would be somewhat similar to that given by our own Charles II. to his brother James, when the latter remonstrated with the former for heedlessly exposing his life by walking unguarded about the London parks. "Brother," replied the merry monarchy "don't distress yourself! Rest assured that my subjects will never take my life to make you king!"

It may suffice to recur to the formidable Sikh invasion of 1845-46, and our subsequent desperate struggles with that nation in 1848-49, which offered such favourable opportunities to our native subjects for revolt, had any such disposition been widely prevalent; yet, even with such tempting opportunities, they remained perfectly quiescent. No stronger proof could be required that, for the mere alternative of a change of masters (and that a change for the worse), an insurrectionary movement, as an aid to invasion, would be a very unwise and unsafe dependence.

Doubtless there are, among the millions who populate India, many unwise and ignorant bigots, both Muhammadan and Hindú to whom a Christian and foreign rule must be distasteful, and numberless reckless and unruly spirits who sigh for the good old times of anarchy and universal plunder, such as existed when we first took the field to repress the marauding Mahrattas who levied black mail throughout the best part of Hindústán, and aimed at its universal conquest. But, on the whole, I believe that India has never been so wisely, unselfishly, and beneficently governed as since our gracious Queen assumed the supreme sway. Never has there been manifested such an earnest and universal desire to do justice to its people, by improving their general condition, by elevating them in the moral and social scale of being, and so preparing the way for their gradual admission to offices of trust and power.

The storm of the great mutiny of 1857 has effected wonders in clearing the political atmosphere, and in giving an impulse to civilization, with its beneficent train of material blessings, such as the natives are fast learning to appreciate, and which can scarce fail to render them more and more contented with our sway. Well may they pause and reflect whether it is likely that Russia, similarly circumstanced and with her well-known antecedents in an opposite direction, either would or could do as much.

It cannot, however, be denied that the Russian progress in Central Asia since the Crimean war, and especially during the last ten years, has been of a startling and even of an aggressive character, so far as British India is concerned. But the conditions of warfare and the capacity of India to resist an invader have materially altered since Timúr and Bábar obtained their easy triumphs, at the head of rude, undisciplined Tátár hordes. They had no siege guns, with their cumbrous appendages of heavy ordnance-stores, to impede their progress across the long succession of mountain ranges that intervene between Central Asia and the British Indian possessions; and those who venture to predict a successful issue to any modem invading force from that quarter must altogether ignore or undervalue not only the formidable physical difficulties but also the strength and efficiency of our magnificent army in India, which I believe to be more than a match for the best troops that could be brought into the field against us.

To attack a country so situated, with any chance of success, an overwhelming force would be necessary, accompanied by heavy artillery, and with supports and arsenals within moderate distance in its rear. But it has been well said by an able writer in the *Edinburgh Review*, when referring to the difficulty of conducting military operations in Afghánistán: "Take a small force, and you are beaten; take a large one, and you are starved." The stern lesson enforced by the Russians on the great Napoleon at Moscow will scarcely be lost upon themselves. Afghánistán is the great breakwater established by nature against an inundation of northern forces in these times.

Lord Napier's success in surmounting the physical difficulties of Abyssinia furnishes no practical precedent, inasmuch as his march was almost unopposed; but the small bill of nine millions sterling which accrued, notwithstanding this favourable circumstance, ought to operate as a caution to rulers ambitious of invading the north-west frontier of India, by even the easiest route available.

By general consent such a route is most likely to be found in the direction of Merv, and thence by Hirát to Kandahár, and should Russia show unmistakable indications of aggressive intentions in the direction of Persia and Hirát, it may serve as a fresh stimulus for us to strengthen to the utmost that double line of barrier which is so fortunately within our grasp in the Sulaimán range and in the River Indus behind it, and calmly and fearlessly defy the foe, should he really undertake so vast and so perilous an expedition. Happy shall we then be if, in addition to our physical sources of strength, we are reinforced by a third *moral* barrier behind us—the barrier of a loyal and contented people!

At the same time, viewed apart from international rivalries and jealousies, and those vast schemes of unscrupulous and restless ambition wherewith Russia is accredited by the world at large, it may be fairly admitted, on the other hand, that the legitimate objects of opening out new sources of commerce, and its attendant civilized advantages, are sufficiently worthy in themselves to enlist our sympathy as the consistent advocates of human progress; and in no region of the earth have those blessings been heretofore more at a discount than in the savage wilds and among the cruel slave-making Khanates of Central Asia.

With these advantages secured, and with the increased protection to life and property which the continued presence of a dominant civilized power cannot fail to realize, it may be confidently expected (and we English should rejoice in the expectation) that the long-dormant, though fertile resources of Bukhara, Samarkand, Khukand, and neighbouring states, will be rapidly developed, and therewithal open out new fields for enterprise and new triumphs for civilization.

CHAPTER 3

First Symptoms of Disturbance

When Major-General Elphinstone assumed the command of the troops in Afghánistán in April, 1841, the country enjoyed a state of apparent tranquillity to which it had for many years been a stranger. This remark applies more particularly to those provinces which lie northeast of Ghazní, comprehending Kábul proper, Kohistán, Jallálábád, and the neighbouring districts. The Ghalzí tribes, occupying a large portion of the country between Ghazní and Kandahár, had never been properly subdued, and the permanent occupation of Kalát-i-Ghalzí by our troops had so alarmed their jealous love of independence, as to cause, during the months of July and August, a partial rising of the tribes, which, however, the valour of our Hindústání troops under Colonel Wymer at Haft-asír, and of the 5th Bengal Cavalry under Colonel Chambers at Mukúr, speedily suppressed.

Some of the principal chiefs delivered themselves up as hostages, and quiet was restored. To the west of Kandahár, a notorious freebooter, named Aktar Khán, having collected about seven thousand followers, horse and foot, was signally defeated near Girishk, on the banks of the Hírmand, in the month of July, by a detachment of the *Sháh's* regular troops under Captain Woodburn, consisting of only one infantry regiment, two horse-artillery guns, under Lieutenant Cooper, besides two regiments of *Janbáz*, or Afghán horse: the latter, however, behaved ill, and can hardly be said to have shared in the glory of the unequal conflict. Captain Griffin, with the Bengal 2nd Native Infantry, was, a few days after, equally successful in an attack on the enemy in the same quarter.

Aktar Khán fled to the hills with a few followers, and the land again enjoyed repose. Kohistán, whose wild and turbulent chiefs had sturdily maintained their independence against the late ruler. Dost

Muhammad Khán, seemed at last to have settled down into a state of quiet, though unwilling, subjection to Sháh Shujá. The Nijráo chiefs formed an almost solitary exception to this show of outward submission; and Sir William Macnaghten had strongly urged, at an early period of the year, the expediency of sending a force into that country as soon as practicable. Since our first occupation of Kábul, Nijráo had become a resort for all such restless and discontented characters as had rendered themselves obnoxious to the existing government. The fact of our having permitted them so long to brave us with impunity, had doubtless been regarded by the secret enemies of the new rule as a mark of conscious weakness, and may have encouraged them, in no slight degree, to hatch those treasonable designs against the State which were so suddenly developed in November, 1841, and which were for the time, unhappily, but too successful.

Major Pottinger, having been appointed political agent in Kohistán, arrived from Calcutta in May, 1841, and was one of the first to prognosticate the coming storm. He lost no time in representing to the envoy the insufficiency of our military force in Kohistán, consisting at that time of merely two 6-pounder guns, and the Kohistání regiment raised by Lieutenant Maule, of the Bengal Artillery, which excellent young officer was on the first outbreak of the rebellion cruelly butchered by his own men, or, which is the same thing, with their consent. This regiment was stationed at Chárikár, a post of no strength, and ill adapted for making a protracted defence, as was afterwards proved. The major was, however, considered in the light of an alarmist, and he only succeeded in procuring a few Házirbásh horsemen and a 17-pounder gun, with a small detachment of the Sháh's Artillery, and a very scanty supply of ammunition.

About the end of September, Major Pottinger came to Kábul for the purpose of impressing on the Envoy that, unless strong measures of prevention were speedily adopted, he considered a rise in Kohistán as in the highest degree probable. His apprehensions were considered by the envoy as not altogether unfounded, and he was empowered to retain as hostages the sons of the leading chiefs whose fidelity he suspected. The first interruption to the state of outward tranquillity, which I have described above, occurred early in September. Captain Hay, in command of some *Házirbáshes*, and Lieutenant Maule, with his Kohistání regiment (which had been relieved at Chárikár by the Gúrkha, or 4th Regiment, Shah's Subsidized Force, officered from the line, under Captain Codrington), and two 6-pounder guns, had been sent into the Zurmat valley to collect the annual revenue, with orders likewise to make an attempt to seize certain noted plunderers, among whom were some of the murderers of Colonel Herring, who had long infested the road between Ghazní and Kábul.

The revenue was in the course of being quietly paid, when Captain Hay was mischievously informed by Mullá Mumín, collector of revenue in Zurmat (who shortly after distinguished himself as one of our bitterest foes), that the men whom he wished to seize were harboured in a certain neighbouring fort of no strength whatever, and that the inhabitants would doubtless give them up rather than risk a rupture with the Government. Captain Hay immediately proceeded thither, but found the place much stronger than he had been led to expect, and the people obstinately prepared to resist his demands. On approaching the fort he was fired upon; and finding the 6-pounder shot, of which he gave a few rounds in return, made no impression on the mud walls, he had no alternative but to retreat.

The envoy, on receiving Captain Hay's report, immediately despatched a sufficient force to punish the rebels. It consisted of two hundred of Her Majesty's 44th Infantry, 5th Native Infantry, 6th Regiment Shah's Subsidized Force, four guns of Abbot's battery, two iron 9-pounders Mountain Train, two companies of Sháh's Sappers, and two squadrons of Anderson's Horse. These were under the command of Lieutenant-Colonel Oliver, and were accompanied by Captain G. H. Macgregor,[1] the political agent at Gandámak, who happened to be then at Kábul on business. The force commenced its march on the 27th September, and reached the Zurmat valley without the slightest interruption. On the approach of our troops the rebels had fled to the hills in the greatest consternation, leaving their forts at our mercy. The principal strongholds were destroyed with powder, and the force prepared to return to Kábul.

Meanwhile the hydra of rebellion had reared its head in another far more formidable quarter. Early in October three Ghalzí chiefs of note suddenly quitted Kábul, after plundering a rich *káfila* at Tizín, and took up a strong position in the difficult defile of Khurd-Kábul, about ten miles from the capital, thus blocking up the pass, and cutting off our communication with Hindústán. Intelligence had not very long previously been received that Muhammad Akbar Khán, second son of the ex-ruler Dost Muhammad Khan, had arrived at Bámián from

---

1. Now, (at time of first publication), Major-General Sir George H. Macgregor, K.C.B.

Khulum for the supposed purpose of carrying on intrigues against the Government. It is remarkable that he was nearly connected by marriage with Muhammad Sháh Khan and Dost Muhammad Khan,² also Ghalzís, who almost immediately joined the above-mentioned chiefs. Muhammad Akbar had, since the deposition of his father, never ceased to foster feelings of intense hatred towards the English nation; and, though often urged by the fallen ruler to deliver himself up, had resolutely preferred the life of a houseless exile to one of mean dependence on the bounty of his enemies.

It seems therefore in the highest degree probable that this hostile movement on the part of the Eastern Ghalzí was the result of his influence aver them, combined with other causes which will be hereafter mentioned. The march of General Sale's brigade to their winter quarters at Jallálábád, and ultimately to India, had only been deferred until the return of the force from Zurmat, but was now hastened in consequence of this unwelcome news. On the 9th October the 35th Regiment Native Infantry, under Colonel Monteath, C.B., one hundred of the Shah's Sappers, under Captain G. Broadfoot, a squadron of the 5th Cavalry, under Captain Oldfield, and two guns of Captain Abbot's battery, under Lieutenant Dawes, were sent on in advance to the entrance of the pass at Búta-i-khák, where, on the following night, they were attacked by a large number of rebels, who, taking advantage of the high ground and deep ravines in the neighbourhood of the camp, maintained a sharp fire upon them for several hours, by which thirty-five *sepoys* were killed and wounded.

On the morning of the 11th General Sale marched from Kábul with Her Majesty's 13th Light Infantry to join the camp at Búta-i-khák, and on the following morning the whole proceeded to force the pass of Khurd-Kábul. Intelligence had been received that the enemy, besides occupying the heights of this truly formidable defile, which in many places approach to within fifty yards of each other, rising up almost perpendicularly to an elevation of five hundred or six hundred feet, had erected a *sunga*, or stone breastwork, in the narrowest part of the gorge, flanked by a strong tower. The advance guard, consisting of the Shih's Sappers, a company of Her Majesty's 13th Foot, another of the 35th Native Infantry, and two guns under Lieutenant Dawes, was met about midway through the pass, which is nearly five miles long, by a sharp and continued discharge of *jazáils* from the strong posts of the enemy. This was returned by our men with precision and

---

2. This chief must not be confounded with the ex-ruler of the same name.

effect, notwithstanding the disadvantages of their situation; flanking parties gallantly struggled up the height to dislodge the enemy from thence, while the Sappers rushed on to destroy the above-mentioned breastwork.

Through this, however, the stream which flows down the middle of the defile had already forced a passage, and, as the enemy abandoned it, as well as the flanking tower, on the approach of our troops. Lieutenant Dawes passed his guns through the interval at full speed, getting them under the shelter of a rock beyond the sustained and murderous fire of the enemy's *jazáilchís*, it being impossible to elevate the guns sufficiently to bear upon them. The flankers did their duty nobly, and the fight had lasted for about half an hour, during which the conduct of the Sháh's Sappers, under Captain Broadfoot, was creditable in the highest degree, when the approach of the main column, under General Sale, who had been already shot through the leg, enabled Captain Seaton[3] of the 35th Regiment, who commanded the advance guard, to push on. This he did, running the gauntlet to the end of the pass, by which time the enemy, fearful of being taken in rear, abandoned their position and retired towards Khabar-i-Jabár, on the road to Tizín. The 35th Regiment, Shah's Sappers, Lieutenant Dawes's guns, and a party of *Házirbásh* under Captain Trevor, encamped at Khurd-Kábul, Her Majesty's 13th Light Infantry returning to Búta-i-khák. During their return, parties who still lurked among the rocks fired upon the column, thereby doing some mischief.

In these positions the divided force remained encamped for several days, awaiting the return to Kábul of the troops from Zurmat. During this time several *shab-khúns*, or night attacks, were made on the two camps, that on the 35th Regiment at Khurd-Kábul being peculiarly disastrous from the treachery of the Afghán Horse, who admitted the enemy within their lines, by which our troops were exposed to a fire from the least suspected quarter: many of our gallant *sepoys* and Lieutenant Jenkins thus met their death.

On the 20th October General Sale moved with fait force to Khurd-Kábul, having been previously joined by the 37th Regiment under Major Griffiths, Captain Abbotts guns, the Mountain Train under Captain Backhouse, one hundred of Anderson's Irregular Horse under Lieutenant Mayne, and the remainder of the Sháh's Sappers and Miners. About the 22nd the whole force there assembled, with Captain Macgregor, political agent, marched to Tizín, encountering much

---

3. Afterwards known as Major-General Sir T. Seaton, K. C. B.

determined opposition on the road.

By this time it was too evident that the whole of the eastern Ghalzís had risen in one common league against us. Their governor, or viceroy, Humza Khán, had in the interval gone forth under pretence of bringing .back the chiefs to their allegiance; on his return, however, which took place nearly at the time at which General Sale marched from Khurd-Kábul, the treacherous nature of his proceedings had been discovered, and he was placed by the *Sháh* in confinement; he had been suspected, indeed, before. General Sale remained at Tizín until the 26th October.

It must be remarked that, for some time previous to these overt acts of rebellion, the always strong and ill-repressed personal dislike of the Afgháns towards Europeans had been manifested in a more than usually open manner in and about Kábul. Officers had been insulted and attempts made to assassinate them. Two Europeans had been murdered, as also several camp followers; but these and other signs of the approaching storm had unfortunately been passed over as mere ebullitions of private angry feeling. This incredulity and apathy is the more to be lamented, as it was pretty well known that on the occasion of the *shab-khún*, or first night attack on the 35th Native Infantry at Búta-i-khák, a large portion of our assailants consisted of the armed retainers of the different men of consequence in Kábul itself, large parties of whom had been seen proceeding from the city to the scene of action on the evening of the attack, and afterwards returning. Although these men had to pass either through the heart or round the skirts of our camp at Siyáh Sang, it was not deemed expedient even to question them, far less to detain them.

On the 26th October, General Sale started in the direction of Gandámak,—Captain Macgregor, political agent, having, during the halt at Tizín, half frightened, half cajoled, the refractory Ghalzí chiefs into what the sequel proved to have been a most hollow truce; for the term *treaty* can scarcely be applied to any agreement made with men so proverbially treacherous as the whole race of Afgháns have proved themselves to be from our first knowledge of their existence up to the present moment. Of the difficulties experienced by General Sale during his march to Gandámak, and of the necessity which induced him subsequently to push on to Jallálábád, the public are aware. On the day of his departure from Tizín the 37th Native Infantry, three companies of the Sháh's Sappers, under Captain Walsh, and three guns of the Mountain Train, under Lieutenant Green, retraced their steps towards Kábul, and encamped at Khabar-i-Jabár, to wait as an escort to the sick and convalescent.

The Sappers continued their march back to Kábul unopposed; the rest remained here unmolested until the 1st November, when they broke ground for Khurd-Kábul. Here, in the afternoon of the 2nd, Major Griffiths, who commanded the detachment, received a peremptory order from General Elphinstone to force his way without loss of time to Kábul, where the insurrection had already broken out in all its violence. While striking his camp he was attacked by the mountaineers, who now began to assemble on the neighbouring heights in great numbers, and his march through the pass from Búta-i-khák to Kábul was one continued conflict, nothing saving him from heavy loss but the steadiness and gallantry of his troops, and the excellence of his own dispositions. He arrived in cantonments before daybreak on the morning of the 3rd November.

The two great leaders of the rebellion were Amín-ullah Khán, the chief of Logae, and Abd-ullah Khán, Achakzoe, a chief of great influence, and possessing a large portion of the Pishín valley.

Amín-ullah Khán had, hitherto been considered one of the staunchest friends of the existing Government; and such was the confidence placed in him by the *wazír*, that he had selected him to take charge of Humza Khán, the lately superseded governor of the Ghalzís, as a prisoner to Ghazní. This man now distinguished himself as one of our most inveterate enemies. To illustrate the character of his co-adjutor, Abd-ullah Khán, it will be sufficient to relate the following anecdote. In order to get rid of his elder brother, who stood between him and the inheritance, he caused him to be seized and buried up to the chin in the earth. A rope was then fastened round his neck, and to the end of it was haltered a wild horse: the animal was then driven round in a circle, until the unhappy victim's head was twisted from his shoulders. This same man is also mentioned in terms of just abhorrence by Captain A. Conolly in his *Travels*.

But though the two above-named chiefs took a leading part in the rebellion, there can be little doubt that it had its origin in the deep offence given to the Ghalzís by the ill-advised reduction of their annual stipends—a measure which had apparently been forced upon Sir William Macnaghten by the pecuniary necessities of the king. This they considered, and with some show of justice, as a breach of faith on the part of our Government: at all events, that was surely mistaken economy which raised into hostility men whose determined spirit under a sense of wrong the following anecdote may illustrate. When oppressed by Nádir Sháh, the Ghalzí tribes, rather than succumb to the tyrant's will, took refuge in the mountains amidst the snow, where with their families they fed for months on roots alone: of these they sent a handful to Nádir, with the message, that, so long as such roots could be procured, they would continue to resist his tyranny. Such were many of the men now leagued together by one common feeling of hatred against us.

A passage occurring in a posthumous memorandum by the envoy, now in Lady Macnaghten's possession, requires insertion here.

> The immediate cause of the outbreak in the capital was a seditious letter addressed by Abd-ullah Khán to several chiefs of influence at Kábul, stating that it was the design of the Envoy to seize and send them all to London! The principal rebels met on the previous night, and, relying on the inflammable feelings of the people of Kábul, they pretended that the king had issued an order to put all infidels to death; having previously forged an order from him for our destruction, by the common process of washing out the contents of a genuine paper, with the exception of the seal, and substituting their own wicked inventions.

Such at least is the generally received version of the story, though persons are not wanting who would rashly pronounce the king guilty of the design imputed to him.

But, however that may be, it is certain that the events which I have already narrated ought to have been enough to arouse the authorities from their blind security. It ought, however, to be stated that, alarmed by certain symptoms of disaffection in different parts of the country, and conscious of the inadequacy of the means he then possessed to quell any determined and general insurrection. Sir William had, a few months previously, required the presence of several more regiments: he was, however, induced to cancel this wise precautionary measure. But, even had this additional force arrived, it is next to certain that the loss of British honour, subsequently sustained, could only have been deferred for a period. A fearfully severe lesson was necessary to remove the veil from the eyes of those who, drawing their conclusions from their wishes, *would* consider Afghánistán as a settled country. It is but justice to Sir William Macnaghten to say that such recommendations from him as were incompatible with the retrenching system were not received at headquarters in a way encouraging to him as a public officer.

CHAPTER 4

Popular Outbreak in Kabul

November 2nd, 1841.—At an early hour this morning the startling intelligence was brought from the city that a popular outbreak had taken place; that the shops were all closed; and that a general attack had been made on the houses of all British officers residing in Kábul. About 8 a.m. a hurried note was received, by the envoy in cantonments from Sir Alexander Burnes,[1] stating that the minds of the people had been strongly excited by some mischievous reports, but expressing a hope that he should succeed in quelling the commotion. About 9 a.m., however, a rumour was circulated, which afterwards proved but too well founded, that Sir Alexander had been murdered, and Captain Johnson's treasury plundered. Flames were now seen to issue from that part of the city where they dwelt, and it was too apparent that the endeavour to appease the people by quiet means had failed, and that it would be necessary to have recourse to stronger measures. The report of firearms was incessant, and seemed to extend through the town from end to end.

Sir William Macnaghten now called upon General Elphinstone to act. An order was accordingly sent to Brigadier Shelton, then encamped at Siyáh Sang, about a mile and a half distant from cantonments, to march forthwith to the Bálá Hisár, or royal citadel, where His Majesty Sháh Shujá resided, commanding a large portion of the city, with the following troops, *viz.*, one company of Her Majesty's 44th Foot, a wing of the 54th Regiment Native Infantry under Major Ewart, the 6th Regiment Shah's Infantry under Captain Hopkins, and four Horse Artillery guns under Captain Nicholl; and on arrival there to act according to his own judgment, after consulting with the king.

---

1. The envoy lived in the cantonment, and Sir A. Burnes in the city.

The remainder of the troops encamped at Siyáh Sang were at the same time ordered into cantonments; *viz*.. Her Majesty's 44th Foot under Lieutenant-Colonel Mackerell, two Horse Artillery guns under Lieutenant Waller, and Anderson's Irregular Horse. A messenger was likewise despatched to recall the 37th Native Infantry from Khurd-Kábul without delay.

The troops at this time in cantonments were as follows: *viz.*, 5th Regiment Native Infantry, under Lieutenant-Colonel Oliver; a wing of 54th Native Infantry; five 6-pounder field guns, with a detachment of the Sháh's Artillery, under Lieutenant Warburton; the envoy's body-guard; a troop of Skinner's Horse, and another of local Horse, under Lieutenant Walker; three companies of the Sháh's Sappers, under Captain Walsh; and about twenty men of the Company's Sappers, attached to Captain Paton, assistant quartermaster-general.

Widely spread and formidable as this insurrection proved to be afterwards, it was at first a mere insignificant ebullition of discontent on the part of a few desperate and restless men, which military energy and promptitude ought to have crushed in the bud. Its commencement was an attack by certainly not three hundred men on the dwellings of Sir Alexander Burnes and Captain Johnson, paymaster to the *Sháh's* force; and so little did Sir Alexander himself apprehend serious consequences, that he not only refused, on its first breaking out, to comply with the earnest entreaties of the *wazír* to accompany him to the Bálá Hisár, but actually forbade his guard to fire on the assailants, attempting to check what he supposed to be a mere riot by haranguing the attacking party from the gallery of his house.

The result was fatal to himself; for, in spite of the devoted gallantry of the *sepoys*, who composed his guard and that of the paymaster's office and treasury on the opposite side of the street, who yielded their trust only with their latest breath, the latter were plundered, and his two companions. Lieutenant William Broadfoot, of the Bengal European Regiment, and his brother. Lieutenant Burnes, of the Bombay Army, were massacred, in common with every man, woman, and child found on the premises, by these bloodthirsty miscreants. Lieutenant Broadfoot killed five or six men with his own hand before he was shot down.

No man, surely, in a highly responsible public situation—especially in such a one as that held by the late Sir Alexander Burnes—ought ever to indulge in a state of blind security, or to neglect salutary warnings, however small. It is indisputable that such warnings had been given to him; especially by a respectable Afghán named Táj-Muhammad, on the very previous night, who went in person to Sir A. Burnes to put him on his guard, but retired disgusted by the incredulity with which his assertions were received. It is not for me to comment on his public character. It is the property of the civilized portion of the world; but it is due to another, little known beyond the immediate sphere in which he moved, to say that, had this outbreak been productive of no effects beyond the death of Lieutenant William Broadfoot, it could not be sufficiently deplored: in him was lost to the State not only one of its bravest and most intelligent officers, but a man who for honesty of purpose and soundness of judgment, I may boldly aver, could not be surpassed.

The king, who was in the Bálá Hisár, being somewhat startled by the increasing number of the rioters, although not at the time aware, so far as we can judge, of the assassination of Sir A. Burnes, despatched one of his sons with a number of his immediate Afghán retainers, and that corps of Hindústánís commonly called Campbell's Regiment, with two guns, to restore order: no support, however, was rendered to these by our troops, whose leaders appeared so thunderstruck by the intelligence of the outbreak, as to be incapable of adopting more than the most puerile defensive measures.

Even Sir William Macnaghten seemed, from a note received at this time from him by Captain Trevor, to apprehend little danger, as he therein expressed his perfect confidence as to the speedy and complete success of Campbell's Hindústánís in putting an end to the disturbance. Such, however, was not the case; for the enemy, encouraged by our inaction, increased rapidly in spirit and numbers, and drove back the king's guard with great slaughter, the guns being with difficulty saved.

It must be understood that Captain Trevor lived at this time with his family in a strong *burj*, or tower, situated by the riverside, near the Kazzilbásh quarter, which, on the west, is wholly distinct from the remainder of the city. Within musket shot, on the opposite side of the river, in the direction of the strong and populous village of Dih Afghán, is a fort of some size, then used as a *godown*, or storehouse, by the *Sháh's* commissariat, part of it being occupied by Brigadier Anquetil, commanding the *Sháh's* force. Close to this fort, divided by a narrow watercourse, was the house of Captain Troup, brigade major of the *Sháh's* force, perfectly defensible against musketry. Both Brigadier Anquetil and Captain Troup had gone out on horseback early in the morning towards cantonments, and were unable to return; but the above fort and house contained the usual guard of *sepoys*; and in a garden close at hand, called the *Yábu-Khána*, or lines of the baggage-cattle, was a small detachment of the Sháh's Sappers and Miners, and a party of Captain Perris's *jazailchís*. Captain Trevor's tower was capable of being made good against a much stronger force than the rebels at this present time could have collected, had it been properly garrisoned.

As it was, the *Házirbásh*, or King's Life-guards, were, under Captain Trevor, congregated round their leader, to protect him and his family; which duty, it will be seen, they well performed under very trying circumstances. For what took place in this quarter I beg to refer to a communication made to me at my request by Captain Colin Mackenzie, Assistant Political Agent at Pesháwar, who then occupied the *godown* portion of the fort above mentioned, which will be found hereafter.

I have already stated that Brigadier Shelton was early in the day directed to proceed with part of the Siyáh Sang force to occupy the Bálá Hisár, and, if requisite, to lead his troops against the insurgents. Captain Lawrence, military secretary to the envoy, was at the same time sent forward to prepare the king for that officer's reception. Taking with him four troopers of the Bodyguard, he was galloping along the main road, when, shortly after crossing the river, he was suddenly attacked by an Afghán, who, rushing from behind a wall, made a desperate cut at him with a large two-handed knife. He dexterously avoided the blow by spurring his horse on one side; but, passing onwards, he was fired upon by about fifty men, who, having seen his approach, ran out from the Láhor gate of the city to intercept him. He reached the Bálá Hisár safe, where he found the king apparently in a state of great agitation, he having witnessed the assault from the window of his palace. His Majesty expressed an eager desire to conform to the envoy's wishes in all respects in this emergency.

Captain Lawrence was still conferring with the king, when Lieutenant Sturt, our executive engineer, rushed into the palace, stabbed in three places about the face and neck. He had been sent by Brigadier Shelton to make arrangements for the accommodation of the troops, and had reached the gate of the *Díwán Khána*, or hall of audience, when the attempt at his life was made by someone who had concealed himself there for that purpose, and who immediately effected his escape. The wounds were fortunately not dangerous, and Lieutenant

Sturt was conveyed back to cantonments in the king's own *palanquin*, under a strong escort. Soon after this, Brigadier Shelton's force arrived; but the day was suffered to pass without anything being done demonstrative of British energy and power. The murder of our countrymen, and the spoliation of public and private property, was perpetrated with impunity within a mile of our cantonment, and under the very walls of the Bálá Hisár.

Such an exhibition of weakness on our part taught the enemy their strength—confirmed against us those who, however disposed to join in the rebellion, had hitherto kept aloof from prudential motives, and ultimately encouraged the nation to unite as one man for our destruction.

It was, in fact, the crisis of all others calculated to test the qualities of a military commander, to bring forth genius from its lurking place, or to detect the absence of that rarest of nature's gifts. It would be the height of injustice to a most amiable and gallant officer not to notice the long coarse of painful and wearing illness, which had materially affected the nerves, and probably even the intellect, of General Elphinstone; cruelly incapacitating him, so far as he was personally concerned, from acting in this sudden emergency with the promptitude and vigour necessary for our preservation. Major-General Elphinstone had some time before represented to Lord Auckland the shattered state of his health, stating plainly and honestly that it had unfitted him to continue in command, and requesting permission to resign. Lord Auckland acceded to his wishes; and the General was on the point of returning to India, thence to embark for England, when the rebellion unhappily broke out.

No one, who knew General Elphinstone, could fail to esteem his many excellent qualities both in public and private life. To all under his command, not excepting the youngest subaltern, he was ever accessible, and in the highest degree courteous and considerate: nor did he ever exhibit, either in word or practice, the slightest partiality for officers of his own service over those of the Company. His professional knowledge was extensive; and, before disease had too much impaired his frame for active exertion, he had zealously applied himself to improve and stimulate every branch of the service. He had, indeed, but one unhappy fault as a general—the result, probably, of age and infirmity—and this was a want of confidence in his own judgment, leading him too often to prefer the opinions of others to his own, until, amidst the conflicting views of a multitude of counsellors, he was at a loss which course to take.[2] Hence much of that indecision, procrastination, and want of method which occasionally paralyzed our efforts, gradually disheartened the troops, and ultimately proved a source of calamity to all concerned. I will nevertheless add, that during the siege no one exposed himself more fearlessly or frequently to the enemy's fire than General Elphinstone: but his gallantry was never doubted. Unhappily, Sir William Macnaghten at first made light of the insurrection, and, by his representations as to the general feeling of the people towards us, not only deluded himself, but misled the general in council. The unwelcome truth was soon forced upon us, that in the whole Afghán nation we could not reckon on a single friend.

But though no active measures of aggression were taken, all necessary preparations were made to secure the cantonment against attack. It fell to my own lot to place every available gun in position round the works. Besides the guns already mentioned, we had in the magazine six 9-pounder iron guns, three 24-pounder howitzers, one 12-pounder *ditto,* and three 5½-inch mortars: but the detail of artillerymen fell very short of what was required to man all these efficiently, consisting of only eighty Panjábís belonging to the *Sháh*, under Lieutenant Warburton, very insufficiently instructed, and of doubtful fidelity.

To render our position intelligible, it is necessary to describe the cantonment, or fortified lines so called. It is uncertain to whom the blame justly attaches for the faults which I am about to describe, but the credit of having selected a site for the cantonments, or controlled the execution of its works, is not a distinction now likely to be *claimed* exclusively by *anyone*. But it must always remain a wonder that any Government, or any officer or set of officers, who had either science or experience in the field, should, in a *half*-conquered country, fix their forces (already inadequate to the services to which they might be called) in so extraordinary and injudicious a military position.

Every engineer officer who had been consulted, since the first occupation of Kábul by our troops, had pointed to the Bálá Hisár as the only suitable place for a garrison which was to keep in subjec-

---

2. Lady Sale writes to the same effect:—"We are now in circumstances which require a man of energy to cope with them. Major Thain is said to be a good adviser, but, unfortunately, it is not always in the multitude of counsellors that there is wisdom; and so many proffered their advice and crossed his, that Thain withdrew his, and only now answers such questions as are put to him.".....ced"General Elphinstone vacillates on every point. His own judgement appears to be good, but he is swayed by the last speaker." (*Lady Sale's Afghanistan* by Florentia Sale also published by Leonaur).

tion the city and the surrounding country; but, above all, it was surely the only proper site for the *magazine*, on which the army's efficiency depended. In defiance, however, of rule and precedent, the position eventually fixed upon for our magazine and cantonment was a piece of low swampy ground, commanded on all sides by hills or forts. It consisted of a low rampart and a narrow ditch in the form of a parallelogram, thrown up along the line of the Kohistán road, one thousand yards long and six hundred broad, with round flanking bastions at each corner, every one of which was commanded by some fort or hill. To one end of this work was attached a space nearly half as large again, and surrounded by a simple wall.

This was called the "Mission Compound:" half of it was appropriated for the residence of the envoy, the other half being crowded with buildings, erected without any attempt at regularity, for the accommodation of the officers and assistants of the mission, and the envoy's bodyguard. This large space required in time of siege to be defended, and thus materially weakened the garrison; while its very existence rendered the whole face of the cantonment, to which it was annexed, nugatory for purposes of defence. Besides these disadvantages, the lines were a great deal too extended, so that the ramparts could not be properly manned without harassing the garrison. On the eastern side, about a quarter of a mile off, flowed the Kábul River in a direction parallel with the Kohistán road. Between the river and cantonments, about one hundred and fifty yards from the latter, was a wide canal.

General Elphinstone, on his arrival in April, 1841, perceived at a glance the utter unfitness of the cantonment for purposes of protracted defence, and when a new fort was about to be built for the magazine on the south side, he liberally offered to purchase for the Government, out of his own funds a large portion of the land in the vicinity, with the view of removing some very objectionable inclosures and gardens, which offered shelter to our enemy within two hundred yards of our ramparts; but neither was his offer accepted, nor were his representations on the subject attended with any good result. He lost no time, however, in throwing a bridge over the river, in a direct line between the cantonments and the Siyáh Sang camp, and in rendering the bridge over the canal passable for guns; which judicious measure shortened the distance for artillery and infantry by at least two miles, sparing, too, the necessity which existed previously of moving to and fro by the main road, which was commanded by three or four forts as well as from the city walls.

Moreover, the Kábul River being liable to sudden rises, and almost always unfordable during the rainy season (March and April), it will easily be understood that the erection of this bridge was a work of much importance. But the most unaccountable oversight of all, and that which may be said to have contributed most largely to our subsequent disasters, was that of having *the commissariat stores detached from cantonments*, in an old fort which, in an outbreak, would be almost indefensible. Captain Skinner, the chief commissariat officer, at the time when this arrangement was made, earnestly solicited from the authorities a place *within* the cantonment for his stores, but received for answer that "no such place could be given him, as they were far too busy in erecting barracks for the men, to think of commissariat stores." The envoy himself pressed this point very urgently, but without avail.

At the south-west angle of cantonments was the *bázár* village, surrounded by a low wall, and so crowded with mud huts as to form a perfect maze. Nearly opposite, with only the high road between, was the small fort of Muhammad Sharíf, which perfectly commanded our south-west bastion. Attached to this fort was the *Sháh Bágh*, or king's garden, surrounded by a high wall, and comprising a space of about half a square mile. About two hundred yards higher up the road towards the city, was the commissariat fort, the gate of which stood very nearly opposite the entrance of the *Sháh Bágh*. There were various other forts at different points of our works, which will be mentioned in the course of events.

On the east, at the distance of about a mile, was a range of low hills dividing us from the Siyáh Sang camp; and on the west, about the same distance off, was another somewhat higher range, at the northeast flank of which, by the roadside, was the village of *Bemárú*, commanding a great part of the Mission Compound. In fact, we were so hemmed in on all sides, that, when the rebellion became general, the troops could not move out a dozen paces from either gate, without being exposed to the fire of some neighbouring hostile fort, garrisoned too by marksmen who seldom missed their aim. The country around us was likewise full of impediments to the movements of artillery and cavalry, being in many places flooded, and everywhere closely intersected by deep water-cuts.

I cannot help adding, in conclusion, that almost all the calamities that befell our ill-starred force may be traced more or less to the defects of our position; and that our cantonment at Kábul, whether we look to its situation or construction, must ever be spoken of as discreditable to the military skill and judgment of those responsible for the faults above described.

[The author's description of the faulty and insecure construction and position of the cantonment was fully verified by the present Major-General Sir Frederic Abbot, when serving as Chief Engineer with General Pollock's army, and after a careful survey of the spot in September, 1842. He thus reports upon it:—

> One glance of the accompanying plan is sufficient to show the extreme faultiness of the position. The cantonment appears to have been purposely surrounded with difficulties; indeed, a stranger might suppose that many of the mud forts, approaching so closely to the walls, must have been built for the express purpose of besieging it. With this full knowledge of the difficulties of their position, it is a matter of surprise that our military authorities did not throw themselves into the Bálá Hisár, a movement that might have been effected with little loss at any period of the siege, by holding the heights of Siyáh Sang whilst passing the munitions from place to place; and even had carriage been wanting for the commissariat stores, our troops, holding the town of Kábul at their mercy, could have secured provisions to any amount.

No higher corroborative testimony than the above could be wished or expected. It may, however, now be stated, without hesitation, that what have been deemed "military" errors had a "political" origin, and were the natural result of regarding Afghánistán as a settled country, and the British force as a mere police establishment. When employed against an open enemy in the field, military commanders know what is expected of them, and arrange their plans accordingly, but when their every action, involving expenditure, is subject to civil control, so that not even the simplest field-work can be undertaken without a reference to that controlling power, which, in its turn, must perhaps refer the matter to a thrifty Government some two thousand miles distant, and when they are authoritatively assured that all around them breathes peace and lasting quiet, even the wisest generals may be tempted by a love of ease, or by a distaste for petty interference, to become callous in allowing that which they secretly disapprove; and, being dependent on the civil authorities for information, may be imperceptibly ensnared into a state of fatal security.

And thus it was at Kábul, and to that fruitful source of mischief may be traced those faulty military arrangements whose disastrous tendency was but too truly foreseen and honestly pointed out by Brigadier Roberts and others, while yet there was time to remedy the evil.

When Sir Willoughby Cotton, on his return march from Kábul, met his successor, General Elphinstone, in the Panjáb, he congratulated the latter on having obtained so pleasant a post, where all was in a state of peaceful repose, little dreaming that the paradise of ease and quiet he thus confidently bequeathed was like that of a mine of gunpowder to which the lighted slow-match had already been applied.]

CHAPTER 5

Engagements With Afghan Horse and Foot

November 3rd,—At 3 a.m. the alarm was sounded at the eastern gate of cantonments, in consequence of a brisk file-filing in the direction of Siyáh Sang, which turned out to proceed from the 37th Regiment Native Infantry on its return from Khurd-Kábul, having been closely followed up the whole way by a body of about three thousand Ghalzís. The regiment managed, nevertheless, to save all its baggage excepting a few tents, which were left on the ground for want of carriage, and to bring in all the wounded safe.

A more orderly march was never made under such trying circumstances, and it reflects the highest credit on Major Griffiths and all concerned. This regiment was a valuable acquisition to our garrison, being deservedly esteemed one of the best in the service. Three guns of the Mountain Train, under Lieutenant Green, accompanied them, and were of the greatest use in defending the rear on the line of march. In consequence of their arrival, a reinforcement was sent into the Bálá Hisár, consisting of the left wing 54th Native Infantry, with Lieutenant Green's guns, one iron 9-pounder, one 24-pounder howitzer, two 5½-inch mortars, and a supply of magazine stores. They all reached it in safety, though a few shots were fired at the rearguard from some orchards near the city. Brigadier Shelton was ordered to maintain a sharp fire upon the city from the howitzers and guns, and to endeavour to fire the houses by means of shells and carcasses from the two mortars; should he also find it practicable to send a force into the city, he was to do so.

Early in the afternoon a detachment under Major Swayne, consisting of two companies 5th Native Infantry, one of Her Majesty's 44th, and two Horse Artillery guns under Lieutenant Waller, proceeded out of the western gate towards the city, to effect, if possible, a junction at the Láhor gate with a part of Brigadier Shelton's force from the Bálá Hisár. They drove back and defeated a party of the enemy who occupied the road near the *Sháh Bágh*, but had to encounter a sharp fire from the Kohistán gate of the city, and from the walls of various enclosures, behind which a number of marksmen had concealed themselves, as also from the fort of Mahmúd Khán commanding the road along which they had to pass.

Lieutenant Waller and several *sepoys* were wounded. Major Swayne, observing the whole line of road towards the Láhor gate strongly occupied by some Afghán horse and *jazailchís*, and fearing that he would be unable to effect the object in view with so small a force unsupported by cavalry, retired into cantonments. Shortly after this, a large body of the rebels having issued from the fort of Mahmud Khan, nine hundred yards south-east of cantonments, extended themselves in a line along the bank of the river, displaying a flag; an iron 9-pounder was brought to bear on them from our south-east bastion, and a round or two of shrapnel caused them to seek shelter behind some neighbouring banks, whence, after some desultory firing on both sides, they retired.

Whatever hopes may have been entertained, up to this period, of a speedy termination to the insurrection, they began now to wax fainter every hour, and an order was despatched to the officer commanding at Kandahár to lose no time in sending to our assistance the 16th and 43rd Regiments Native Infantry (which were under orders for India), together with a troop of Horse Artillery, and half a regiment of Cavalry; an order was likewise sent off to recall General Sale with his brigade from Gandámak. Captain John Conolly, political assistant to the envoy, went into the Bálá Hisár early this morning, to remain with the king, and to render every assistance in his power to Brigadier Shelton.

On this day Lieutenant Richard Maule, commanding the Kohistání Regiment, which on its return from Zurmat had been stationed at Kaedara in Kohistán, about twenty miles north-west of Kábul, with the object of keeping down disaffection in that quarter, being deserted by his men, was, together with local Lieutenant Wheeler, his adjutant, barbarously murdered by a band of rebels. They defended themselves resolutely for several minutes, but at length fell under the fire of some *jazails*. Lieutenant Maule had been previously informed of his danger by a friendly native, but chose rather to run the risk of being sacrificed than desert the post assigned him. Thus fell a noble-hearted soldier and a devout Christian.

November 4th.—The enemy having taken strong possession of the *Sháh Bágh*, or King's Garden, and thrown a garrison into the fort of Muhammad Sharíf, nearly opposite the *bázár*, effectually prevented any communication between the cantonment and commissariat fort, the gate of which latter was commanded by the gate of the *Sháh Bágh* on the other side of the road.

Ensign Warren, of the 5th Native Infantry, at this time occupied the commissariat fort with one hundred men, and having reported that he was very hard pressed by the enemy, and in danger of being completely cut off, the general, either forgetful or unaware at the moment of the important fact that upon the possession of this fort we were entirely dependent for provisions, and anxious only to save the lives of men whom he believed to be in imminent perils hastily gave directions that a party under the command of Captain Swayne, of Her Majesty's 44th Regiment, should proceed immediately to bring off Ensign Warren and his garrison to cantonments, abandoning the fort to the enemy. A few minutes previously an attempt to relieve him had been made by Ensign Gordon, with a company of the 37th Native Infantry and eleven camels laden with ammunition; but the party were driven back, and Ensign Gordon killed.

Captain Swayne now accordingly proceeded towards the spot with two companies of Her Majesty's 44th; scarcely had they issued from cantonments ere a sharp and destructive fire was poured upon them from Muhammad Sharíf's fort, which, as they proceeded, was taken up by the marksmen in the *Sháh Bágh*, under whose deadly aim both officers and men suffered severely; Captains Swayne and Robinson of the 44th being killed, and Lieutenants Hallahan, Evans, and Fortye wounded, in this disastrous business. It now seemed, to the officer on whom the command had devolved, impracticable to bring off Ensign Warren's party, without risking the annihilation of his own, which had already sustained so rapid and severe a loss in officers; he therefore returned forthwith to cantonments. In the course of the evening, another attempt was made by a party of the 5th Light Cavalry; but they encountered so severe a fire from the neighbouring enclosures as obliged them to return without effecting their desired object, with the loss of eight troopers killed and fourteen badly wounded.

Captain Boyd, the assistant commissary-general, having meanwhile been made acquainted with the general's intention to give up the fort, hastened to lay before him the disastrous consequences that would ensue from so doing. He stated that the place contained, besides large supplies of wheat and *átá*, all his stores of rum, medicine, clothing, &c., the value of which might be estimated at four *lacs* of *rúpís*: that to abandon such valuable property would not only expose the force to the immediate want of the necessaries of life, but would infallibly inspire the enemy with tenfold courage. He added that we had not above two days' supply of provisions in cantonments, and that neither himself nor Captain Johnson, of the *Shah's* commissariat, had any prospect of procuring them elsewhere under existing circumstances.

In consequence of this strong representation on the part of Captain Boyd, the general sent immediate orders to Ensign Warren to hold out the fort to the last extremity. (Ensign Warren, it must be remarked, denied having received this note.) Early in the night a letter was received from him to the effect that he believed the enemy were busily engaged in mining one of the towers, and that such was the alarm among the *sepoys* that several of them had actually made their escape over the wall to cantonments; that the enemy were making preparations to burn down the gate; and that, considering the temper of his men, he did not expect to be able to hold out many hours longer, unless reinforced without delay. In reply to this he was informed that he would be reinforced by 2 a.m.

At about 9 o'clock p.m. there was an assembly of staff and other officers at the general's house, when the envoy came in and expressed his serious conviction that, unless Muhammad Sharíf's fort were taken that very night, we should lose the commissariat fort, or at all events be unable to bring out of it provisions for the troops. The disaster of the morning rendered the general extremely unwilling to expose his officers and men to any similar peril; but, on the other hand, it was urged that the darkness of the night would nullify the enemy's fire, who would also most likely be taken unawares, as it was not the custom of the Afgháns to maintain a very strict watch at night. A man in Captain Johnson's employ was accordingly sent oat to reconnoitre the place; he returned in a few minutes with the intelligence that about twenty men were seated outside the fort near the gate, smoking and talking; and from what he overheard of their conversation, he judged the garrison to be very small, and unable to resist a sudden onset.

The debate was now resumed, but another hour passed and the

general could not make up his mind. A second spy was despatched, whose report tended to corroborate what the first had said. I was then sent to Lieutenant Sturt, the engineer, who was nearly recovered from his wounds, for his opinion. He at first expressed himself in favour of an immediate attack, but, on hearing that some of the enemy were on the watch at the gate, he judged it prudent to defer the assault till an early hour in the morning: this decided the general, though not before several hours had slipped away in fruitless discussion.

Orders were at last given for a detachment to be in readiness at 4 a.m. at the Kohistán gate; and Captain Bellew, deputy assistant quartermaster-general, volunteered to blow open the gate; another party of Her Majesty's 44th were at the same time to issue by a cut in the south face of the rampart, and march simultaneously towards the commissariat fort, to reinforce the garrison. Morning had, however, well dawned ere the men could be got under arms; and they were on the point of marching off, when it was reported that Ensign Warren had just arrived in cantonments with his garrison, having evacuated the fort.

It seems that the enemy had actually set fire to the gate; and Ensign Warren, seeing no prospect of a reinforcement, and expecting the enemy every moment to rush in, led out his men by a hole which he had prepared in the wall. Being called upon in a public letter from the assistant adjutant-general to state his reasons for abandoning his post, he replied that he was ready to do so before a court of inquiry, which he requested might be assembled to investigate his conduct; it was not, however, deemed expedient to comply with his request.

It is beyond a doubt that our feeble and ineffectual defence of this fort, and the valuable booty it yielded, was the first *fatal* blow to our supremacy at Kábul, and at once determined those chiefs—and more particularly the Kazzilbáshes—who had hitherto remained neutral, to join in the general combination to drive us from the country.

Captain Trevor, having held out his house against the rebels until all hope of relief was at an end, was safely escorted into cantonments this morning, with his wife and seven children, by his *Házirbásh* horsemen, who behaved faithfully, but now, out of regard for their families, dispersed to their houses. Captain Mackenzie, likewise, after defending his fort until his ammunition was expended, fought his way into cantonments late last night, having received a slight wound on the road. His men had behaved with the utmost bravery, and made several successful sallies. (See his own account.)

November 5th.—It no sooner became generally known that the commissariat fort, upon which we were dependent for supplies, had been abandoned, than one universal feeling of indignation pervaded the garrison; nor can I describe the impatience of the troops, but especially the native portion, to be led out for its recapture—a feeling that was by no means diminished by their seeing the Afgháns crossing and re-crossing the road between the commissariat fort and the gate of the *Sháh Bágh*, laden with the provisions upon which had depended our ability to make a protracted defence. Observing this disposition among the troops, and feeling the importance of checking the triumph of the enemy in its infancy, I strenuously urged the general to send out a party to capture Muhammad Sharíf's fort by blowing open the gate, and volunteered myself to keep the road clear from any sudden advance of cavalry, with two Horse Artillery guns, under cover of whose fire the storming party could advance along the road, protected from the fire of the fort by a low wall, which lined the road the whole way.

The general agreed; a storming party from the 5th Native Infantry was ordered; the powder bags were got ready; and at about 12 midday we issued from the western gate: the guns led the way, and were brought into action under the partial cover of some trees, within one hundred yards of the fort. For the space of twenty minutes the artillery continued to work the guns under an excessively sharp fire from the walls of the fort; but the storming party, probably in uncertainty as to an entrance having been secured, had in the meantime remained stationary under cover of the wall by the road side. The general, who was watching proceedings from the gateway, observing that the gun ammunition was running short, and that the troops had from some unknown cause failed to take advantage of the best opportunity for advancing, recalled us into cantonments: thus the enemy enjoyed their triumph undiminished.

November 6th.—It was now determined to take the fort of Muhammad Sharíf by regular breach and assault. At an early hour, three iron 9-pounder guns were brought to bear upon its north-east bastion, and two howitzers upon the contiguous curtain. I took charge of the former, and Lieutenant Warburton of the latter. In the space of about two hours a practicable breach was effected, during which time a hot fire was poured upon the artillerymen from the enemy's sharpshooters, stationed in a couple of high towers which completely commanded the battery, whereby, as the embrasures crumbled away from the constant concussion, it became at length a difficult task to work the guns. A storming party, composed of three companies, *viz.* one company of Her Majesty's 44th under Ensign Raban, one company 5th Native Infantry under Lieutenant Deas, one company 37th under Lieutenant Steer, the whole commanded by Major Griffiths, speedily carried the place. Poor Raban was shot through the hearty when conspicuously waving a flag on the summit of the breach.

As this fort adjoined the *Sháh Bágh*, it was deemed advisable to dislodge the enemy from the latter, if possible. Learning that there was a large opening in the wall in the north side of the garden, and being left to exercise my own discretion, I took a 6-pounder gun thither, and fired several rounds of grape and shrapnel upon parties of the enemy, assembled within under the trees, which speedily drove them out; and had a detachment of infantry been ordered to take advantage of the opportunity thus afforded to throw themselves into the building at the principal entrance by the road side, the place might have been easily carried permanently, and immediate repossession could have been then taken of the commissariat fort opposite, which had not yet been emptied of half its contents.

While this was going on, a reconnoitring party under Major Thain, *aide-de-camp*, consisting of one Horse Artillery gun, one troop 5th Cavalry, and two companies of infantry, scoured the plain to the west of cantonments; and having driven the enemy from several enclosures, were returning homeward, when large numbers of Afghán horse and foot were observed to proceed from the direction of the city towards the south-west extremity of a hill, which runs in a diagonal direction from north-east to south-west across the plain, to the west of cantonments. A *risálah* of Anderson's Horse had been stationed on the summit of this hill all the morning as a picket, whence they had just been recalled, when a large body of the enemy's horse reached the base, and proceeded to crown the summit. Major Thain's party, observing this, came to a halt; and a few minutes afterwards a reinforcement opportunely arrived, consisting of one *risálah* of Irregular Horse under Captain Anderson, one troop of *ditto* under Lieutenant Walker, and two troops 5th Cavalry under Captains Collyer and Bott.

I now considered it my duty to join the Horse Artillery gun, which had no officer with it, and I accordingly left the 6-pounder gun under the protection of Captain Mackenzie, who, with a few of his *jazailchís*, had now joined me, having been engaged in skirmishing across the plain towards the west end of the *Sháh Bágh*, where, finding an opening, he had crept in with his men, and cleared that part of the garden, but, not being supported, had been obliged to retire with a loss of fifteen killed out of ninety-five.

I now advanced with the Horse Artillery gun, supported by a troop of the 5th Cavalry, to the foot of the hill, and opened fire upon the enemy, while the rest of the cavalry, headed by Anderson's Horse, rode briskly up the slope to force them off. The officers gallantly headed their men, and encountered about an equal number of the enemy, who advanced to meet them, A hand-to-hand encounter now took place, which ended in the Afghán Horse retreating to the plain, leaving the hill in our possession. In this affair Captain Anderson personally engaged, and slew the brother-in-law of Abd-ullah Khán. Meanwhile the enemy began to muster strong on the plain to the west of the *Sháh Bágh*, whence they appeared to be gradually extending themselves towards the cantonments, as if to intercept our return; it was therefore deemed prudent to recall the cavalry from the height, and show front in the plain, where they could act with more effect.

A reinforcement of two companies of infantry and one Horse Artillery gun was sent out, and the whole force was drawn up in order of battle, anticipating an attack, with one gun on either flank. In this position a distant fire was kept up by the enemy's *jazailchís*, which was answered principally by discharges of shrapnel and round shot from the guns; the heights, too, were again crowned by the Afghán horse, but no disposition was manifested by them to encounter us in open fight, and, as the night gradually closed in, they slowly retired to the city. On this occasion about one hundred of the enemy fell on the hill, while the loss on our side was eight troopers killed and fourteen wounded.

It will be remembered that I left a 6-pounder gun at the opening in the wall of the *Sháh Bágh*. After my departure, large numbers of the enemy's infantry had filled the west end of the *Sháh Bágh*, and, stealing up among the trees, and close to the high wall, towards the gun, kept up so hot and precise a fire as to render its removal absolutely necessary. Captain Mackenzie had been joined by a party of Her Majesty's 44th; with whom, and with a few of his own men, he endeavoured to cover the operation, which was extremely difficult, it being necessary to drag the gun by hand over bad ground. Several of the *Sháh's* gunners were killed, and many of the covering party knocked over, the gun being barely saved. I may here add, that from this time forward the *jazailchís,* under the able direction of Captain Mackenzie, who volunteered to lead them, were forward to distinguish themselves on all occasions, and continued to the very last a most useful part of our force.

November 8th,—An attempt was made by the enemy to mine one of the towers of the fort we captured on the 6th, which could not have happened had we taken possession of the gate of the *Sháh Bágh* at the same time. Our chief cause of anxiety now was the empty state of our granary. Even with high bribes and liberal payment, the Envoy could only procure a scanty supply, insufficient for daily consumption, from the village of Bemárú, about half a mile down the Kohistán road, to the north. The object of the enemy undoubtedly was to starve us out; to effect which, the chiefs exerted their whole influence to prevent our being supplied from any of the neighbouring forts. Their game was a sure one; and so long as they held firmly together, it could not fail to be sooner or later successful.

During the short interval of quiet which ensued after our capture of the fort, the rebels managed to rig out a couple of guns which they procured from the work-yard of Lieutenant Warburton (in charge of the *Sháh's* guns), situated, unfortunately, in the city. These they placed in a position near Mahmud Khán's fort, opposite the south-east bastion of cantonments. All this time a cannonade was daily kept up on the town by Captain Nicholl of the Horse Artillery in the Bálá Hisár; but, though considerable damage was thereby done, and many of the enemy killed, it required a much more powerful battery than he possessed to ruin a place of such extent.

On the morning of the 2nd, when the rebellion commenced, the two guns, which were sent with Campbell's Hindústánís into the city, had been left outside the gate of the Bálá Hisár in the confusion and hurry of retreat, where they had ever since remained. So jealous a watch was kept over these by the enemy from the houses of the Sháh Bázár, that it was found impossible to get them back into the fort; and it was necessary for our troops to maintain an equally strict watch to prevent their being removed by the enemy, who made several desperate efforts to obtain them. An attempt of this kind took place today, when the rebels were driven back into the city with considerable loss.

November 9th.—The general's weak state of health rendering the presence of a coadjutor absolutely necessary, to relieve him from the command of the garrison. Brigadier Shelton, the second in command, was, at the earnest request of the Envoy, summoned in from the Bálá Hisár, in the hope that, by heartily co-operating with the envoy and general, he would strengthen their hands and rouse the sinking confidence of the troops. He entered cantonments this morning, bringing with him one Horse Artillery gun, one Mountain Train *ditto*, one company of Her Majesty's 44th, the Shah's 6th Infantry, and a small supply of *átá*.

[The following memorandum of Brigadier Shelton's services, extracted from the *Naval and Military Gazette* of the following year, bears strong evidence of his previous experience in war, and gallantry in the field:—

> General Shelton entered the Army in November, 1805. In 1808, he was present at the battles of Roleiça and Vimiera. In 1809, in the retreat to Corunna and in the expedition to Walcheren. In 1810, at the Battle of Busaco. In 1811-12, at the sieges of Badajos. In 1812, at the Battle of Salamanca, the taking of Madrid, and in the retreat from Burgos. In 1813, at the Battle of Vittoria, and at the siege of San Sebastian, where he lost his right arm. In 1814, in operations before Bayonne. In Canada (Lake Ontario). In 1824, employed in the operations and capture of Arracan. In 1841, he marched with a brigade to Afghánistán, and in February was despatched to the Nazian Valley, and undertook military operations there, after which he marched to Kábul. Except three months, leave on account of his wound, he served during the whole of the Peninsular war; and, as he was a Captain in 1812, he had more than *Subaltern* experience in that war! At the end of the war he went to Sandhurst, and obtained the usual certificate. He has been twenty years in India.]

CHAPTER 6

Further Engagements With the Enemy

November 10th.—Henceforward Brigadier Shelton bore a conspicuous part in the drama upon the issue of which so much depended. He had, however, from the very first, seemed to despair of the force being able to hold out the winter at Kábul, and strenuously advocated an immediate retreat to Jallálábád.

Sir William Macnaghten and his suite were altogether opposed to Brigadier Shelton in this matter, it being in his (the envoy's) estimation a duty we owed the Government to retain our post, at whatsoever risk. This difference of opinion, on a question of such vital importance, was attended with unhappy results, inasmuch as it deprived the general, in his hour of need, of the strength which unanimity imparts, and produced an uncommunicative and disheartening reserve in an emergency which demanded the freest interchange of counsel and ideas.

[Acting on the principle "*audi alteram partem*," I here insert the arguments used by one of Brigadier Shelton's ablest apologists:—

> We are told that he from the first advocated an immediate retreat to Jallálábád, and that Sir William Macnaghten and his suite were altogether opposed to Brigadier Shelton in this matter. We find General Shelton never altering this opinion, but at last Lieutenant Sturt, upon 20th December, and Major Pottinger, 26th December, advocating it, the chief military authorities having also adopted it. The Envoy had, however, opposed it— and Lieutenant Eyre condemns it. But the Duke of Wellington is reported to have said in the House of Lords:

'*After the first few days*, particularly after the negotiations at Kábul had commenced, it became hopeless for him (General Elphinstone) to maintain his position: it became evident that sooner or later a movement, which might possibly fail, to march the troops from Kábul, must be undertaken, and that an attempt must be made to move them to a place of safety.'

Hear, also, what that gallant soldier, Sir Robert Sale, says, who had a few days previously left Kábul, and evidently knew that such a move ought to have been made on Jallálábád, for in page 17 of the Blue. Book, he writes from that place, so early as the 15th November:

'*Under these circumstances, a regard for the honour and interest of our Government compels me to adhere to my plan, already formed, of putting this place into a state of defence, and holding it, if possible, until the Kábul force falls back upon me.*'

The natural conclusion of the above is, that had General Shelton been in command, he would, regardless of the opinion of the envoy, have retreated at an early period on Jallálábád, and there is every reason to believe that he would have saved the greater part of the force.

The facts appear to be these—Brigadier Shelton was ordered into the cantonment by his superior officer, Major-General Elphinstone, when the difficulties, dangers, and deranged discipline of the force under that officer's command appear to have already attained a power beyond the energies of his failing health to contend with; but the Major-General did not resign his command nor quit the cantonment; and, although the Brigadier's advice may have been asked, and even taken, yet no responsibility could have justly attached to that advice, even though it were bad and unsound, so long as his superior officer continued in the command.

The great fault attending the fearful crisis appears to have been (what in moments of hazard and danger is almost always the case) too many advisers; and it is a surprise to me that the step was not taken of removing all the non-effectives to the Bálá Hisár. At the head of these was Sir W. Macnaghten. Why was His Excellency in the military cantonment instead of being at the *Darbár* of Sháh Shujá-ul-Mulk, at which he was the representative of Her Majesty? Had the sick general, the envoy, and all the women and children, been removed, as so many embarrassments to a place already exposed to the constant attacks of a vigorous enemy, discipline might have been restored to the British forces; but was the Brigadier in a situation to adopt this energetic step? or, had he suggested it, is there any reason to believe that it would have been obeyed?

Some say the Brigadier ought to have assumed the command. If the envoy thought so, he might have interfered. The assuming command must be at the risk of an officer's commission, if he fails! The defect in the general, Lieutenant Eyre points out; before Brigadier Shelton was consulted all our supplies were gone—the enemy were on the 9th November too strong to be attacked and the cantonment defended at the same time. Let people recollect *Buenos Ayres*, in 1807, and a crowded city; Kábul having, also, flat-roofed houses—fancy three thousand men even (Whitelocke had a much larger force), entering a city, with twenty thousand to thirty thousand men, armed to the teeth—guns could not fire on those on the tops of houses—the streets might be clear, but even at Ghazní it was so—but the house-tops were crowded with men—*we* took *them* by surprise.

We had enriched the people, and the chiefs, become rich, could pay numerous followers; the feeling against us was too strong to be changed after eight days of rebellion; and soldiers become dispirited when they find the prospect of starvation, and no means of averting their destruction. The delay of Sir John Moore's retreat, and through a dreadful winter,—because political expediency advised a march on Madrid,—in the horrors of which General Shelton shared, and the terrible retreat from Moscow, must have been in his recollection; and he therefore wished to retreat before the snow should fall, and before the last day's provisions were served out.]

But I am digressing.—About 9 a.m. on the 10th the enemy crowned the heights to the west in great force, and almost simultaneously a large body of horse and foot, supposed to be Ghalzís, who had just arrived, made their appearance on the Siyáh Sang hills to the east, and, after firing a *feu-de-joie,* set up a loud shout, which was answered in a similar way by those on the opposite side of us. This was supposed to be a preconcerted signal for a joint attack on the cantonments. No movement was, however, made on the western side to molest us, but on the eastern quarter parties of the enemy, moving down into the plain, took possession of all the forts in that direction. One of these, called the Riká-báshí Fort, was situated directly opposite the Mission Compound, at the north-east angle of cantonments, within musket-shot of our works, into which the enemy soon began to pour a very annoying fire; a party of sharp-shooters at the same time, concealing themselves among the ruins of a house immediately opposite the north-east bastion, took deadly aim at the European artillerymen who were working the guns, one poor fellow being shot through the temple in the act of sponging. From two howitzers and a 5½-inch mortar, a discharge of shells into the fort was kept up for two hours.

At this time not above two days' supply of provisions remained in garrison, and it was very clear that, unless the enemy were quickly driven out from their new possession, we should soon be completely hemmed in on all sides. At the Envoy's urgent desire, he taking the entire responsibility on himself, the general ordered a force to hold themselves in readiness, under Brigadier Shelton, to storm the Riká-báshí Fort. About 12 a.m. the following troops assembled at the eastern gate:—two Horse Artillery guns, one Mountain Train gun. Walker's Horse, Her Majesty's 44th Foot under Colonel Mackerell, 37th Native Infantry under Major Griffiths, 6th Regiment of *Sháh's* force under Captain Hopkins. The whole issued from cantonments, a storming party consisting of two companies from each regiment taking the lead, preceded by Captain Bellew, who hurried forward to blow open the gate.

Missing the gate, however, he blew open a wicket of such small dimensions as to render it impossible for more than two or three men to enter abreast, and these in a stooping posture. This, it will be seen, was one cause of discomfiture in the first instance; for the hearts of the men failed them when they saw their foremost comrades struck down, endeavouring to force an entrance under such disadvantageous circumstances, without being able to help them. The signal, however, was given for the storming party, headed by Colonel Mackerell. On nearing the wicket, the detachment encountered an excessively sharp fire from the walls, and the small passage, through which they endeavoured to rush in, merely served to expose the bravest to almost certain death from the hot fire of the defenders. Colonel Mackerell, however, and Lieutenant Bird of Shah's 6th Infantry, accompanied by a handful of Europeans and a few *sepoys*, forced their way in; Captain Westmacott of the 37th being shot down outside, and Captain M'Crae sabred in the entrance.

The garrison, supposing that these few gallant men were backed by the whole attacking party, fled in consternation out of the gate, which was on the opposite side of the fort, and which ought to have been the point assailed. Unfortunately, at this instant a number of the Afghán cavalry charged suddenly round the comer of the fort next the wicket: the cry of "Cavalry!" was raised; a bugler sounded the retreat, and it became for the time a scene of *sauve qui peut.* The officers, knowing the fearful predicament of their commander, exhorted their men to charge forward; but a private of the 44th, named Steward, who was afterwards promoted for his gallantry, alone obeyed the call.

At this critical juncture Brigadier Shelton's acknowledged courage redeemed the day; for, exposing his own person to a hot fire, he stood firm amidst the crowd of fugitives, and by his exhortations and example at last rallied them; advancing again to the attack, again our men faltered, notwithstanding that the fire of the great guns from the cantonments, and that of Captain Mackenzie's *jazailchís* from the north-east angle of the Mission Compound, together with a demonstration on the part of our cavalry, had greatly abated the ardour of the Afghán horse. A third time did the Brigadier bring on his men to the assault, which now proved successful. We became masters of the fort.[1]

But what, in the meantime, had been passing inside the fort, where, it will be remembered, several of our brave brethren had been shut up, as it were, in the lion's den?

On the first retreat of our men. Lieutenant Bird, with Colonel Mackerell and several Europeans, had hastily shut the gate by which the garrison had for the most part evacuated the place, securing the

---

1. The following remarks of the *Naval and Military Gazette* are worthy of consideration:—"We would here observe, with respect to the panic amongst the troops at the Riká-báshí Fort, although not immediately connected with our subject, that, whilst it is the especial office of discipline to correct the tendency to such disasters, instances of the sort may be adduced, even in the ranks of the bravest of the brave. Napier tells us, 'that no age, no nation, ever sent forth braver troops to battle than those who stormed Badajos.' Yet, the same eminent writer relates, that, during the raging of that storm, 'some of the soldiers, perceiving a lighted match on the ground, cried out, "A mine!" At that word, such is the power of imagination, those troops whom neither the strong barrier, nor deep ditch, nor the high walls, nor the deadly fire of the enemy, could stop, staggered back, appalled by a chimera of their own raising; and, in this disorder, a French reserve drove on them with a firm and rapid charge, and pitching some men over the walls, and killing others outright again cleared the ramparts, even to the St. Vincent.'"

chain with a bayonet; the repulse outside, however, encouraged the enemy to return in great numbers, and, it being impossible to remain near the gate on account of the hot fire poured in through the crevices, our few heroes speedily had the mortification to see their foes not only re-entering the wicket, but, having drawn the bayonet, rush in with loud shouts through the now reopened gate. Poor Mackerell, having fallen, was literally hacked to pieces, although still alive at the termination of the contest. Lieutenant Bird, with two *sepoys*, retreated into a stable, the door of which they closed; all the rest of the men, endeavouring to escape through the wicket, were met and slaughtered.

Bird's place of concealment at first, in the confusion, escaped the observation of the temporarily triumphant Afgháns; at last it was discovered, and an attack commenced at the door. This, being barricaded with logs of wood, and whatever else the tenants of the stable could find, resisted their efforts, while Bird and his now solitary companion, a *sepoy* of the 37th Native Infantry (the other having been struck down), maintained as hot afire as they could, each shot taking deadly effect from the proximity of the party engaged. The fall of their companions deterred the mass of the assailants from a simultaneous rush, which must have succeeded; and thus that truly chivalrous young officer stood at bay with his equally brave comrade for upwards of a quarter of an hour, when, having only five cartridges left, in spite of having rifled the pouch of the dead man, they were rescued as related above. Our troops literally found the pair "grim and lonely there," upwards of thirty of the enemy having fallen by their unassisted prowess.[2]

Our loss on this occasion was not less than two hundred killed and wounded. Four neighbouring forts were immediately evacuated by the enemy, and occupied by our troops: they were found to contain about one thousand four hundred *maunds* of grain; in removing which no time was lost, but as it was not found practicable to bring off more than half before nightfall Captain Boyd, the assistant commissary-general, requested Brigadier Shelton that a guard might be thrown into a small fort, where it must be left for the night; this was, however, refused, and on the following morning, as might have been expected, the grain was all gone: permanent possession was, however, taken of the Riká-báshí and Zulfikár Forts, the towers of the remainder being blown up on the following day.

---

2. Lieutenant Bird's promising career was tragically closed on the subsequent retreat, when almost within sight of Jallálábád.

Numbers of Ghalzí horse and foot still maintaining their position on the Siyáh Sang heights. Brigadier Shelton moved his force towards that quarter. On reaching the base of the hill, fire was opened from, the two Horse Artillery guns, which, with the firm front presented by our troops, caused the enemy shortly to retire towards the city, and ere we turned homeward not a man remained in sight.

November 13th.—The enemy appeared in great force on the western heights, where, having posted two guns, they fired into cantonments with considerable precision. At the earnest entreaty of the envoy, it was determined that a party, under Brigadier Shelton, should sally forth to attack them, and, if possible, capture their guns.

[Lady Sale observes:—
It was with great difficulty the envoy persuaded the general and Brigadier to consent to a force going out; and it was late before the troops were ready.". . . . "The general again (as in the late attack on the Riká-báshí Fort) asked the envoy if he would take the responsibility of sending out the troops on himself; and, on his conceding, the force was sent. The envoy had also much angry discussion on this point with Brigadier Shelton.
But all these delays of conference lost much time, and it was between 4 and 5 p.m. before operations commenced.]

The force ordered for this service was not ready until 3 p.m. It consisted of the following troops:—two squadrons 5th Light Cavalry, under Colonel Chambers; one squadron Shah's 2nd Irregular Horse, under Lieutenant Le Geyt; one troop of Skinner's Horse, under Lieutenant Walker; the Body Guard; six companies Her Majesty's 44th, under Major Scott; six companies 37th, under Major Swayne; four companies Shah's 6th Infantry, under Captain Hopkins; and one Horse Artillery gun and one Mountain Train *do.* under myself, escorted by a company of 6th Shah's under Captain Marshall. After quitting cantonments, the troops took the direction of a gorge between the two hills bounding the plain, distant about a mile (the enemy's horse crowning that to the left), and advanced in separate columns at so brisk a pace, that it seemed a race which should arrive first at the scene of action.

The infantry had actually reached the foot of the hill, and were on the point of ascending to the charge, ere the Horse Artillery gun, which had been detained in the rear by sticking fast in a canal, could be got ready for action; nor had more than one round of grape been fired, ere the advance, led on by the gallant Major Thain, had closed upon the foe, who resolutely stood their ground on the summit of the ridge, and unflinchingly received the discharge of our musketry, which, strange to say, even at the short range of ten or twelve yards, seemed to do little execution! From this cause the enemy, growing bolder every moment, advanced close up to the bayonets of our infantry, upon whom they pressed so perseveringly, as to succeed in driving them backwards to the foot of the hill, wounding Major Thain on the left shoulder and sabring several of the men. Several rounds of grape and shrapnel were now poured in, and threw them into some confusion, whereupon a timely charge of our cavalry, Anderson's Horse taking the lead, drove them again up the hill, when our infantry once more advancing carried the height, the enemy retreating along the ridge, closely followed by our troops, and abandoning their guns to us. The Horse Artillery gun now took up a position in the middle of the gorge, whence it played with effect on a large body of horse assembled on the plain west of the hill, who forthwith retreated to a distance.

> [Lady Sale, eye-witness to this scene, writes thus:—
> The Afghán cavalry charged furiously down the hill upon our troops in close column. The 37th Native Infantry were leadings the 44th in the centre, and the Sháh's 6th in the rear. No square or balls were formed to receive them. All was a regular confusion; *my very heart felt as if it leapt to my teeth when I saw the Afgháns ride clean through them.* The onset was fearful. They looked like a cluster of bees; but we beat them, and drove them up again.
> The 5th Cavalry and Anderson's Horse charged them up the hill again, and drove them along the ridge. Lieutenant Eyre quickly got the Horse Artillery gun into the gorge, between the Bemárú hills and that to the left (the gorge leading to the plain towards the lake). From this position, he soon cleared that plain, which was covered with horsemen.]

Our troops had now got into ground where it was impracticable for Horse Artillery to follow. I accordingly pushed forward with one artilleryman and a supply of drag-ropes and spikes, to look out for the deserted guns of the enemy; one of these, a 4-pounder, was easily removed along the ridge by a party of the Sháh's 8th Infantry; but the other, a 6-pounder, was awkwardly situated in a ravine half-way down the side of the hill, our troops, with the Mountain Train 3-pounder, being drawn up along the ridge just above it. The evening was now fast closing in, and a large body of Afghán infantry occupied some enclosures on the plain below, whence they kept up so hot a fire upon the gun, as to render its removal by no means an easy task; but the envoy having sent us a message of entreaty that no exertions might be spared to complete the triumph of the day by bringing off *both* the enemy's guns, and the further detention of the troops being attended with risk, as the enemy, though driven from the hill, still maintained a threatening attitude below, I descended with the Horse Artillery gunner, and, having driven in a spike, returned to assist in making sure of the captured 4-pounder.

This, from the steepness of the hill, and the numerous water-cuts which everywhere intersected the plain, proved a somewhat troublesome business. Lieutenant Macartney, however, with a company of the Sháh's 6th Infantry, urged on his men with zeal, and we at last had the satisfaction to deposit our prize safe within the cantonment gates. Meanwhile the enemy, favoured by the darkness, pressed hard upon our returning troops, and by dint of incessant firing and shouting rendered their homeward march somewhat disorderly, effecting, however, but little damage.

It was no small disadvantage under which we laboured, that no temporary success of our troops over those of the enemy could be followed up, nor even possession be retained of the ground gained by us at the point of the bayonet, owing to the necessity of withdrawing our men into their quarters at night. On reaching the cantonment, we found the garrison in a state of considerable alarm, and a continual blaze of musketry illuminating the whole line of rampart. This had arisen from a demonstration of attack having been made by the enemy on the south-west bastion, which had been immediately checked by a few rounds of grape from the guns, and by a well-directed fire from the *jazailchís* under Captain Mackenzie; but it was long ere quiet could be restored, the men continuing to discharge their pieces at they knew not what.

Our infantry soldiers, both European and Native, might have taken a salutary lesson from the Afgháns in the use of their firearms; the latter, as a general rule, taking steady deliberate aim, and seldom throwing away a single shot; whereas our men seemed to fire entirely at random, without any aim at all; hence the impunity with which the Afghán horsemen braved the discharge of our musketry in this day's action within twelve yards, not one shot, to all appearance, taking effect.

[Lady Sale remarks as follows:—
There is also a peculiarity in the Afghán mode of fighting—that of every horseman carrying a foot-soldier behind him to the scene of action, where he is dropped, without the fatigue of walking to his post. The horsemen have two or three matchlocks or *jazails* each, slung at their backs, and are very expert in firing at the gallop. These *jazails* carry much further than our muskets.]³

In this affair Captain Paton, assistant quartermaster-general, had the misfortune to receive a wound in the left arm, which rendered amputation necessary, and the valuable services of one of our most efficient staff officers were thus lost. This was the last success our arms were destined to experience. Henceforward it becomes my weary task to relate a catalogue of misfortunes and difficulties, which, following close upon each other, disheartened our officers and soldiers, and finally sunk us all into irretrievable ruin, as though Heaven itself, for its own inscrutable purposes, had doomed our downfall. But here it is fit I should relate the scenes that had all this while been enacting at our solitary outpost in Kohistán.

3. *Lady Sale's Afghanistan* by Florentia Sale also published by Leonaur.

CHAPTER 7

Treachery of the Nijrao Chiefs

On the 15th November, Major Pottinger, C.B., and Lieutenant Haughton, Adjutant of the Sháh's 4th or Gúrkah Regiment, came in from Chárikár, both severely wounded, the former in the leg, and the latter having had his right hand amputated, besides several cuts in the neck and left arm. Their escape was wonderful. The following is an outline of what had taken place in Kohistán, from the commencement of the insurrection up to the present date.

It appears, from Major Pottinger's account of the transactions of that period, that it was not without reason he had so urgently applied to Sir William Macnaghten for reinforcements. Towards the end of October, premonitory signs of the coming tempest had become so unequivocally threatening as to confirm Major Pottinger in his worst suspicions, and in his conviction that order could not possibly be restored without a departure on the part of Government from the long-suffering system which had been obstinately pursued with respect to Nijráo in particular; but his conviction alone could do little to stem the torrent of coming events.

About this time Mír Masjídí, a contumacious rebel against the *Sháh's* authority, who had been expelled from Kohistán during General Sale's campaign in that country in 1840, and who had taken refuge in Nijráo after the fashion of many other men of similar stamp, obstinately refusing to make his submission to the *Sháh* even upon the most favourable terms, openly put himself at the head of a powerful and well-organized party, with the avowed intention of expelling the *Firingís* and overturning the existing government. He was speedily joined by the most influential of the Nijráo chiefs. A few of these made their appearance before Laghmání, where Major Pottinger resided, and proffered their services towards the maintenance of the public tranquillity. It will be seen that their object was the blackest treachery.

I shall here relate Major Pottinger's story, almost in his own words, as given to me.

In the course of the forenoon of the 3rd of November, Major Pottinger had an interview with a number of the more influential chiefs in his house or fort, and, about noon, went into the garden to receive those of inferior rank, accompanied by his visitors: here they were joined by Lieutenant Charles Rattray, Major Pottinger's Assistant. In discussing the question of the rewards to which their services might entitle them, the head men declared that, although *they* were willing to agree to Major Pottinger's propositions, they could not answer for their clansmen, and the above-mentioned petty chiefs, who were awaiting the expected conference at some little distance. Mr. Rattray, accordingly, in company with several of the principal, joined the latter, and, shortly after, proceeded with them to an adjoining field, where numbers of their armed retainers were assembled, for the purpose of ascertaining their sentiments on the subject of the conference.

While thus engaged, this most promising and brave young officer apparently became aware of intended foul play, and turned to leave the field, when he was immediately shot down. At this time Major Pottinger was still sitting in his garden, in company with several of the above-mentioned chiefs, and had just received intelligence of the purposed treachery from Muhammad Kásim Khán, a *díbáshí* of Házirbásh, a small detachment of which composed a part of his escort: he had with difficulty comprehended the man's meaning, which was conveyed by hints, when the sound of firing was heard:—the chief that were with him rose and fled, and he escaped into the fort by the postern gate; which having secured, he, from the *terre-plein* of the rampart, saw poor Mr. Rattray lying badly wounded in the field at the distance of some three hundred yards, and the late pretended negotiators making off in all directions with the plunder of the camp of the Házirbásh detachment. Of these plunderers a party passing close to Mr. Rattray, and observing that life was not extinct, one of them put his gun close to his head, and blew his brains out,—several others discharging their pieces into different parts of his body.

Major Pottinger's guard, being by this time on the alert, opened a fire, which speedily cleared the open space; but the enemy, seeking shelter in the numerous watercourses, and under the low walls surrounding the fort, harassed them incessantly until the appearance of

Lieutenant Haughton, Adjutant of the Gúrkah Regiment, who, advancing from Chárikár, where the corps was cantoned, distant about three miles, speedily drove the assailants from their cover. Captain Codrington, who commanded the regiment, chanced to be in Laghmání at this very time; and, on Mr. Haughton's approach, he led out a sortie and joined him: the skirmish was sharp, and the enemy suffered severely. Captain Codrington remaining in possession of an adjacent canal, the bank of which was immediately cut to supply the tank of the fort with water in case of accidents.

The evening had now closed in. and the enemy had retired, taking up a position which seemed to threaten the Chárikár road. Captain Codrington accordingly left Laghmání in haste, strengthening Major Pottinger's party to about one hundred men, these having to garrison four small forts. He promised, however, to relieve them the next morning, and to send a further supply of ammunition, of which there only remained one thousand five hundred rounds. Captain Codrington reached Chárikár unmolested; and the enemy, returning to their former point of attack, carried off their dead with impunity, the garrison being too weak to make a sally. On the morning of the 4th, Captain Codrington despatched four companies with a 6-pounder gun, according to promise. Their march caused numbers of the enemy now assembled on all sides to retreat; but one large body remained in position on the skirts of the mountain, range to their right, and threatened their flank.

Lieutenant Haughton, who commanded, detached Ensign Salusbury with a company to disperse them, which, in spite of the disparity of numbers, was effected in good style. Unhappily the Gúrkahs, being young soldiers, and flushed with success, pressed forward in pursuit with too much eagerness, regardless of the recalling bugle, when at last Mr. Salusbury with difficulty halted them, and endeavoured to retrace his steps. The enemy, observing the error they had committed in separating themselves too far from their main body, rallied and followed them in their retreat so closely, as to oblige Mr. Salusbury to halt his little band frequently, and face about. Lieutenant Haughton, consequently, in order to extricate the compromised company, halted his convoy, and despatched the greatest part of his men in the direction of the skirmish.

All this encouraged the other parties of the enemy who had retired to return, against whom, in numbers not less than four thousand men, Haughton maintained his ground until rejoined by his subaltern, when, seeing the hopelessness of making good his way to Laghmání, he retreated, and regained in safety the fortified barracks at Chárikár. Many of the men fell in this expedition, which would have proved infinitely more disastrous, from the number of the enemy's cavalry, who latterly seemed to gain confidence at every stage, but for the extraordinary gallantry and conduct of Lieutenant Haughton, who, with a handful of men and a gun, protected the rear of our over-matched troops. Mr. Salusbury was mortally wounded, and the trail of the gun gave way just as the party reached Chárikár.

This disappointment led Major Pottinger to believe that no second attempt would be made to relieve them; and as he had no ammunition beyond the supply in the men's pouches, he determined to retreat on Chárikár after dark: the better to hide his intention, he ordered, grain to be brought into the fort. Meantime the Chárikár cantonment was attacked on all sides, and in the afternoon large bodies of the enemy were detached thence, and joining others from that part of the valley, recommenced their investment of Laghmání. That part of the major's garrison, which occupied the small fort to the east of the principal one, defended by himself, although their orders were not to vacate their posts until after dark, being panic-stricken, did so at once, gaining the stronger position, but leaving behind several wounded comrades and their *havildár*, who remained staunch to his duty: these, however, were brought off.

Major Pottinger then strengthened the garrison of a cluster of adjacent huts, which, being surrounded by a sort of rude fortification, formed a tolerably good outwork; but the want of European officers to control the men was soon lamentably apparent, and in a short time the Gúrkahs, headed by their native officer, abandoned the hamlet, followed as a matter of course by the few Afghán soldiers attached to Captain Codrington's person, who had remained faithful until then. This last misfortune gave the enemy cover up to the very gate of the main stronghold, and before dark they had succeeded in getting possession of a gun-shed built against its outer wall, whence they commenced mining.

As soon as night had fairly closed in, Major Pottinger drew together the Gúrkah garrison outside the postern gate, under pretence of making a sortie, and thus separated them from the Afgháns and their followers, who remained inside; he then marched for Chárikár, the garrison of the remaining fort joining him as he drew on; he passed by the investing posts in perfect silence, taking his route along the skirts of the mountains to avoid the main road, and arrived in safety at Chárikár. In Laghmání he abandoned the hostages whom he had taken from the Kohistán chiefs, two boxes of treasure containing two thousand *rupees*, about sixty stand of *jazails*, all his office records, Mr. Rattray's, Dr. Grant's, and his own personal property, and a number of horses belonging to himself, and the above-mentioned two officers, and to some horsemen who had not deserted; for the greater part of his mounted escort had fled in the beginning of the affray. The Hirátís, and seven or eight Peshawarís, were the only Afgháns who adhered to him; the Kábulís had deserted to a man immediately on the murder of Mr. Rattray; they had been much disgusted the preceding month, as well as their comrades who proved unfaithful too, by the sudden reduction of a portion of his escort; which naturally led them to apprehend that their livelihood from the British service was of a precarious nature.

On the morning of 5th November large bodies of the enemy closed in round the Chárikár barracks, and about 7 o'clock they attacked the outposts with a spirit engendered by the success of the preceding evening. Captain Codrington requested Major Pottinger to take charge of what artillery he had, and to move a squadron in support of the skirmishers, which he did. The skirmishers were driven in, and, while retreating, Major Pottinger was wounded in the leg by a musket-shot. Encouraged by this, and by the unfinished state of the works round the barracks, in the entrance of which there was no gate, the enemy advanced with great determination to the attack, and dislodged the Gúrkahs from some mud huts outside, which were still occupied by a part of the regiment.

In this affair Captain Codrington, an officer of whose merits it is difficult to speak too highly, fell mortally wounded. The main post was, however, successfully defended, and the enemy driven back with considerable loss; upon which Lieutenant Haughton (who had now succeeded to the command, the only remaining officer being Mr. Rose, a mere youth), made a sortie and drove the enemy out of the gardens occupied by them in the morning, maintaining his ground against their most desperate efforts until after dark. Belief was then sent to the garrison (consisting of about fifty men) of Khoja Mír's fort, which it had been found expedient to occupy previously, because it commanded the interior of the barracks on the southern side.

From this time the unfortunate horses and cattle of the garrison were obliged to endure the extremity of thirsty there being *no* water for *them*, and the supply for even the fighting-men scanty in the extreme, obtained only from a few pools in the ditch of the rampart, which had been formed by a seasonable fall of rain. During the 6th the enemy renewed their attack in augmented numbers, the whole population of the country apparently swarming to the scene of action. Notwithstanding two successful sorties, all the outposts were driven in by dark, and thenceforth the garrison was confined to the barrack itself.

On the 7th the enemy got possession of Khoja Mir's fort: the regimental *múnshí* had been gained over, and through him the native officer was induced to surrender. From the towers of that fort, on the 8th, the enemy offered terms, on the condition that all the *infidels* should embrace Muhammadanism. Major Pottinger replied that they had come to aid a Muhammadan sovereign in the recovery of his rights; that they consequently were within the pale of Islám, and exempt from coercion on the score of religion. The enemy rejoined, that the king himself had ordered them to attack the *Káfirs*, and wished to know if Major Pottinger would yield on receiving an order. He refused to do so, except on the production of a written document. All this time the garrison was sorely galled from the post of vantage in possession of the enemy.

On the 9th, the enemy were enabled by the carelessness of the guard to blow up a part of the south-west tower of the barracks; but, before they could profit by the breach and the panic of the men, Mr. Haughton rallied the fugitives, and, leading them back, secured the top of the parapet wall with a barricade of boards and sand-bags.

On the 10th, the officers drew their last pool of water, and served out *half a wineglass* to each fighting-man.

On the 11th, all could not share even in that miserable proportion, and their sufferings from thirst were dreadful. During the night a sortie, was made, and some of the followers brought in a little water from a distant place, the sight of which only served to aggravate the distress of the majority; still, however, the fortitude of these brave and hardy soldiers remained unshaken, although apathy, the result of intense suffering, especially among Hindús, began to benumb their faculties.

On the 12th, after dark, Mr. Haughton ordered out a party to cover the water-carriers in an attempt to obtain a supply; but the over-harassed *sepoys*, unable to restrain themselves, dashed out of the ranks on approaching the coveted element, instead of standing to their arms to repel the enemy, and, consequently, the expedition failed in its object. Another sortie, consisting of two companies under Ensign Rose, was then ordered out, one of which, having separated from the other, dispersed in search of water; that under Mr. Rose himself fell on a post of the besiegers, every man of which they bayoneted; but, being unaccountably struck with a panic, the men fled back to the barracks, leaving Mr. Rose almost alone, who was then obliged to return, having accomplished his object but partially.

These circumstances were communicated by Mr. Haughton to Major Pottinger (whose wound had disabled him from active bodily co-operation in these last events), together with the startling intelligence that the corps was almost wholly disorganized from the large amount of killed and wounded, the hardships it had undergone, the utter inefficiency of the native officers, who had no sort of control over the soldiers, the exhaustion of the men from constant duty, and the total want of water and provisions.

Relief from Kábul, for which Major Pottinger had written repeatedly, seemed now hopeless, and an attempt at protracted defence of the post appeared likely to ensure the destruction of its brave defenders. Major Pottinger considered that the only remaining chance of saving any portion of the regiment was a retreat to Kábul; and, although that was abundantly perilous, he entertained a hope that a few of the most active men who were not encumbered with wives and children might escape. Then was felt most bitterly the impolicy of the encouragement which had been held out to all the recruits to bring their families with them, on what, even at the time of their being raised, was looked on by the most able officers as likely to prove a campaign of several years. Mr. Haughton coincided in the Major's views, and it was agreed, to ensure secrecy, that the men should not be informed of their intentions until paraded for the march.

This wretched state of things continued until the afternoon of the 13th, when Mr. Haughton discovered amongst the Panjábí artillerymen two who had deserted a few days previously, and who apparently had returned for the purpose of seducing their comrades. He immediately seized them; but, while he was in the act of their apprehension, the *jemadár* of the artillery, himself a Panjábí Mussulman, snatched a sword from a bystander, and cut down that officer, repeating his blows as he lay on the ground. Before the astonished Gúrkahs could draw their knives or handle their muskets, this miscreant, followed by all the artillery-men and the greater number of the Muhammadans in the barracks, rushed out of the gate and escaped.

The tumult and confusion occasioned by this impressed Major Pottinger with the idea that the enemy had driven the men from the walls; under this impression he caused himself to be carried to the main gate, but on his arrival he found that Dr. Grant had secured that point, and rallied the men. The native officers immediately gathered round him, with many of the *sepoys*, to assert their fidelity; but demoralization had evidently progressed fearfully, as may be judged from the fact that the garrison had plundered the treasure and the quarters of the deceased Captain Codrington the instant the major had left them, and that in the face of the enemy's fire they had pulled down the officers' boxes, which had been piled up as traverses to protect the doorway, broken them open, and pillaged them.

Dr. Grant then amputated Mr. Haughton's right hand, and hastily dressed the severe wounds which he had received on his left arm and on his neck. In the evening the doctor spiked all the guns with his own hands, and the garrison then left the barracks by the postern gate. The advance was led by Major Pottinger (Mr. Haughton, who accompanied him, being unable to do more than sit passively on his horse). Dr. Grant brought out the main body, and Ensign Rose, with the quartermaster sergeant, commanded the rear.

Notwithstanding the previous sufferings of these unfortunate men, it may be said that here commenced their real disasters. In vain did Major Pottinger attempt to lead his men to seize a building generally occupied by the enemy after nightfall, by the possession of which the exit of the main body from the barracks might be covered. In fact, it was with much difficulty that he eventually succeeded in halting them at about half a mile from the barracks until the main body and rear should close up. The men were naturally occupied entirely with their families, and such property as it had been impossible to prevent their bringing away; and discipline, the only source of hope under such circumstances, was at an end.

After the junction of the main body and rear, Dr. Grant suddenly disappeared, and was not afterwards seen.

The regiment then proceeded along the road to Sinjit Dara, where Major Pottinger knew that water could be procured. On reaching the first stream the last remnant of control over this disorderly mob was lost; much delay took place, and, in moving on, the advance became suddenly separated from the main body. After an anxious search Major Pottinger effected a rejunction.

At Sinjit Dara they quitted the road, to avoid alarming the villages and any outposts that might be stationed there; and much time, was lost in regaining the track from the other side; at Istálif the same manoeuvre was practised. Major Pottinger now found very few inclined to push on; exhaustion from the pain of his wound precluded the possibility of his being of any further use as a leader; and he determined to push on with Mr. Haughton towards Kábul, although with faint hope that the strength of either would prove adequate to the exertion. Having no guide, they got into many difficulties; and day was breaking by the time they reached the range of mountains half way between Chárikár and Kábul.

Men and horses were by this time incapable of further endurance: the latter, it must be remembered, had been ten days without water previously to starlings and five days without food; they were still upwards of twenty miles from any place of safety; their sufferings from their wounds, fatigue, hunger, and thirst, made life a burden, and at this time despair had almost obtained a victory—but God sustained them. By Mr. Haughton's advice they sought shelter in a very deep but dry ravine, close to a small village, hoping that their proximity to danger might prove a source of safety; as it was probable that the inhabitants, who by this time must have been on the alert, would scarcely think of looking for their prey close to their own doors. The companions of Major Pottinger and Mr. Haughton were a *sepoy* of the regiment, a *múnshí*, and the regimental *baniah*. In the forenoon they were alarmed by a firing on the mountains above them; the cause of this, as it appeared afterwards, was that a few of the fugitive Gúrkahs had ascended the hills for safety (which, indeed, it was Major Pottinger's wish to do, until he yielded to the arguments of his companion), whither they were pursued and massacred by the country people.

The rest of the day passed in tranquillity; and again, under the friendly shroud of darkness, having previously calculated their exact position, did this sorely-bestead little party resume their dangerous route. It was providential that Major Pottinger had, from his habits as a traveller through unknown and difficult regions, accustomed himself to ascertain and remember the bearings of the most conspicuous landmarks of the countries he traversed, it was therefore comparatively easy for him to lead the way over the steep and rugged peaks, by which alone they might hope to find a safe path,—for the main road, and even the more accessible tracks across the tops of the mountains, were closely beset, and watch-fires gleamed in all directions.

Indeed Ghulám-Muyan ud-dír, a distinguished partisan in the

service of the rebels, had been despatched from Kábul, with a number of his most active followers, purposely to intercept and seize the major, of whose flight intelligence had been early received, and actually was at that time patrolling those very heights over which the fugitives passed. But the protecting hand of Providence was displayed not only in leading them unharmed through the midst of their enemies, but in supplying them with mental fortitude and bodily strength. Weak and exhausted, their hardy and usually sure-footed Turkmán horses could scarcely strain up the almost impracticable side of the mountain, or preserve their equilibrium in the sharp, sudden descents which they encountered, for path there was none.

On one occasion Mr Haughton, whose desperate wounds I have already described, fell off, and, being unable to rise, declared his determination of awaiting his fate where he lay. The major refused to desert him, and both slept for about one hour, when, nature being a little restored, they pushed on until they descended into the plain of Alifát, which they crossed, avoiding the fort of that name, and struggling up the remaining ridge that separated them from the plain of Kábul, they entered it by the southern end of the Kábul lake. Intending now to cross the cultivation, and to reach cantonments by the back of the *Sháh's* garden, Major Pottinger missed his road close to Qila-i-buland, and found himself within the enemy's sentries; but being unwilling to alarm them by retracing his steps, after discovering his mistake, he led the way towards Dih Afghán. Here they were challenged by various outposts, to whom they answered after the fashion of Afghán horsemen; but they were compelled, in order to avoid suspicion, actually to enter the city of Kábul, their only hope now being in the slumberous security of the inhabitants at that hour (it being now about 3 a.m.), and in the protection of their Afghán dress and equipments.

The Gúrkah *sepoy*, who, strange to say, had kept up with them *on foot*, had his outward man concealed by a large *posthin*, or sheep-skin cloak. They pursued their way through the lanes and *bázár* of the city, without any interruption, except the occasional gruff challenge of a sleepy watchman, until they gained the skirts of the city. There they were like to have been stopped by a picket which lay between them and the cantonment. The disposition to a relaxation of vigilance as the morning approaches, which marks the Afghán soldier, again befriended them; they had nearly passed the post before they were pursued. Desperation enabled them to urge their wearied horses into a pace, which barely gave them the advantage over their enemies who were on foot;

and they escaped with a volley from the now aroused picket, the little Gúrkah freshening his way in the most surprising manner, considering his previous journey. A few hundred yards further brought them within the ramparts of our cantonment, where they were received by their brethren in arms as men risen from the dead.

[The gallant Haughton still survives, (as at time of first publication), as a Major-General and "Companion of the Star of India," in the Bengal Staff Corps, having filled with great credit several important posts.

Major Eldred Pottinger, C.B., the hero of Hirát, having been compelled by failing health to seek a change of climate, was attacked by malignant fever at Hong-Kong, where he died, aged 32, on the 13th November 1843, the anniversary of his retreat from Chárikár. A monument was erected to his memory, in the cathedral of Bombay, by public subscription, "in token of the admiration and respect in which his character as a soldier and his conduct as a man are held by his friends in the Presidency."]

CHAPTER 8

Unprofitable Operations at the Village of Bemaru

November 16th.—The impression made on the enemy by the action of the 13th was so far salutary, that they did not venture to annoy us again for several days. Advantage was taken of this respite to throw magazine supplies from time to time into the Bálá Hisár, a duty which was ably performed by Lieutenant Walker, with a *risálah* of Irregular Horse under cover of night. But even in this short interval of comparative rest, such was the wretched construction of the cantonment, that the mere ordinary routine of garrison duty, and the necessity of closely manning our long line of rampart both by day and night, was a severe trial to the health and patience of the troops; especially now that the winter began to show symptoms of unusual severity. There seemed, indeed, every probability of an early fall of snow, to which all looked forward with dread, as the harbinger of fresh difficulties and of augmented suffering.

These considerations, and the manifest superiority of the Bálá Hisár as a military position, led to the early discussion of the expediency of abandoning the cantonment and consolidating our forces in the above-mentioned stronghold. The envoy himself was, from the first, greatly in favour of this move, until over-ruled by the many objections urged against it by the military authorities; to which, as will be seen by a letter from him presently quoted, he learnt by degrees to attach some weight himself; but to the very last it was a measure that had many advocates, and I venture to state my own firm belief that, had we at this time moved into the Bálá Hisár, Kábul might have been still in our possession. The chief objections urged were:

1st, the difficulty of conveying our sick and wounded;
2ndly, the want of firewood;

3rdly, the want of forage for the cavalry;

4thly, the triumph that our abandonment of cantonments would afford the enemy;

5thly, the risk of defeat on the way thither.

On the other hand it was advanced:

1st, that, though to carry the sick would be *difficult,* it still was not *impossible*; for so short a distance two, or even three, men could be conveyed on each *dúlí*; some might manage to walk, and the rest could be mounted on the *yábús* and camels, on top of their loads;

2ndly, although wood was scarce in the Bálá Hisár, there was enough for purposes of cooking, and for the want of fires the troops would be amply compensated by the comparative ease and comfort they would enjoy in other respects;

3rdly, the horses must, in the case of there being no forage, have been shot; but the want of cavalry would have been little felt in such a situtation;

4thly, as we should have destroyed all that was valuable before leaving, the supposed triumph of the enemy would have been very short-lived, and would soon have given way to a feeling of disappointment at the valueless nature of their acquisition, and of dismay at the strength and security of our new position;

5thly, the distance did not exceed two miles, and one-half of that distance was protected by the guns of the Bálá Hisár. If we had occupied the Siyáh Sang hills with a strong party, placing guns there to sweep the plain on the cantonment side, the enemy could have done little to impede our march, without risking a battle with our whole force in a fair field, to which they were generally averse, but which would, perhaps, have been the *best* mode for *us* of deciding the struggle.

To remove so large a force, clogged with so many thousands of camp followers, without loss of some kind, was, of course, next to impossible; but ought such considerations to have interfered with a step which would have been attended in the long run with such great military and political advantages? Our troops, once collected in the Bálá Hisár, could have been spared for offensive operations against the city and the neighbouring forts, by which means plenty of food and forage would in all probability have been readily procured, while the commanding nature of the position would have caused the enemy to despair of driving us out, and a large party would probably have been ere long formed in our favour. Such were the chief arguments employed on either side; but Brigadier Shelton having firmly set his face against the movement from the first moment of its proposition, all serious idea of it was gradually abandoned, though it continued to the very last a subject of common discussion.

November 18th.—Accounts were this day received from Jallálábád, that General Sale, having sallied from the town, had repulsed the enemy with considerable loss. At the beginning of the insurrection. General Sale's brigade was at Gandámak; and I have already mentioned, that an order recalling it to Kábul was immediately despatched by the envoy. General Sale, on receipt of it, summoned a council of war, by which it was unanimously agreed to be impracticable to obey the order. The circumstances of his march to Jallálábád are already well known to the public. The hope of his return had tended much to support our spirits; our disappointment was therefore great to learn that all expectation of aid from that quarter was at an end. Our eyes were now turned towards the Kandahár force as our last resource, though an advance from that quarter seemed scarcely practicable so late in the year.

Much discussion took place this evening regarding the expediency of taking Mahmud Khán's fort. There were many reasons to urge in favour of making the attempt. It was one of the chief resorts of the rebels during the day, and they had established a battery of two guns under the walls, from which they constantly fired upon our foraging parties, and upon the south-east bastion of cantonments. It was about nine hundred yards distant from our rampart, which was too far for breaching with the 9-pounders, but a dry canal, which ran towards it in a zigzag direction, afforded facilities for a regular approach within three hundred yards, of which advantage might have been taken to enable the artillery to make a breach.

Secondly, this fort commanded the road all the way up to the Bálá Hisár and the possession of it would at once have secured to us an easy communication with that place, and with the city. Thirdly, the envoy declared his opinion that the moral effect derived from its possession would be more likely to create a diversion in our favour, than any other blow we could strike, as the Afgháns had always attached great importance to its occupation and had a superstitious opinion that whatever party held possession of it were sure to be masters of Kábul. These considerations had decided the general in favour of making the attempt this very night, by blowing open the gate, and a storming party was actually warned for the duty; but some sudden objections being raised, the plan was given up, and never afterwards resumed by the military.

It was, however, the cause of no small astonishment to the officers in the Bálá Hisár, who, from their commanding situation, could observe all that took place on both sides, that Mahmud Khán's fort should have been suffered to remain in the hands of the enemy, though at night it was often garrisoned by a mere handful of men. This fort, nevertheless, gave abundant occupation to the artillery, who, when nothing else was going on, were frequently employed in disturbing the enemy in that quarter with one of the iron 9-pounders, and an occasional shelling from the mortar.

November 19th.—A letter was this day received by the general from the envoy to the following effect:—

"That, all hope of assistance from Jallálábád being over, it behoved us to take our future proceedings into consideration. He himself conceived it our imperative duty to hold on as long as possible in our present position, and he thought we might even struggle through the whole winter by making the Mahomedans and Christians live chiefly upon flesh, supposing our supplies of grain to fail; by which means, as the essentials of wood and water were abundant, he considered our position might be rendered impregnable. A retreat towards Jallálábád would teem not only with disaster, but dishonour, and ought not to be contemplated until the very last extremity. In eight or ten days we should be better able to judge whether such extremity should be resorted to.

In that case, we should have to sacrifice not only the valuable properly of Government, but His Majesty Shah Shujá, to support whose authority we were employed by Government; and even were we to make good our retreat to Jallálábád, we should have no shelter for our troops, and our camp followers would all be sacrificed. He had frequently thought of negotiating, but there was no party of sufficient power and influence to protect us. Another alternative would to be throw ourselves into the Bálá Hisár; but he feared that would be also a disastrous retreat, to effect which much property must be necessarily sacrificed. Our heavy guns might be turned against us, and food and fuel might be scarce, for a farther supply of which we might be dependent on sorties into the city, in which, if beaten, we must of course be ruined. On the whole, he was decidedly of opinion that we should hold out; it was still possible that reinforcements might arrive from Kandahár, or something might turn up in our favour; there were hopes, too, that on the setting in of winter the enemy would disperse. He had been long disposed to recommend a blow being struck to retrieve our fortunes such as taking Mahmud Khán's fort; but he had since reason to believe this would not answer. In eight or ten days, he concluded, it would remain for the military authorities to determine whether there was any chance of improving our position, and to decide whether it would be more prudent to attempt a retreat to Jallálábád, or to the Bálá Hisár. If provision sufficient for the winter could be procured, on no account would he leave the cantonment."

November 22nd.—The village of Bemárú (or *"husbandless,"* from a beautiful virgin who was buried there) was situated about half a mile to the north of cantonments, on the Kohistán road, at the northeast extremity of a hill which bounded the plain to the west. As it was built on a slope, and within musket-shot, the upper houses commanded a large portion of the Mission Compound. From this village we for a long time drew supplies, the envoy largely bribing the proprietor, to which, however, the enemy in some measure put a stop, by taking possession of it every day. This morning, large bodies of Afghán horse and foot, having again issued from the city, proceeded to crown the summit of the above-mentioned hill. It was determined, at the recommendation of the envoy, to send a party of our troops to forestall the enemy in the occupation of the village, and Major Swayne, 5th Native Infantry, was appointed to that duty, with a detachment composed as follows:—a Wing 5th Native Infantry, two *risálas* Irregular Horse, one *risála* 5th Light Cavalry, and one Mountain Train gun.

The party had already reached the village, when it was deemed proper to send after it a Horse Artillery gun, which I was requested by the General to accompany. Major Swayne, however, it would seem, found the village already occupied by a body of Kohistánís, and the entrance blocked up in such a manner that he considered it out of his power to force a passage. On arriving at the place with the Horse Artillery gun, I found him in an orchard on the roadside, the trees of which partially protected the men from a very sharp fire, poured in amongst them from the houses. There being no shelter for the gun here, nor any mode of employing it to advantage, it was ordered to cross some fields to the right, and take up a position where it could best fire upon the village, and upon the heights above it, which were now crowded with the enemy's infantry.

In order to protect the horses, I drew up the gun near the fort of Zulfa Khán, under the walls of which they had shelter; but for the gun itself no other position could be found than in the open field, where it was exposed to the full fire of the enemy posted in the tillage and behind the neighbouring , walls. The Mountain Train gun was also with me, and both did some execution among the people on the summit of the hill, though to little purpose.

Major Swayne, whose orders were to storm the village, would neither go forward nor retire; but concealing his men under the cover of some low wall, he all day long maintained a musketry fire on the houses of Bemárú, but without satisfactory result. The cavalry were drawn up in rear of the gun on the open plain, as a conspicuous mark for the Kohistánís, and where, as there was nothing for them to do, they accordingly did nothing. Thus we remained for five or six hours, during which time the artillery stood exposed to the deliberate aim of the numerous marksmen who occupied the village and its immediate vicinity, whose bullets continually sang in our ears, often striking the gun, and grazing the ground on which we stood. Only two gunners, however, out of six were wounded, but the cavalry in our rear had many casualties both among men and horses.

Late in the evening, a party of Afghán horse moving round from behind Bemárú, proceeded towards a fort in our rear, whence a cross fire was opened upon us. Brigadier Shelton now joined, bringing with him a reinforcement from the 5th Native Infantry, under Colonel Oliver. Major Swayne, with two companies, was then sent to reconnoitre the fort whence the fire proceeded, and the Horse Artillery gun was at the same time moved round, so as to bear upon the Afghán cavalry, who hovered among the trees in the same quarter. While engaged in this operation, I received a bullet through the left hand, which for the present terminated my active services. Shortly after this the troops were recalled into cantonments.

It was worthy of note, that Muhammad Akbar Khán, second son of the late Amir Dost Muhammad Khán, arrived in Kábul this night from Bámíán. This man was destined to exercise an evil influence over our future fortunes. The crisis of our struggle was already nigh at hand.

CHAPTER 9

Our Force Driven Back With Severe Loss

November 23rd.—This day decided the fate of the Kábul force. At a council held at the general's house on the night of the 22nd it was determined, on the special recommendation of the envoy, that, in consequence of the inconvenience sustained by the enemy so frequently taking possession of Bemárú, and interrupting our foraging parties, a force, under Brigadier Shelton, should on the following morning take the village by assault, and maintain the hill above it against whatever number of the enemy might appear.

Accordingly, at 2 a.m. the under-mentioned troops[1] moved out of cantonments in perfect silence by the Kohistán gate, and skirting the *masjid* immediately opposite, which was held by a company of Her Majesty's 44th, took the direction of the gorge at the further extremity of the Bemárú hill, which they ascended, dragging the gun to the top with great difficulty, from the rugged and steep nature of the side, which labour was greatly facilitated by the exertions of two hundred commissariat *sarwúns*, who had volunteered for the occasion. The whole force then moved to the knoll at the northeast extremity of the hill, which overhung the village of Bemárú.

The gun was placed in position commanding an inclosure in the village, which, from its fires, was judged to be the principal bivouac of the enemy, and a sharp fire of grape commenced, which evidently created great confusion, but it was presently answered by a discharge of

---

1. 1 H. A. gun, under Sergt. Mulhal. 5 Cos. H. M. 44th, under Capt. Leighton. 6 Cos. 5th N. I., under Lieut.-Col. Oliver. 6 Cos. 37th N.I., under Major Kershaw, H. M. 13th. Sappers, 100 men, under Lieut. Laing. 1 Squadron 5th Lt. Cav., under Capt. Bott. 1 *Do*. Irregular Horse, under Lieut. Walker. 100 men, Anderson's Horse.

jazails; the enemy forsaking the open space, and covering themselves in the houses and towers: to this we replied in the intervals of the cannonade by discharges of musketry. It was suggested by Captain Bellew and others to Brigadier Shelton to storm the village, while the evident panic of the enemy lasted, under cover of the darkness, there being no moon: to this the Brigadier did not accede.

When the day broke, parties of the enemy were descried hurrying from the village, and making across the plain towards the distant fort, their fire having previously slackened from the failure of their ammunition. At this time, certainly, not above forty men remained in the village. A storming party, consisting of two companies 37th Native Infantry, and some Europeans, under Majors Swayne and Kershaw, were ordered to carry the village; but Major Swayne, taking a wrong direction, missed the principal entrance, which was open, and arrived at a small *khirkhí*, or wicket, which was barricaded, and which he had no means of forcing, so that he was obliged to cover himself and his men as well as he could from the sure aim of the enemy's marksmen, by whose fire his party suffered considerably, himself being shot through the neck.

After remaining thus for about half an hour, he was recalled by the Brigadier, who observed large bodies of armed men pouring out from the city towards the scene of conflict. Meanwhile Lieutenant Walker had been directed to lead his Irregular Horse down into the plain on the west side of the hill, to cut off such fugitives from the village as he might be able to intercept, and to cover himself from the fire of infantry under the walls of an old fort not far from the base of the hill. Brigadier Shelton, leaving three companies of the 37th Native Infantry in the knoll above Bemárú as a reserve, under Major Kershaw, moved back with the troops and guns to the part of the hill which overlooked the gorge.

Shortly after this it was suggested to raise a *sanga*, or stone breastwork, for the protection of the troops wholly exposed to the distant fire of the enemy's *jazails*, but this proposition was not acted on. Immense numbers of the enemy, issuing from the city, had now crowned the summits of the hill opposite the gorge,—in all, probably ten thousand men. The plain on the west of the two hills was swept by swarms of their cavalry, who evidently designed to cut off the small party of Irregular Horse under Lieutenant Walker; while the failure of our attempt to storm the village had rendered it easy for the enemy to throw strong reinforcements into it, and to supply the ammunition of which they had been in great want.

About 7 a.m. the fire from the enemy's hill was so galling that the few skirmishers sent to the brow of our hill could with difficulty retain their posts. As an instance of the backwardness which now began to develop itself among our men, it must be mentioned that Lieutenant-Colonel Oliver endeavoured to induce a party of his own regiment to follow him to the brow of the hill, to keep down the sharp fire of a number of the enemy, who had ensconced themselves in a small ravine commanding the foremost square; not a man would follow him,—and it was only after that brave officer had gone forward himself into the thickest of the fire, saying, "Although my men desert me, I myself will do my duty," that about a dozen were shamed into performing theirs.

The remainder of the troops (the infantry formed into two squares, and the cavalry being drawn up *en masse* immediately in their rear,) suffered severely without being able to retaliate, from the comparatively short range of the musket. Our single gun maintained as hot a fire on the masses of the enemy as possible, doing great execution; but the want of a second gun to take up the fire was sensibly felt, inasmuch as after a short time the vent became too hot for the artillerymen to serve. This state of things continued until between 9 and 10 o'clock, when a large party of the enemy's cavalry threatened our right flank, and, to prevent his destruction. Lieutenant Walker was recalled. This demonstration, however, was repulsed by a well-directed discharge of shrapnel from the Horse Artillery gun, by one of which a chief of consequence, supposed to be Abd-ullah Khán, Achakzae, was mortally wounded.

By the recall of Lieutenant Walker the enemy were enabled to surround our position at all points, except that facing the cantonments; our gun ammunition was almost expended, and the men were faint with fatigue and thirst (no water being procurable), while the number of killed and wounded was swelled every instant.

About this time (between 10 and 11 a.m.) large bodies of the enemy's infantry advanced across the plain from the *Sháh Bágh* to the end of the hill, to cut off the supplies of ammunition coming from cantonments, as also the *dhúlís* on which we endeavoured to send off a few of the wounded. These, however, were checked by a party of our troops in the *masjid*, opposite the Kohistán gate, and by about fifty *jazailchís* under the temporary command of Captain Trevor, (Captain Mackenzie, their leader, having been requested by Brigadier Shelton to act as one of the staff for the day,) who lined some low walls and watercourses, as well as by frequent discharges of round shot and shrapnel from the cantonment guns under Lieutenant Warburton.

Previously to this, numbers of the most daring Gházís had descended into the gorge, and, taking advantage of some hillocks on the ascent towards our position, had crept gradually up, maintaining a deadly fire on our skirmishers, who were, unfortunately, wholly exposed; they became at length disheartened, and gave way. At this moment the Brigadier offered a reward of one hundred *rúpís* to any man who should take a flag of the enemy which had been planted behind a tumulus about thirty yards in front of the square, and he fruitlessly endeavoured to induce the men to charge bayonets; several of the officers at the same time advanced to the front, and actually pelted the enemy with stones.

All attempts, however, to encourage our men were in vain. The attacking party were now emboldened to make a rush upon our gun; our cavalry were ordered to charge, but again in vain, for the men would not follow their officers. The panic spread, and our troops gave way, except the second square, which had been formed about two hundred yards in the rear, and three companies under Major Kershaw at the other extremity of the hill; behind this second square the officers with great difficulty rallied the fugitives, leaving the gun in the hands of the enemy, who lost no time in walking off with the limber and horses.

By this time the news of Abd-ullah Khán's wound had spread among the ranks of the enemy, causing great confusion, which extended to the Gházís now in possession of the gun. This, and the tolerably firm attitude resumed by our troops, induced them to content themselves with the limber and horses, and retire. Their retreat gave fresh courage to our disheartened soldiers, who again took possession of the gun, and advanced to the brow of the hill, where were found the bodies of Captain Macintosh and Lieutenant Laing, as well as those of the soldiers slain in the onset, including two Horse Artillery men, who, with a devotedness worthy of British soldiers, had perished while vainly endeavouring to defend their charge.

Some fresh gun-ammunition having now arrived from cantonments, carried by *lascars*, a fire was again opened on the ranks of the enemy; but we were unable to push the advantage gained by the momentary disorder alluded to above, because, in fact, the cavalry would not act. In the observations on this action, made hereafter, there will be found some palliation for the backwardness of the cavalry on this occasion, in spite of the gallant bearing of their leaders; the infantry were too few, and too much worn out and disheartened, to be able to make a forward movement. The consequence was, that not only did the whole force of the enemy come on with renewed vigour and spirits, maintaining at the same time the fatal *jazail* fire which had already so grievously thinned our ranks, but fresh numbers poured out of the city, and from the surrounding villages, until the hill occupied by them scarcely afforded room for them to stand.

This unequal conflict having lasted until past noon, during which period reinforcements and an additional gun had been in vain solicited from the cantonments, Brigadier Shelton sent Captain Mackenzie to request Major Kershaw to move up his reserve (which could scarcely so be called, having been the whole day hard pressed by large bodies of the enemy in the village, and by parties occupying ruins and broken ground on the skirts of his position). The major, fearing that, if he abandoned the knoll on which he had been stationed, our retreat to the cantonments (then becoming more and more imperatively necessary) might be cut off, made answer, that "he begged to suggest that the Brigadier should fall back upon him." Before this message could be delivered, the front ranks of the advanced square, at the Brigadier's extremity of the hill, had been literally mowed down;—most of the artillerymen, who performed their duty in a manner which is beyond praise, shared the same fate.

The manoeuvre practised by the Ghāzīs previously was repeated by still greater numbers. The evident unsteadiness of our troops, and the imminent danger to which the gun was a second time exposed, induced the Brigadier, after repeated suggestions from Sergeant Mulhall, who commanded the battery, to order the gun to be limbered up—a second limber having arrived from cantonments—and to retire towards Major Kershaw's position. Scarcely had this movement been commenced, when a rush from the Ghāzīs completely broke the square;—all order was at an end:—the entreaties and commands of the officers, endeavouring to rally the men, were not even listened to, and an utter rout ensued down the hill in the direction of cantonments, the enemy closely following, whose cavalry, in particular, made a fearful slaughter among the unresisting fugitives.

Major Kershaw's party, perceiving this disaster, endeavoured to escape; but strong parties, issuing from the village, cut off their retreat, and thus great numbers of our *sepoys* perished: the grenadier company, especially, was all but annihilated. The mingled tide of flight and pursuit seemed, to those who manned the walls of cantonment, to be about to enter the gate together; and, by some fatality, the ammunition of the great guns in battery within the cantonments was almost expended. A heavy fire, however, was opened from the Sháh's 5th Infantry in the Mission Compound; a fresh troop of the 5th Cavalry, under Lieutenant Hardyman, charged across the plain towards the enemy, joined by Lieutenant Walker, who had rallied fifteen or twenty of his own men; during which gallant effort this most promising and brave young officer received a mortal wound.

These operations, assisted by a sharp discharge from the *jazailchís* under Captain Trevor, contributed to check the pursuit; and it was observed at the time, and afterwards ascertained to be correct, that a chief (Usmán Khán) voluntarily halted his followers, who were among the foremost, and led them off; which may be reckoned, indeed, the chief reason why the mass of our people who on that day went forth to battle were not destroyed. Our loss was tremendous; the principal part of the wounded having been left in the field, including Lieutenant-Colonel Oliver, where they were miserably cut to pieces. Our gun and second limber, which, while endeavouring to gallop down the hill, had overturned on rough ground, we had the mortification to behold triumphantly carried off by the enemy.

About half an hour previous to the flight of our troops, a note had been written to the assistant adjutant-general by Captain Troup, earnestly requesting that the Mountain Train gun, which had by that time been repaired, might be sent out with the least possible delay, and the first idea that suggested itself to that officer after our defeat was, that by quickly bringing this gun to bear upon the Horse Artillery gun, then in the hands of the enemy, the latter might still be saved. He therefore galloped with speed to cantonments, where finding the Mountain Train gun just ready to start, he was on the point of leading it out of the gate, when his progress was interrupted by the assistant adjutant-general, on the plea that it would now be of no use.

This is the more to be lamented, as from the spot occupied by Captain Trevor's *jazailchís*, who, protected by a low wall, still kept up a sharp and effectual fire on the enemy, the range to the side of the hill whence the Afgháns were endeavouring to carry off the captured gun, about which they clustered in thousands was so short, that grape, even from a small calibre, must have prevented the execution of their intentions. Had the company of fresh infantry which was drawn up outside the gate, under command of Lieutenant Alexander, moved forward in company with the mountain gun to the support of the above gallant handful of *jazailchís,* excellent service might have been rendered. But it seemed as if we were under the ban of Heaven.

Observations.

In this miserable and disastrous affair no less than six great errors must present themselves, even to the most unpractised military eye, each of which contributed in no slight degree to the defeat of our troops, opposed as they were by overwhelming numbers.

1st. The first and perhaps most fatal mistake of all was the taking out a *single* gun. The General Order by the Marquess of Hastings, expressly forbidding less than two guns to take the field, under any circumstances or on any pretence whatever, when another is available, must be well known at least to every officer who has served in India. This positive prohibition was the offspring of dearly-bought experience, and the action of Bemárú affords another convincing example of the risk to which a single gun is exposed when unsupported by the fire of a second. It was certainly the Brigadier's intention to take the mountain gun also; but this had unfortunately been disabled on the previous day, and it had been twice specially reported, both to the Brigadier and to the General the foregoing night, by Captain Troup, that it could not be got ready before 12 a.m. on the following day.

2ndly. The second error is scarcely less evident than the first. Had immediate advantage been taken of the panic which our unexpected cannonade created among the possessors of the village, whose slack fire afforded sufficient evidence of the actual fact that they were not only contemptible in numbers, but short of ammunition, had, I say, a storming party been led to the attack under cover of the darkness, which would have nullified the advantage they possessed in being under cover, the place must inevitably have fallen into our hands, and thus would the principal object of the sally have been gained, and a good line of retreat secured for our troops in case of necessity.

3rdly. The third error was so manifest as to be quite unaccountable. A party of one hundred sappers had accompanied the force for the express purpose of raising a *sanga.* The fittest place for such a work would have been half-way along the ridge occupied by us, where our troops would then have been wholly protected from the fire of the *jazails* from the opposite hill, while the enemy could not have advanced to the attack without exposing themselves to the full effects of our musketry and grape. It would, in fact, have infused into our troops a sense of security from any sudden charge of the enemy's horse, and at the same time have enabled our own cavalry to issue forth with the assurance of having in their rear a place of defence on which to fall back if hard pressed by the enemy. It has been seen that no such defence was raised.

4thly. All have heard of the British squares at *Waterloo*, which defied the repeated desperate onsets of Napoleon's choicest *cavalry*. At Bemárú we formed squares to resist the *distant fire of infantry*, thus presenting a solid mass against the aim of perhaps the best marksmen in the worlds the said squares being securely perched cm the summit of a steep and narrow ridge up which no cavalry *could* charge with effect. A Peninsular General would consider this to be a novel fashion; yet Brigadier Shelton had the benefit of Peninsular experience in his younger days, and, it must be owned, was never surpassed in dauntless bravery.

5thly. Our cavalry, instead of being found upon the plain, where they might have been useful in protecting our line of communications with the cantonments, and would have been able to advance readily to any point where their services might have been required, were hemmed in between two infantry squares, and exposed for several hours to a destructive fire from the enemy's *jazails*, on ground where, even under the most favourable circumstances, they could not have acted with effect. This false and unsatisfactory position of course discouraged the troopers; and, when the infantry finally gave way, the two arms of the service became mixed up in a way that greatly increased the general confusion, and rendered it impossible for the infantry to rally, even had they been so disposed. The truth is, that the cavalry were not allowed fair play, and such a position must have disgusted and dispirited any troops.

6thly. Shortly after our regaining possession of the gun, one of the Brigadier's staff. Captain Mackenzie, feeling convinced that, from the temper of the troops and from the impossibility of rectifying the false position in which the force was placed, not only was success beyond hope, but that defeat in its most disastrous shape was fast approaching, proposed to the Brigadier to endeavour to effect a retreat while it was yet in his power to do so with comparative impunity. His reply was, "Oh, no I we will hold the hill some time longer."

At that time, even if the slaughter of the soldiery, the loss of officers, the evident panic in our ranks, and the worse than false nature of our position, had not been sufficient to open all eyes as to the impossibility even of partial success, (for the real object of the expedition, *viz.* the possession of the village of Bemárú, had been, as it were, abandoned from the very firsts) the weakness and exhaustion of both men and horses, who were not only worn out by bodily fatigue, but suffering grievously from extreme thirst and the debility attendant on long fasting, ought to have banished all idea of further delaying a movement in which alone lay the slightest chance of preserving to their country lives, by the eventual sacrifice of which not even the only solace to the soldier in the hour of misfortune, the consciousness of unimpaired honour, was likely to be gained.

[These criticisms gave rise to much discussion in the English papers. On behalf of Brigadier Shelton they may be summed up as follows:—

1. It is admitted in the narrative that the Brigadier *"in vain solicited an additional gun"* to be sent from cantonments, and ought not therefore to be held responsible on that score. Owing to the paucity of European Artillery gunners only one of the Horse Artillery guns could be manned for field operations at one time, as it was considered by the General essential to retain a small reserve of European artillerymen for defensive purposes within the long extent of ramparts. Hence the Mountain Train gun was usually substituted, but chanced on this occasion to be out of repair.

2. The Brigadier seems to have objected to risk a night attack, on principle, and cannot be held responsible for the failure of the storming party at daybreak, which arose solely from missing the proper entrance to the village, which was open, and time was thus given to the enemy to pour forth from the city in overwhelming numbers.

3. With regard to the omission to raise a *"sanga,"* or breastwork, for which purpose one hundred sappers had been sent out with the force, it has been alleged that *"these men were too busily employed in fighting to be available for such a work."*

4 and *5.* It has been asserted that what the author has termed *"Squares"* were not squares at all. "The enemy were trying to turn our flanks, and the Afghán horsemen were pushing up hill, so *the flanks were thrown back to give a flunking fire"*—the odds against us being about 15,000 to 800!

On the other hand Lady Sale, who was an eye-witness of the day's proceedings, describes what occurred as follows:—

I had taken up my post of observation, as usual, on the top of the house, whence I had a fine view of the field of action, and where, by keeping behind the chimneys, I escaped the bullets that continually whizzed past me. Brigadier Shelton having brought forward skirmishers to the brow of the hill, formed the remainder of his infantry into two squares—the one about two hundred yards in rear of the other, the intervening space being crammed with our cavalry, who, from the nature of the ground, were exposed to the full fire of the enemy without being able to act themselves.

The number of the enemy's footmen must have been upwards of ten thousand (some say fifteen thousand), and the plain, on the north-west of the hills, was swept by not less than three thousand or four thousand Afghán cavalry.... The fight continued till about 10 o'clock, by which time our killed and wounded became very numerous. In spite of the execution done by our shrapnel, the fire of the enemy told considerably more than ours did, from the superiority of their *jazails* and *jingals* over our muskets.... They also fought from behind *sangas* and hillocks, whilst our men were perfectly exposed; our troops also labouring under the disadvantage of being drawn up in square, from an apprehension of an attack from the Afghán cavalry

The vent of the gun became too hot for the artillerymen to serve it.

At this time (half-past 9 a.m.) a party of Gházíás ascended the brow of the hill.... It is possible that the Brigadier might not have seen their advance; but when they had nearly attained the summit, they had an evident advantage over us, as their shots generally told in fixing up at our men, whose persons were wholly exposed, whilst only a few of their heads were visible to our troops, *and the old fault of firing too high most probably sent all our shots harmlessly over their heads,* for to hit them it was requisite to fire on the ground. When they fairly appeared above ground, it was very evident that our men were not inclined to meet them. Every field-glass was now pointed to the hill with intense anxiety by us in cantonments, and we saw the officers urging their men to advance on the enemy. Most conspicuous were Mackintosh, Laing, Troup, Mackenzie, and Layton; who, to encourage the men, pelted the Gházíás with stones as they climbed the hill; and, *to do the fanatics justice, they returned the as-*

sault with the same weapons. Nothing would do; our men would not advance, though this party did not appear to be a hundred and fifty in number.

At length one of the Gházíás rushed forward, waving his sword over his head; a *sipáhi* of the 37th darted forth and met him with his bayonet; but instead of a straight charge, he gave him a kind of side stroke with it, and they both fell, and both rose again. Both were killed eventually, the Gházíá was shot by another man. It was very like the scenes depicted in the battles of the Crusaders. The enemy rushed on—drove our men before them very like a flock of sheep, with a wolf at their heels. They captured one gun. The artillerymen fought like heroes; two were killed at the gun; Sergeant Mulhall received three wounds, poor Laing was shot whilst waving his sword over the gun, and cheering the men. . . . Brigadier Shelton says that when our men ran he ordered the halt to be sounded; at which the troops mechanically arrested their flight, and fell into their places!

They ran till they gained the second square, which had not broken; and the men finding a stand, turned about, gave a shout, and then the Gházíás were, in their turn, panic-struck, abandoned the gun, but made off with the limber and horses. On this we retook the gun, without resistance. . . . At this time I was standing on the ramparts, and heard the envoy, in my presence, ask the General (Elphinstone) to pursue the flying troops into the city, which he refused, saying, 'it was a wild scheme, and not feasible.'

This account coincides exactly with the statements made by those officers engaged in the action whom I had opportunities of consulting. The reader can therefore form his own judgment.

6. It must be admitted, in Brigadier Shelton's favour, that the odds were fearfully against him, although had reinforcements been sent out to his aid at the critical time the result might have been widely different, and he would have been deservedly extolled as a hero.]

CHAPTER 10

Conferences and Negotiations With the Insurgent Chiefs

November 24th.—Our troops had now lost all confidence; and even such of the officers as had hitherto indulged the hope of a favourable turn in our affairs, began at last reluctantly to entertain gloomy forebodings as to our future fate. Our force resembled a ship in danger of wrecking among rocks and shoals, for want of an able pilot to guide it safely through them. Even now, at the eleventh hour, had the helm of affairs been grasped by a hand competent to the important task, we might perhaps have steered clear of destruction; but, in the absence of any such deliverer, it was but too evident that Heaven alone could save us by some unforeseen interposition.

I have already mentioned the new bridge thrown over the river by General Elphinstone: this the enemy, advancing up the bed of the river under cover of the bank, today began to demolish. I must do Brigadier Shelton the justice to say that, he seeing the vast importance of the bridge in case of a retreat (an alternative of which he never lost sight), had strongly urged the erection of a field-work for its protection; in fact there was a small unfinished fort near at hand, which one night's work of the sappers would have rendered fit for the purpose, and a small detachment thrown into it would have perfectly commanded the bridge. But this simple precaution was neglected, and the result will be seen in the sequel.

Captain Conolly now wrote in from the Bálá Hisár, strongly advising an immediate retreat thither, on which movement several of the chief military and all the political officers considered our only hope of holding out through the winter to depend. But the old objections were still urged against the measure by Brigadier Shelton and others;

and the general, in a letter this day addressed to the envoy, expressed his opinion that:

> .... the movement, if not altogether impossible, would be attended with great difficulty, encumbered as we should be with numerous sick and wounded. The enemy would doubtless oppose us with their whole force, and the greater part of the troops would be required to cover the operation, thus leaving the cantonments imperfectly defended; that the men were harassed, dispirited, and greatly reduced in numbers; and failure would be attended with certain destruction to the whole force. To remove the ammunition and stores would be the work of several days, during which the enemy would hover around, and offer every obstacle to our operations. Our wounded were increased, whilst our means of conveying them were diminished. Would the Bálá Hisár hold the force with all the followers? Water was already said to be selling there at a high price.[1] We had barely twenty days, supply of provisions in the cantonments; and, even supposing we could find means to carry it with us, there was no prospect of obtaining more in the Bálá Hisár. A retreat thence would be worse than from our present position, after having abandoned our cattle; and the sick and wounded must be left behind us.

In these opinions Brigadier Shelton entirely concurred. An appalling list of objections, it must be confessed, but insufficient to shake my belief that a removal of the force into the Bálá Hisár was not only practicable but necessary for our safety and honour, while the risks attending it, though formidable, were only such as we ought, as soldiers, to have unhesitatingly incurred. Sháh Shujá had moreover declared himself impatient to receive us; and, even had the dreaded ruin overwhelmed us in the attempt, would it not have been a more manly and honourable course, than the inglorious treaty we shortly afterwards entered into with a treacherous band of rebels, by which we deserted the sovereign whom it was our duty to protect to the last drop of our blood? Had we boldly sallied forth, preferring death to dishonour, would not the fate of our poor fellows have been a hundredfold happier than that they subsequently experienced, in their miserable retreat, inasmuch as they would have died in the consciousness of having bravely done their duty? Never were troops exposed to

---

1. This report was entirely untrue.

greater hardships and dangers; yet, sad to say, never did soldiers shed their blood with less beneficial result than during the investment of the British lines at Kábul.

But, to return to my narrative.

A letter to the address of the envoy was this day received from Usmán Khán,[2] Bárakzí, a near relative of the new king, and generally supposed to have a favourable leaning towards us, wherein he took credit to himself for having:

.... checked the ardour of his followers in their pursuit of our flying troops on the preceding day, when, by following up their success, the loss of our cantonments and the destruction of our force was inevitable; but that it was not the wish of the chiefs to proceed to such dreadful extremities, their sole desire being that we should quietly evacuate the country, leaving them to govern it according to their own rules, and with a king of their own choosing.

On the receipt of this friendly communication, the envoy requested the general to state his opinion regarding the possibility, in a military point of view, of retaining our position in the cantonments; as, in case of a negative reply, he might be able to enter into negotiations with the existing rulers of the country.

The general replied to the effect that:

.... we had now been in a state of siege for three weeks; our provisions were nearly expended, and our forage entirely consumed, without the prospect of procuring a fresh supply; that our troops were much reduced by casualties, and the large number of sick and wounded increased almost daily; and that, considering the difficulty of defending the extensive and ill-situated cantonment, the near approach of winter, the fact of our communications being cut off, and that we had no prospect of reinforcement, with the whole country in arms against us; he did not think it possible to retain our present position in the country, and therefore thought the envoy ought to avail himself of the offer to negotiate, which had been made him.

November 27th.—Nothing else of consequence took place until this mornings when two deputies from the assembled chiefs, having

---

2. This chief had sheltered Captain Drummond in his own house since the first day of the outbreak.

made their appearance at the bridge, were ushered into cantonments by Captains Lawrence and Trevor, the envoy having agreed to confer with them, on condition that nothing should be proposed which it would be derogatory in him to consider. The interview took place in the officers' guard-room at the eastern gate; the exact particulars did not transpire, but the demands made by the chiefs were such as it was impossible to comply with, and the deputies took leave of the envoy with the exclamation that "we should meet again in battle!"

"We shall at all events meet," replied Sir William, "at the day of judgement." At night the envoy received a letter from the chiefs proposing terms of so disgraceful and insulting a nature, as seemed at once to preclude all hope of terminating our difficulties by treaty. The tenor of them was as follows:

> That we should deliver up Shih Shujá and his whole family; lay down our arms; and make an unconditional surrender; when they might perhaps be induced to spare our lives, and allow us to leave the country on condition of never returning.

The envoy's reply was such as well became the representative of his country's honour.

> He was astonished, (he said), at their departing from that good faith for which he had given them credit, by violating the conditions on which he had been led to entertain proposals for a pacific arrangement; that the terms they proposed were too dishonourable to be entertained for a moment; and that, if they persisted in them, he must again appeal to arms, leaving the result to the God of battles.

December 1st,—No active renewal of hostilities took place until today, when a desperate effort was made by the enemy to gain possession of the Bálá Hisár, which they endeavoured to effect by a night attack, in the first instance, on the *Búrj-i-lákh*, an isolated tower forming an outwork to the fortress, and from its elevated position commanding almost the entire works. This point was, however, strongly reinforced without delay by Major Ewart, commanding the garrison, and notwithstanding the determined spirit exhibited by the enemy, who made repeated charges up the hill, they were repulsed with considerable slaughter.

December 4th.—At an early hour the enemy moved out in force from the city, and, having crowned the Bemárú hills, posted two guns in the gorge, from which they maintained a tolerably brisk fire for several hours into the cantonments, effecting fortunately but little mischief; in the evening they, as usual, retired to their respective haunts. During the night a rush was suddenly made by a party of Afgháns to the gate of Muhammad Sharíf's fort, garrisoned by our troops, which they attempted, in imitation of our own method at the taking of Ghazní, to blow open with powder bags, but without success.

December 5th.—This day the enemy completed the destruction of our bridge over the river, which they commenced on the 24th *ult.*, no precaution having been taken to prevent the evil. Day after day we quietly looked on without an effort to save it, orders being in vain *solicited* by various officers for preventive measures to be adopted. In consequence of the enemy having commenced mining one of the towers of Muhammad Sharíf's fort, the garrison was reinforced, and Lieutenant Sturt succeeded during the night in destroying the mine. This, however, could only be effected at the expense of opening a passage under the walls, which it became necessary to barricade; and although this measure of precaution was efficiently executed, such was the nervous state of the party composing the garrison, that no reliance could be placed on their stability in case of an attack.

December 6th.—The garrison of Muhammad Sharíf's fort was relieved at an early hour by one company of Her Majesty's 44th, under Lieutenant Grey, and one company 37th Native Infantry, under Lieutenant Hawtrey, an amply sufficient force for the defence of the place against any sudden onset; but, unhappily, the fears of the old garrison were communicated to the new, and, owing to the representations of Lieutenant Hawtrey, the defences were minutely examined by Lieutenant Sturt, the garrison engineer, and by him pronounced to be complete. Scarcely, however, had that officer returned to cantonments, ere information was conveyed to the general that the detachment, having been seized with a panic, had taken flight over the walls, and abandoned the fort to the enemy.

It would appear that a small party of *jazailchís*, having crept up to the undermined tower under cover of the trees in the *Sháh Bágh*, had fired upon the garrison through the barricaded breach which I have above described, unfortunately wounding Lieutenant Grey, upon whose departure for medical aid, the Europeans, deprived of their officer, lost what little confidence they had before possessed, and collecting their bedding under the walls, betrayed symptoms of an intention to retreat. The enemy meanwhile, emboldened by the slackened fire of the defenders, approached momentarily nearer to the walls, and, making a sudden rush to the barricade, completed the panic of the garrison, who now made their escape over the walls in the greatest consternation, deaf to the remonstrances of their gallant commander. The *sepoys*, who at first remained staunch, contaminated by the bad example set them, refused to rally: and Lieutenant Hawtrey, finding himself deserted by all, was obliged reluctantly to follow, being the last to leave the fort.

The enemy, though at first few in numbers, were not slow to avail themselves of the advantage afforded them, and their banner was soon planted in triumph on the walls.

December 7th.—The European garrison was this day withdrawn from the *bázár*, and three companies of the 37th Native Infantry substituted in their room.

[This deplorable affair of Muhammad Sharíf's fort was made the subject of much censorious comment and of mutual recrimination at the time; and writings as I did, before the excitement caused by these disastrous events had been calmed down, and when it seemed inevitable that nothing less would satisfy the public mind than a thorough sifting of facts, I felt in a manner compelled, as a faithful narrator of events, and in the cause of truth and justice, to lay bare what then seemed a serious evil, regardless of unpleasant consequences. But now the case is altogether different, and I feel that I should not be justified in reviving needlessly an ungracious topic which had best be forgotten.

Moreover, while looking back calmly, through a long vista of years, on those sad events of my younger days, and with a more ripe military experience than I then could boast, I feel persuaded that there was a natural tendency among the actors in those trying scenes (myself included) to view what were in reality accidental and exceptional errors or backslidings, on the part of officers or men, through an exaggerated medium. For, after all, there was nothing very surprising in the occupants of a small fortified outpost being seized with a temporary panic on discovering that their enemies outside were secretly undermining the walls, with the probable intent to blow up the interior garrison at any moment!

Such incidents are by no means so rare as might be supposed in time of war, even among the bravest troops in the world, and when we consider the continuous hardships and trials which these harassed and half-starved soldiers had undergone during the previous seven weeks, we ought not to marvel if their nervous system had become temporarily unstrung. Let it the rather be remembered, to their lasting credit, how these self-same men fought their way, only a few days subsequently, under the personal leading of their brave brigadier, during the fatal and ever-memorable retreat from Kábul, through a long series of difficult mountain passes, and opposed on all sides by a countless host of fanatical Afgháns, as hereafter recorded in these pages; and—let the voice of a worn-out opprobrium be silenced for evermore![3]

The alarming discovery having been made that our supply of provisions had been materially over-rated, and that not even a sufficiency for one day remained in store. Captain Hay was despatched with a convoy of military stores into the Bálá Hisár, with orders to bring back the animals laden with grain. He started several hours before daybreak, but on reaching the Siyáh Sang hill, a few straggling shots being fired upon his rear, the men riding the laden *yábús* (Afghán ponies) were panic-stricken, and, hastily casting the loads to the ground, galloped for safety to the front.

Much private property was lost at the same time, for, notwithstanding all the opposition that had been made to the proposal of a retreat to the Bálá Hisár, the general in some degree deferred to the opinions of those who favoured the movement, by adopting the half-measure of sending in magazine supplies from time to time by driblets. This led many to suppose that the whole force would sooner or later retreat thither, and accordingly advantage was taken of every opportunity to send in a few private necessaries in advance. On this occasion the attempt failed in the manner I have above related; but Captain Hay nevertheless accomplished the primary object of his journey, by bringing back as much provisions as could be collected on so short a notice.

December 8th,—The envoy, having addressed a public letter to the general, requested him to state "whether or not it was his opinion that any further attempt to hold out against the enemy would merely have the effect of sacrificing both His Majesty Sháh Shujá and ourselves; and whether, supposing this to be so, the only alternative left was not to negotiate for our safe retreat out of the country, on the most favourable terms possible?"

---

3. Though somewhat late in the day, I rejoice in the opportunity now afforded me of offering the above tribute of the respect due alike to the dead and to the living.

The general, in reply, stated his conviction that:

.....the present situation of the troops was such, from the want of provisions and the impracticability of procuring more, that no time ought to be lost in entering into negotiations for a safe retreat from the country: That, as regarded the troops at Kandahár, and the rumours of their approach to our assistance, he would be sorry, in the absence of all authentic information, to risk the sacrifice of the troops by waiting for their arrival, when we were ignorant even of their having commenced their march, and were reduced to three days, supply of provisions for our *sepoys* at half rations, and almost without any forage for our horses and cattle: That our number of sick and wounded in hospital exceeded six hundred, and our means for their transport were far from adequate, owing to the death by starvation of so many of our camels, from which cause also we should be obliged, at this inclement season, to leave their tents and bedding behind, with such a march before us:

That, as regarded the king, he must be excused from entering upon that point of the envoy's letter, and leave its consideration to his better knowledge and judgment; but he might be allowed to say that it little became him, as commanding the British troops in Afghánistan, to regard the necessity of negotiation in any other light than as concerned *their* honour and welfare, for both of which he should be answerable, by a farther stay here, after the sudden and universal rebellion against His Majesty's authority which had taken place throughout his dominions: That the whole of the grain and forage in the vicinity was exhausted, and the defence of the extensive and ill-selected cantonment would not admit of distant expeditions to obtain supplies from the strongly fortified dwellings of an armed and hostile population; our present numbers being insufficient for its defence, and obliging the whole of the troops to be almost constantly under arms.

In conclusion, he could only repeat his opinion that the envoy should lose no time in entering into negotiations.

This letter was countersigned by Brigadiers Shelton and Anquetil, and Colonel Chambers, who entirely concurred in the opinions it expressed. Meanwhile starvation stared us in the face, and it became necessary to adopt immediate measures for obtaining a further supply of provisions. A consultation was accordingly held with this object at the general's house, and it was determined that an attack should be made on the neighbouring fort of *Khoja Ruwash* at an early hour the following morning.

December 9th,—The morning dawned, but no signs of preparation appeared for the proposed enterprise; no bridge was laid down for the passage of the guns and cavalry; no troops were in readiness to march; and it was plain that either no orders had been given, or no attention had been paid to them. Thus, notwithstanding the importance of its object, the expedition was suffered to die a natural death.

Upon this subject I shall only remark that Brigadier Shelton commanded the garrison, and that with him the necessary arrangements rested.

[The following explanation has since been given in an English paper:—
The real fact is, the Envoy found from his informant that there were plenty of provisions in the village, (and in another, *Khadabad*, near it,) but it was fully armed, and it was declared that the whole armed force of the city would sally out to resist our march to the place; and hence the *Envoy* and *General* decided on the force not being sent. Was this the Brigadier's fault?]

Intelligence having been this day received of a decisive victory gained over the enemy by General Sale at Jallálábád, the envoy conceived it might have the effect of modifying the general's opinion regarding the immediate necessity of negotiating with the rebel chiefs, and addressed him a letter on the subject. The general, however, declared in reply, that, pleasing as the intelligence was, it could not in the slightest degree influence our position, so as to affect the expediency of our treating; in forming which opinion he was much influenced by the joint representations that had been just made to him by Captains Boyd and Johnson, the respective heads of the Company's and *Sháh's* commissariat, wherein they declared their utter inability to procure grain or forage within three or four miles, and that, although three days' supply of *átá* (ground wheat) might still be procurable from the Bálá Hisár, yet every additional day's delay now crippled the cattle more and more, and rendered our position more perilous. Notwithstanding these apparently conclusive arguments, there existed strong grounds for believing that the Bálá Hisár contained a much larger supply of provisions than was generally supposed.

December 10th.—Another convoy of military stores was despatched to the Bálá Hisár this morning under command of Lieutenant Le Geyt, by whom a further supply of *átá* was brought back in return.

December 11th.—The rebel chiefs having manifested an inclination to treat, the envoy, accompanied by Captains Lawrence, Mackenzie, and Trevor, went out to meet them on the plain towards Siyáh Sang. There were present Muhammad Akbar Khán, Usmán Khán, Muhammad Khán Naib Amír (commonly called Naib Amír), Bdrakzis;—Muhammad Sháh Khán, Hamza Khán, Khuda Khán, Ghalzís;—Jayat Ulal Khán, Pupalzí;—Khán Sharín Khán, Kazilbásh;—and several others of inferior note, but all heads of tribes. After the exchange of salutations. Sir William addressed the assembled Kháns, alluding to past times, during which relations of perfect cordiality and friendship had existed between them and the English. He greatly lamented that feelings of so pleasant and mutually beneficial a nature should have been thus rudely interrupted; but professed himself wholly ignorant of the causes of such interruption.

He proceeded to state that sentiments of good will towards the Afghán nation had principally induced the British Government to lend their aid, in restoring to the seat of his ancestors a king, who, notwithstanding his misfortunes, originating in causes to which he would not then allude, had ever reigned in the hearts of the mass of his people; that the restoration of their monarch had apparently given the utmost satisfaction to all classes throughout his dominions. If, however, that satisfaction had passed away, and given place to emotions of a wholly contrary nature (and he supposed that the assembled *sirdars* and *Kháns* might be considered the mouth-piece of the people), it no longer became the British Government to persist in a course so displeasing to those chiefly interested in the result.

On this account he was willing to enter into negotiations, for the smoothing over of present difficulties, and for the adopting of such measures as were likely to be the most conducive towards the re-establishment of that mutual friendship between the British and Afghán Governments, the maintenance of which, he felt assured, must be earnestly desired by both parties. To all these propositions Muhammad Akbar Khán and Usmán Khán, as the principal personages present, expressed, with the hearty concurrence of the inferior chiefs, their entire assent, adding many expressions of their personal esteem for the envoy himself, and their gratitude for the way in which the exiled *amír* had been used.

The envoy then requested permission to read to them a paper containing a general sketch of the proposed treaty. This being agreed to, the articles of the treaty were read and discussed. Their general purport was to the effect—That the British should evacuate Afghánistán, including Kandahár, Ghazní, Kábul, Jallálábád, and all the other stations absolutely within the limits of the country so called;—that they should be permitted to return not only unmolested to India, but that supplies of every description should be afforded them in their road thither, certain men of consequence accompanying them as hostages;—that the Amír Dost Muhammad Khán, his family, and every Afghán now in exile for political offences, should be allowed to return to their country;—that Sháh Shujá and his family should be allowed the option of remaining at Kábul or proceeding with the British troops to Ludiána, in either case receiving from the Afghán Government a pension of one *lakh* of *rúpís per annum*;—that means of transport for the conveyance of our baggage, stores, &c., including that required by the royal family, in case of their adopting the latter alternative, should be furnished by the existing Afghán Government ;—that an amnesty should be granted to all those who had made themselves obnoxious on account of their attachment to Sháh Shujá and his allies, the British;—that all prisoners should be released;—that no British force should be ever again sent into Afghánistán, unless called for by the Afghán Government, between whom and the British nation perpetual friendship should be established on the sure foundation of mutual good offices.

To all these terms the chiefs cordially agreed, with the exception of Muhammad Akbar, who cavilled at several, especially that of the amnesty, but was over-ruled by his coadjutors. He positively refused to permit the garrison to be supplied with provisions until it had quitted cantonments, which movement he clamorously demanded should take place the following morning. His violence caused some confusion; but the more temperate of his party having interfered, it was finally agreed that our evacuation of the cantonments should take place in three days—that provisions should be supplied—and that to all the above-mentioned articles of this new treaty a formal assent in writing should be sent, with all the usual forms of a restored peace. The chiefs, on returning to the city, took with them Captain Trevor as a hostage for the sincerity of the envoy.

During the whole of this interview, which took place not far from the bottom of the Siyáh Sang hills, great anxiety was felt in the cantonments from the apparent danger to which the envoy was exposed,— he being accompanied only by a few troopers of the Body-guard,— and from the circumstance of large bodies of the enemy's horse and foot being seen to pass towards the scene of conference from the city, their leaders evidently with much difficulty restraining their advance beyond a certain point. Sir William, however, although not unaware of the perfidious nature of those he had to deal with, nor insensible to the risk he ran, (a shot, in fact, from the fanatic multitude, having whistled over the heads of the gentlemen in attendance on him, as they advanced towards the rendezvous,) wisely imagined that a display of confidence was the best mode of begetting good faith.

It is, however, pretty certain that the tumultuary movements of the Afghán troops, whose presence was in direct violation of the stipulations under which the conference was held, were not without their cause, it having been the earnest desire of Muhammad Akbar to seize upon the envoy's person at that very meeting, from which step he was with difficulty restrained by the other *Kháns*. But no sense of personal danger could have deterred a man of Sir William's truly chivalrous and undaunted character from the performance of any duty, private or public.

Would that he had been more alive to the apprehensions which influenced common men! We might not then have to mourn over the untimely fate of one whose memory must be ever cherished in the hearts of all who knew and were capable of appreciating him, notwithstanding the disastrous termination of his political career, as that of a good, and, in many essential points, a great man.

CHAPTER 11

Preparations for Evacuating

December 12th,—It is undeniable that Sir William Macnaghten was forced into this treaty with men whose power he despised, and whose treachery was proverbial, against his own judgment, by the pressing representations of our military heads. It is no less true that, whatever may have been his political remissness or want of foresight before the rebellion broke out, he had, throughout the perils that afterwards beset us, displayed a truly British spirit of unflinching fortitude and indefatigable energy, calculated, under more auspicious leaders, to have stimulated the zeal and valour of the troops, and to have cheered them under the trials and hardships they were called on to endure; and I can safely add, without fear of contradiction, that scarcely an enterprise was undertaken throughout the siege but at the suggestion, and even the entreaties, of the envoy, he volunteering to take on himself the entire responsibility.

Justice demands this tribute to the memory of one, whose acts, as they will assuredly undergo the severe scrutiny of his countrymen, it therefore becomes the duty of every eye-witness, who bears testimony on the subject, not only to shield from misrepresentation, but, where they are deserving of it, to hold up to public admiration. I am led to write this solely by my public knowledge of the man. If I could bring myself, on matters of such vital importance, to follow the dictates of mere private feeling, my bias would be altogether on the side of my late lamented military chief, and for whose infirmities every allowance ought, in common justice, to be made. With a mind and talents of no ordinary stamp, and a hitherto unsullied fame, he committed the fatal error of transporting himself suddenly from a state of prolonged luxurious repose, at an advanced age, to undertake the fatigues and cares inseparable from high military command, in a foreign, uncongenial climate; he thus not only ruined his already shattered health, but (which to a soldier was a far worse calamity) grievously damaged that high reputation which his early services had secured for him.

The terms of the new treaty were immediately made known to Sháh Shujá, by which that unfortunate monarch found himself once more doomed to an old age of exile and degradation. The first step towards its fulfilment was the withdrawal of our troops from the Bálá Hisár, which was to have taken place this very day, but was postponed for a short time longer to admit of the necessary preparations being made. A deputation of chiefs had an interview in the close of the day, who were the bearers of a most unexpected proposition, to the effect that Shah Shujá should continue king, on condition of intermarrying his daughters with the leading Afghán chiefs, and abandoning the offensive practice of keeping the chief nobles of his kingdom waiting for hours at his gate in expectation of audience. The Afgháns hate ceremony, which Sháh Shujá, carried at all times to an absurd extent, hence much of his unpopularity. This arrangement was not intended to annul those parts of the treaty which related to our immediate evacuation of the country, for the fulfilment of which some married families were demanded as hostages.

December 13th,—Such was the inveterate pride of the king, that he yielded a most reluctant consent to the above-mentioned proposals, notwithstanding that the only alternative was the instant resignation of his kingdom. Little confidence was, however, placed by the envoy in the sincerity of the chiefs, whose hatred of the Dúrání ruler was notorious. As our retreat was now fully decided on, and our well-stocked magazine was shortly to fall a prey to our enemies, the General ordered that some ammunition should be distributed to certain of the camp-followers; and commanding officers were directed to indent for new arms and accoutrements, in exchange for such as were old and damaged. The reins of discipline had, however, by this time become so terribly relaxed, and so little attention was paid to superior orders by either officers or men, that many of the officers in command of companies rested content with sending their men to the magazine, to help themselves at will, the stores being unfortunately, in the absence of any finished building for their reception, arranged under the trees of an orchard, in charge of a small guard.

The consequence was, as might have been expected, a scene of confusion and plunder, which was rendered worse by a rush of camp-followers, who, imagining that a licence had been given for everyone to take whatever he pleased, flocked in hundreds to the spot, and terribly increased the tumult; insomuch that the authority of several officers, who, observing what was going on, exerted themselves to restore order, was for several minutes set at naught. At last, however, the place was cleared of the intruders, and the greater portion of the stolen articles was recovered the same evening. But this event may be taken as an instance of the unsteadiness of the troops, and of the recklessness that now began to extend itself amongst all ranks of the force.

At 2 p. m. the troops in the Bálá Hisár, consisting of the 54th N. I., half of Captain Nicholl's troop of horse artillery, and a detachment of the mountain train, with two howitzers, under Lieutenant Green, commenced their evacuation of that fortress. They were also encumbered with an iron nine-pounder gun, and a twenty-four pounder brass howitzer, drawn by bullocks, which it was the general's wish should have been left behind, but his order to that effect had by some accident missed its destination. As the utmost scarcity of provisions prevailed in cantonments, Captain Kirby, the commissariat officer, had zealously exerted himself to collect a supply of about 1600 *maunds* of wheat and flour to carry thither.

Much delay, however, occurred in packing and loading; and the best part of the day being nearly spent ere one third of that quantity was ready, Major Ewart deemed it advisable to move off without further loss. He found Muhammad Akbar Khán in waiting with a small body of followers outside the gate, for the purpose of escorting him to cantonments; and, as evening drew nigh, a dense crowd of armed Afgháns had been observed to collect on the Siyáh Sang Hill, along the base of which our troops must pass, giving rise to suspicions of some meditated treachery. While the rearguard, with the Mountain-train gun and a portion of the baggage, was leaving the gate, some of Muhammad Akbar's followers, pushing quietly past them, endeavoured to effect an entrance into the fort; but on their being recognised by the king's guard, the gates were immediately shut, and a round or two of grape fired upon the intruders, with so indiscriminate an aim as to endanger the lives of Captain Conolly and several of the *sepoys*, of whom some were severely wounded.

It can scarcely be doubted that Muhammad Akbar's intention was to have seized the gate with a few of his men, until a rush of the Afgháns from the hill should have enabled him to carry the body of the place by storm. The vigilance of the garrison having defeated this plan, the wily chief, imagining that the gates would again be opened to readmit our troops, informed Major Ewart that, owing to the lateness of the hour and the threatening attitude assumed by the crowd on the hill, it would be necessary to postpone his inarch until the following morning. In consequence of this sudden ill-timed announcement, Major Ewart applied to the king for the immediate readmission of his troops for shelter during the night; but the monarch, whose suspicions of foul play on the part of Muhammad Akbar were now fully awakened, positively refused to accede to the request. The prospect of passing the night in the low marshy ground under the walls, without tents, bedding, firewood, or food, for officers or men, was sufficiently cheerless; while the fear of treachery on the part of Muhammad Akbar, and the dangerous vicinity of an armed multitude, whose watch-fires already gleamed on the adjacent hills, tended but little to relieve the discomforts of such a situation. The cold was intensely bitter, and perhaps so miserable a night had never before been spent by Indian troops.

December 14th.—At an early hour this morning, Muhammad Akbar having declared his readiness to proceed, the troops commenced their march. The advance-guard was suffered to proceed unmolested; but the rearguard, on reaching the base of the Siyáh Sang hill, was fired upon by the enemy, who crowned the ridge; and the iron 9-pounder being for a few moments accidentally separated from the column in crossing a water-cut, an instantaneous rush was made upon it by a number of Afgháns, and a poor sick European artilleryman, who for want of a more suitable conveyance had been lashed to the gun, was unmercifully butchered. The approach of the rearguard, and a round or two of grape from the Mountain Train howitzer, drove off the assailants; and they were restrained from offering any additional annoyance by the exertions of Muhammad Akbar himself, who, galloping in amongst them with a few followers, threatened to cut down any who dared to be guilty of further opposition to the progress of the detachment, which accordingly reached cantonments safe at about 9 a.m.

December 16th,—Sháh Shujá having, for reasons best known to himself, withdrawn his consent to the arrangement which was to have continued him in the possession of his rights, the treaty resumed its original form; but the chiefs positively refused to supply provisions or forage, until we should further assure them of our sincerity by giving up every fort in the immediate vicinity of cantonments. Forage had for many days been so scarce, that the horses and cattle were kept alive by paring off the bark of trees, and by eating their own dung over and over again, which was regularly collected and spread before them. The camp-followers were destitute of other food than the flesh of animals which expired daily from starvation and cold. The daily consumption of *átá* by the fighting-men was about one hundred and fifty *maunds*, and not above two days, supply remained in store. By giving up the forts in question, all of which commanded the cantonment, we should place ourselves entirely at the mercy of the enemy, who could at any time render our position untenable.

But our leaders now seemed to consider that we had no other chance left than to concede to the demands of the chiefs, however unreason- able; and our troops were accordingly withdrawn from the Riká-báshí, Magazine, and Zulfikár's Forts, and from the *masjid* opposite the western gate, all of which were forthwith occupied by the Afgháns, who, on their part, sent in Nassar-ullah Khán, a brother of Nawáb Zamán Khán, as a hostage, and a supply of about one hundred and fifty *maunds* of *átá* for the troops. They likewise promised us two thousand camels and four hundred *yábús* for the march to Jallálábád.

December 18th.—The delay of the chiefs in furnishing the necessary carriage, and the *Sháh's* dilatoriness in deciding on his future course, compelled us from day to day to postpone our departure. Meanwhile the increasing severity of the winter rendered every hour's procrastination of the utmost consequence; and this morning our situation was rendered more desperate than ever by a heavy fall of snow, which covered the ground to the depth of five inches, and never afterwards disappeared. Thus a new enemy entered on the scene, which we were destined to find even more formidable than an army of rebels.

December 19th,—The envoy wrote an order for the evacuation of Ghazní, and it was arranged that the 27th Native Infantry, which garrisoned the place, should march through the Zurmat valley, and pursue the route of Derá Ishmaíl Khán. The 22nd was fixed for our departure.

December 20th.—The envoy had an interview with the chiefs, who now demanded that a portion of our guns and ammunition should be immediately given up. They also required Brigadier Shelton as a hostage. It was proposed by Lieutenant Sturt to the General to break off the treaty, and march forthwith to Jallálábád, devoting all the means of transport we possessed to the service of the sick, and the conveyance of such public stores as were absolutely necessary. But neither the general nor his immediate advisers could bring themselves to adopt a course which would have saved the national honour, at the risk of sacrificing our whole force.

It has been truly said that a council of war never fights. A door of hope had, until this day, still remained open to us in the approach of Colonel Maclaren's force to our assistance from Kandahár; we now heard with despair of its retreat from Tází, in consequence of the snow.

December 21st.—The envoy met Usmán Khán and Muhammad Akbar Khán on the plain, when four hostages were fixed upon, two of whom (Captains Conolly and Airey) were at once given over. Brigadier Shelton, having expressed a decided objection to undertake the duty, was not insisted upon. In the evening Captains Trevor and Drummond were permitted to return to cantonments, the latter officer having been concealed in the city since the 2nd of November.

December 22nd.—I was ordered to conduct an officer of Nawáb Zamán Khán over the magazine, that he might make choice of such stores as would be most acceptable to the chiefs. I recommended a large pile of 8-inch shells to his notice, which I knew would be of no use to the chiefs, as the mortars were with Captain Abbott's battery at Jallálábád. He eagerly seized the bait, and departed in great glee, with his prize laden on some old ammunition-waggons.

The envoy at the same time sent his carriage as a present to Muhammad Akbar Khán. That same night the last-named chief spread the net, into which Sir William Macnaghten was, on the following day, so miserably lured to his destruction. Captain Skinner, at this time living under Muhammad Akbar's protection, was made the bearer of proposals to the envoy, of so advantageous a nature, as to prove, in his forlorn circumstances, irresistibly tempting.

Amin-ullah Khán, the most influential of the rebels, was to be seized on the following day, and delivered up to us as a prisoner. Muhammad Khán's fort was to be immediately occupied by one of our regiments, and the Bálá Hisár, by another. Sháh Shujá was to continue king; Muhammad Akbar was to become his *wazír*, and our troops were to remain in their present position until the following spring. That a scheme like this, bearing impracticability on its very face, should have for a moment deceived a man of Sir William's usual intelligence and penetration, is indeed an extraordinary instance of infatuation, that can only be accounted for on the principle that a drowning man will catch at a straw.

Our fortunes were now at their lowest ebb; the chiefs were apparently delaying our departure until the snow should have formed an impassable barrier to the removal of our troops, who, even in the absence of an enemy, would but too probably perish from cold and famine. A treaty formed with men famed for falsehood and treachery, and who had already shown an utter disregard of some of its most important stipulations, could be regarded as little better than so much waste paper; added to which considerations, Sir William felt that his own fame was deeply involved in the issue of that policy,[1] of which he had from the very first been the prime advocate and upholder, and that with it he must stand or fall.

The specious project of Muhammad Akbar offered a solution to the difficulties that beset his path, at which he grasped with an eagerness engendered by despair. The strength of the rebels had hitherto lain in their unanimity; the proposed stroke of policy would at once dissolve the confederacy, and open a road by which to retrieve our ruined fortunes. On either hand there was danger; and, miserable as Sir William's life had been for the past six weeks, he was willing to stake his all on the issue of a plan which seemed to offer a faint hope of recovering the ground we had lost.

In a fatal hour he signed his name to a paper consenting to the arrangement. His doom was sealed. The whole was a scheme got up by the chiefs, to test his sincerity.

December 23rd.—At about noon Sir William Macnaghten, attended by Captains Lawrence, Trevor, and Mackenzie, left the mission-house to attend a conference with Muhammad Akbar Khán on the plain towards Siyáh Sang. Previously to this he had requested the general that two regiments and two guns might be in readiness for secret service, and that, as the interview would be of a critical nature, the garrison might be kept well on the alert, and the walls strongly manned. In leaving the cantonments, Sir William expressed his disappointment at the paucity of men on the ramparts, and the apparent inertness of the garrison at such a critical moment, saying, "However, it is all of a piece with the military arrangements throughout the siege." On his leaving the gate only sixteen troopers of the Body-guard were in attendance, but the remainder shortly afterwards joined, under Lieuten-

---

1. That of invading Afghánistán for the purpose of restoring Sháh Shujá as king.

ant Le Geyt.

Sir William now for the first time explained to the officers who accompanied him the objects of the present conference, and Captain Lawrence was warned to be in readiness to gallop to the Bálá Hisár, to prepare the king for the approach of a regiment.

Apprehensions being expressed of the danger to which the scheme might expose him, in case of treachery on the part of Muhammad Akbar, he replied, "Dangerous it is; but if it succeeds, it is worth all risks: the rebels have not fulfilled even one article of the treaty, and I have no confidence in them; and if by it we can only save our honour, all will be well. At any rate, I would rather suffer a hundred deaths than live the last six weeks over again."

Meanwhile crowds of armed Afgháns were observed hovering near the cantonment and about Muhammad Khán's fort, causing misgivings in the minds of all but the envoy himself, whose confidence remained unshaken. On arriving near the bridge, they were met by Muhammad Akbar Khán, Muhammad Sháh Khán, Dost Muhammad Khán, Khuda Baksh Khán, Azád Khán, and other chiefs, amongst whom was the brother of Amin-ullah Khán, whose presence might have been sufficient to convince Sir William that he had been duped.

The usual civilities having passed, the envoy presented Akbar Khán, with a valuable Arab horse, which had only that morning been purchased for three thousand *rúpís*. The whole party then sat down near some rising ground, which partially concealed them from cantonments.

Captain Lawrence having called attention to the number of inferior followers around them, with a view to their being ordered to a distance, Muhammad Akbar exclaimed, "No, they are all in the secret;" which words had scarcely been uttered, when Sir William and his three companions found themselves suddenly grasped firmly by the hands from behind, whilst their swords and pistols were rudely snatched away by the chiefs and their followers. The three officers were immediately pulled forcibly along and compelled to mount on horseback, each behind a Ghalzí chief, escorted by a number of armed retainers, who with difficulty repelled the efforts of a crowd of fanatic Gházís, who, on seeing the affray, had rushed to the spot, calling aloud for the blood of the hated *infidels*, aiming at them desperate blows with their long knives and other weapons, and only deterred from firing by the fear of killing a chief. The unfortunate envoy was last seen struggling violently with Muhammad Akbar, "consternation and horror depicted on his countenance."

On their nearing Muhammad Khán's fort, renewed attempts were made to assassinate the three captive officers by the crowd there assembled. Captain Trevor, who was seated behind Dost Muhammad Khán, unhappily fell to the ground, and was instantly slain. Captains Lawrence and Mackenzie reached the fort in safety, but the latter was much bruised in various parts of his body, and both were greatly exhausted from the excitement they had undergone.

At the entrance of the fort, a furious cut was aimed at Captain Mackenzie's head by a ruffian named Mullah Múmin, which was warded off by Muhammad Sháh Khán, that chief receiving the blow on his own shoulder: Being taken into a small room, they found themselves still in continual jeopardy from repeated assaults of the Gházís without, who were with the greatest difficulty restrained from shooting them through the window, where the hand of some recent European victim (afterwards ascertained to be that of the envoy himself) was insultingly held up to their view.

Throughout this trying scene they received repeated assurances of protection from the Ghalzí chiefs; but Amín-ullah Khán coming in gave vent to a torrent of angry abuse, and even threatened to blow them from a gun. It is deserving of notice, that, amidst the congratulations which on all sides met the ear of Muhammad Sháh Khán on the events of the day, the solitary voice of an aged *Mullá* was raised in condemnation of the deed, which he solemnly pronounced to be "foul" and calculated to cast a lasting disgrace on the religion of Muhammad. At midnight they were removed to the house of Muhammad Akbar Khán. As they passed through the streets of Kábul, notwithstanding the excitement that had prevailed throughout the day, it resembled a city of the dead; nor did they meet a single soul.

By Akbar Khán they were received courteously, and were now informed for the first time by Captain Skinner of the murder of the envoy and Captain Trevor. That Sir William Macnaghten met his death at the hands of Muhammad Akbar himself there can be no reasonable doubt. That chief had pledged himself to his coadjutors to seize the envoy that day, and bring him into the city, when the chiefs hoped to have been able to dictate their own terms, retaining him as a hostage for their fulfilment. Finding it impossible, from the strenuous resistance Sir William offered, to carry him off alive, and yet determined not to disappoint the public expectation altogether,—influenced also by his tiger passions, and the remembrance of his father's wrongs,—Muhammad Akbar drew a pistol, the envoy's own gift a few hours before, and shot him through the body, which was immediately hacked to pieces by the ferocious Gházís, by whom the dismembered trunk was afterwards carried to the city, and publicly exposed in the Chár Chauk, or principal mart. The head was taken to the house of Nawáb Zamán Khán, where it was triumphantly exhibited to Captain Conolly.

Such was the cruel fate of Sir William Macnaghten, the accomplished scholar, the distinguished politician, and the representative of Great Britain at the court of Sháh Shujá-ul-Mulk.

It cannot but be acceptable to my readers, if I here present entire the interesting and important letters of Captains Mackenzie and Lawrence on this melancholy subject.

LETTER ADDRESSED BY CAPTAIN C. MACKENZIE TO LIEUTENANT VINCENT EYRE.

My Dear Eyre,

You ask for a minute account of the circumstances attending the assassination of the late Sir William Macnaghten, and my own detention and imprisonment on that occasion. You may remember that, for many days previous to the fatal 23rd December, the poor Envoy had been subjected to more wear and tear, both of body and mind, than it was possible for the most iron frame and the strongest intellect to bear without deeply feeling its effects. He had fulfilled all the preliminary conditions of the treaty which had been proposed between the British and the Afghán insurgents, whereas the *Kháns* had in no one particular adhered to their engagements. Bad faith was evident in all their proceedings, and our condition was a desperate one; more especially as Sir William had ascertained, by bitter experience, that no hope remained in the energies and resources of our military leaders, who had formally protested that they could do nothing more.

Beset by this disgraceful imbecility on the one hand, and by systematic treachery on the other, the unfortunate envoy was driven to his wits' end, and, as will be seen, forgot, in a fatal moment, the wholesome rule which he had theretofore laid down for himself, of refusing to hold communication with individuals of the rebel party, especially with him who was notorious, even amongst his villainous countrymen, for ferocity and treachery, to wit, Muhammad Akbar Khán.

Late in the evening of the 22nd December, Captain James Skinner, who, after having been concealed in Kábul during the greater part of the siege, had latterly been the guest of Muhammad Akbar, arrived in cantonments, accompanied by Muhammad Sadíq Khán, a first cousin of Muhammad Akbar, and by Sirwár Khán, the Arhání merchant who in the beginning of the campaign had furnished the army with camels, and who had been much in the confidence of Sir A. Burnes, being in fact one of our staunchest friends. The two latter remained in a different apartment, while Skinner dined with the envoy. During dinner, Skinner jestingly remarked that he felt as if laden with combustibles, being charged with a message from Muhammad Akbar to the envoy of a most portentous nature.

Even then I remarked that the envoy's eye glanced eagerly towards Skinner with an expression of hope. In fact, he was like a drowning man catching at straws. Skinner, however, referred him to his Afghán companions, and after dinner the four retired into a room by themselves. My knowledge of what there took place is gained from poor Skinner's own relation, as given during my subsequent captivity with him in Akbar's house. Muhammad Sadíq disclosed Muhammad Akbar's proposition to the envoy, which was, that the following day Sir William should meet him (Muhammad Akbar) and a few of his immediate friends, *viz.* the chiefs of the Eastern Ghalzís, outside the cantonments, when a final agreement should be made, so as to be fully understood by both parties; that Sir William should have a considerable body of troops in readiness, which, on a given signal, were to join with those of Muhammad Akbar and the Ghalzís, assault and take Mahmúd Khán's fort, and secure the person of Amín-ullah.

At this stage of the proposition Muhammad Sadíq signified that, for a certain sum of money, the head of Amín-ullah should be presented to the envoy; but from this Sir William shrunk with abhorrence, declaring that it was neither his custom nor that of his country to give a price for blood. Muhammad Sadíq then went on to say, that, after having subdued the rest of the *Kháns*, the English should be permitted to remain in the country eight months longer, so as to save their *purdah* (veil, or credit), but that they were then to evacuate Afghánistán, as if of their own accord; that Sháh Shujá was to continue king of the country, and that Muhammad Akbar was to be his *wazír*. As a further reward for his (Muhammad Akbar's) assistance, the British Government were to pay him thirty *lacs* of *rupees*, and four *lacs* of *rupees per annum* during his life!

To this extraordinary and wild proposal, Sir William gave ear with an eagerness which nothing can account for but the supposition, confirmed by many other circumstances, that his strong mind had been harassed, until it had, in some degree, lost its equipoise; and he not only assented fully to these terms, but actually gave a Persian paper to that effect, written in his own hand, declaring as his motives that it was not only an excellent opportunity to carry into effect the real wishes of Government, which were to evacuate the country with as much credit to ourselves as possible, but that it would give England time to enter into, a treaty with Russia, defining the bounds beyond which neither were to pass in Central Asia.

So ended this fatal conference, the nature and result of which, contrary to his usual custom. Sir William communicated to none of those who, on all former occasions, were fully in his confidence, *viz*. Trevor, Lawrence, and myself. It seemed as if he feared that we might insist on the impracticability of the plan, which he must have studiously concealed from himself. All the following morning his manner was distracted and hurried in a way that none of us had ever before witnessed. It seems that Muhammad Akbar had demanded a favourite Arab horse, belonging to Captain Grant, assistant adjutant-general of the force.

To avoid the necessity of parting with the animal, Captain Grant had fixed his price at the exorbitant sum of five thousand *rupees*; unwilling to give so large a price, but determined to gratify the *sirdár*, Sir William sent me to Captain Grant to prevail upon him to take a smaller sum, but with orders that if he were peremptory, the five thousand *rupees* should be given. I obtained the horse for three thousand *rupees*, and Sir William appeared much pleased with the prospect of gratifying Muhammad Akbar by the present.

After breakfast, Trevor, Lawrence, and myself were summoned to attend the envoy during his conference with Muhammad Akbar Khán. I found him alone, when, for the first time, he disclosed to me the nature of the transaction he was engaged in. I immediately warned him that it was a plot against him. He replied hastily, "A plot! let me alone for that, trust me for that!" and I consequently offered no further remonstrance. Sir William then arranged with General Elphinstone that the 54th Regiment, under Major Ewart, should be held in readiness for immediate service.

The Sháh's 6th, and two guns, were also warned. It is a curious circumstance, and betrays the unhappy vacillation of poor Elphinstone, that, after Sir William had actually quitted the cantonment in full expectation that everything had been arranged according to his desire, he (the General) addressed a letter to him, which never reached him, remonstrating on the danger of the proposed attack, and strongly objecting to the employment of the two above regiments. About 12 o'clock Sir William, Trevor, Lawrence, and myself set forth on our ill-omened expedition. As we approached the Siyáh Sang gate. Sir William observed with much vexation that the troops were not in readiness, protesting at the same time, however, that, desperate as the proposed attempt was, it was better that it should be made, and that a thousand deaths were preferable to the life he had lately led.

After passing the gate, he remembered the horse which he had intended as a present for Akbar, and sent me back for it. When I rejoined him I found that the small number of the body-guard who had accompanied him, had been ordered to halt, and that he, Trevor, and Lawrence, had advanced in the direction of Mahmúd Khán's fort, being some five hundred or six hundred yards from the eastern rampart, and were there awaiting the approach of Muhammad Akbar and his party, who now made their appearance. Close by were some hillocks, on the further side of which from the cantonment a carpet was spread where the snow lay least thick, and there the *Kháns* and Sir William sat down to hold their conference.

Men talk of presentiment; I suppose it was something of the kind which came over me, for I could scarcely prevail upon myself to quit my horse. I did so, however, and was invited to sit down among the *sirdárs*. After the usual salutations Muhammad Akbar commenced business, by asking the envoy if he was perfectly ready to carry into effect the proposition of the preceding night? The envoy replied, "Why not?" My attention was then called off by an old Afghán acquaintance of mine, formerly chief of the Kábul police, by name Ghulám Muyan-ud-dín. I rose from my recumbent posture, and stood apart with him conversing. I afterwards remembered that my friend betrayed much anxiety as to where my pistols were, and why I did not carry them on my person. I answered that although I wore my sword for form, it was not necessary at a friendly conference to be armed *cap-a-pie*.

His discourse was also full of extravagant compliments, I suppose for the purpose of lulling me to sleep. At length my attention was called off from what he was saying, by observing that a number of men, armed to the teeth, had gradually approached to the scene of conference, and were drawing round in a sort of circle. This Lawrence and myself pointed out to some of the chief men, who affected at first to drive them off with whips; but Muhammad Akbar observed that it was of no consequence, as they were in the secret. I again resumed my conversation with Ghulám Muyan-ud-dín, when suddenly I heard Muhammad Akbar call out, "*Bigir! Bigir!*" (seize! seize!), and turning round, I saw him grasp the envoy's left hand with an expression in his face of the most diabolical ferocity.

I think it was Sultán Ján who laid hold of the envoy's right hand. They dragged him in a stooping posture down the hillock, the only words I heard poor Sir William utter being "*Az baráí Khudá!*" (for God's sake!) I saw his face however, and it was full of horror and astonishment. I did not see what became of Trevor, but Lawrence was dragged past me by several Afgháns, whom I saw wrest his weapons from him. Up to this moment I was so engrossed in observing what was taking place, that I actually was not aware that my own right arm was mastered, that my urbane friend held a pistol to my temple, and that I was surrounded by a circle of Gházís with drawn swords and cocked *jazails*.

Resistance was in vain, so listening to the exhortations of Ghulám Muyan-ud-dín, which were enforced by the whistling of divers bullets over my head, I hurried through the snow with him to the place where his horse was standing, being despoiled *en route* of my sabre, and narrowly escaping divers attempts made on my life. As I mounted behind my captor, now my energetic defender, the crowd increased around us, the cries of "Kill the

Káfir" became more vehement, and, although we hurried on at a fast canter, it was with the utmost difficulty Ghulám Muyan-ud-dín, although assisted by one or two friends or followers, could ward off and avoid the sword cuts aimed at me, the rascals being afraid to fire lest they should kill my conductor.

Indeed he was obliged to wheel his horse round once, and taking off his turban (the last appeal a Mussulman can make), to implore them for God's sake to respect the life of his friend. At last, ascending a slippery bank, the horse fell. My cap had been snatched off, and I now received a heavy blow on the head from a bludgeon, which fortunately did not quite deprive me of my senses. I had sufficient sense left to shoot ahead of the fallen horse, where my protector with another man joined me, and clasping me in their arms, hurried me towards the wall of Muhammad Khán's fort.

How I reached the spot where Muhammad Akbar was receiving the gratulations of the multitude, I know not, but I remember a fanatic rushing on me and twisting his hand in my collar until I became exhausted from suffocation. I must do Muhammad Akbar the justice to say, that, finding the Gházís bent on my slaughter, even after I had reached his stirrup, he drew his sword and laid about him right manfully, for my conductor and Mirza Bahá-ud-dín Khán were obliged to press me up against the wall, covering me with their own bodies, and protesting that no blow should reach me, but through their persons.

Pride, however, overcame Muhammad Akbar's sense of courtesy, when he thought I was safe, for he then turned round to me, and repeatedly said in a tone of triumphant derision, "*Shumá mulk-i-má me-gíred!*" (*You'll* seize my country, will you!) He then rode off, and I was hurried towards the gate of the fort. Here new dangers awaited me, for Mullá Múmin, fresh from the slaughter of poor Trevor, who was killed riding close behind me—Sultán Ján having the credit of having given him the first sabre cut,—stood here with his followers, whom he exhorted to slay me, setting them the example by cutting fiercely at me himself. Fortunately a gun stood between us, but still he would have effected his purpose, had not Muhammad Sháh Khán at that instant, with some followers, come to my assistance. These drew their swords in my defence, the chief himself throwing his arm round my neck, and receiving on his shoulder a cut aimed by Mullá Múmin at my head.

During the bustle I pushed forward into the fort, and was immediately taken to a sort of dungeon, where I found Lawrence safe, but somewhat exhausted by his hideous ride and the violence he had sustained, although unwounded. Here the Ghalzí chiefs, Muhammad Sháh Khán, and his brother Dost Muhammad Khán, presently joined us, and endeavoured to cheer up our flagging spirits, assuring us that the envoy and Trevor were not dead, but on the contrary quite well. They stayed with us during the afternoon, their presence being absolutely necessary for our protection. Many attempts were made by the fanatics to force the door, to accomplish our destruction. Others spit at us and abused us through a small window, through which one fellow levelled a blunderbuss at us, which was struck up by our keepers and himself thrust back.

At last Amín-ullah made his appearance, and threatened us with instant death. Some of his people most officiously advanced to make good his word, until pushed back by the Ghalzí chiefs, who remonstrated with this iniquitous old monster, their master, whom they persuaded to relieve us from his hateful presence. During the afternoon a human hand was held up in mockery to us at the window. We said that it had belonged to an European, but were not aware at the time that it was actually the hand of the poor envoy.

Of all the Muhammadans assembled in the room discussing the events of the day, one only, an old *Mullá*, openly and fearlessly condemned the acts of his brethren, declaring that the treachery was abominable, and a disgrace to Islám. At night they brought us food, and gave us each a *postín* to sleep on. At midnight we were awakened to go to the house of Muhammad Akbar in the city. Muhammad Sháh Khán then, with the meanness common to all Afgháns of rank, robbed Lawrence of his watch, while his brother did me a similar favour. I had been plundered of my rings and everything else, previously, by the under-strappers.

Reaching Muhammad Akbar's abode, we were shown into the room where he lay in bed. He received us with great outward show of courtesy, assuring us of the welfare of the envoy and Trevor, but there was a constraint in his manner for which I could not account. We were shortly taken to another apartment, where we found Skinner, who had returned, being on parole, early in the morning. Doubt and gloom marked our meeting, and the latter was fearfully deepened by the intelligence which we now received from our fellow-captive of the base murder of Sir William and Trevor. He informed us that the head of the former had been carried about the city in triumph. We of course spent a miserable night.

The next day we were taken under a strong guard to the house of Zamán Khán, where a council of the *Kháns* was being held. Here we found Captains Conolly and Airey, who had some days previously been sent to the *Nawáb's* house as hostage for the performance of certain parts of the treaty which was to have been entered into. A violent discussion took place, in which Muhammad Akbar bore the most prominent part. We were vehemently accused of treachery, and everything that was bad, and told that the whole of the transactions of the night previous had been a trick of Muhammad Akbar, and Amínullah, to ascertain the envoy's sincerity. They declared that they would now grant us no terms, save on the surrender of the whole of the married families as hostages, all the guns, ammunition, and treasure.

At this time Conolly told me that on the preceding day the envoy's head had been paraded about in the courtyard; that his and Trevor's bodies had been hung up in the public *bazár*, or *chauk*; and that it was with the greatest difficulty that the old *Nawáb*, Zamán Khán, had saved him and Airey from being murdered by a body of fanatics, who had attempted to rush into the room where they were. Also that previous to the arrival of Lawrence, Skinner, and myself, Muhammad Akbar had been relating the events of the preceding day to the *Jirga*, or council, and that he had unguardedly avowed having, while endeavouring to force the envoy either to mount on horseback or to move more quickly, *struck* him, and that, seeing Conolly's eye fastened upon him with an expression of intense indignation, he had altered the phrase and said, "I mean I pushed him."

After an immense deal of gabble, a proposal for a renewal of the treaty, not, however, demanding all the guns, was determined to be sent to the cantonments, and Skinner, Lawrence, and myself, were marched back to Akbar's house, enduring en route all manner of threats and insults. Here we were closely confined in an inner apartment, which was indeed necessary for our safety.

That evening we received a visit from Muhammad Akbar, Sultan Jan, and several other Afgháns. Muhammad Akbar exhibited his double-barrelled pistols to us, which he had worn the previous day, requesting us to put their locks to rights, something being amiss. *Two of the barrels had been recently discharged*, which he endeavoured, in a most confused way, to account for by saying that he had been charged by a *havildár* of the escort, and had fired both barrels at him.

Now, all the escort had run away without even attempting to charge, the only man who advanced to the rescue having been a Hindú *Jemadár* of Chaprásís, who was instantly cut to pieces by the assembled Gházís, This defence he made without any accusation on our part, betraying the anxiety of a liar to be believed. On the 26th, Captain Lawrence was taken to the house of Amín-ullah, whence he did not return to us. Captain Skinner and myself remained in Akbar's house until the 30th. During this time we were civilly treated, and conversed with numbers of Afghán gentlemen who came to visit us. Some of them asserted that the envoy had been murdered by the unruly soldiery. Others could not deny that Akbar himself was the assassin.

For two or three days we had a fellow-prisoner in poor Sirwár Khán, who had been deceived throughout the whole matter, and out of whom they were then endeavouring to screw money. He of course was aware from his countrymen that, not only had Akbar committed the murder, but that he protested to the Gházís that he gloried in the deed. On one occasion a *múnshí* of Major Pottinger, who had escaped from Chárikár, named Mohan Bír, came direct from the presence of Muhammad Akbar to visit us. He told us that Muhammad Akbar had begun to see the impolicy of having murdered the Envoy, which fact he had just avowed to him, shedding many tears either of pretended remorse, or of real vexation, at having committed himself.

On several occasions Muhammad Akbar personally, and by deputy, besought Skinner and myself to give him advice as to how he was to extricate himself from the dilemma in which he was placed, more than once endeavouring to excuse himself for not having effectually protected the envoy, by saying that Sir William had drawn a sword-stick upon him.

It seems that meanwhile the renewed negotiations with Major

Pottinger, who had assumed the envoy's place in cantonments, had been brought to a head, for, on the night of the 30th, Akbar furnished me with an Afghán dress (Skinner already wore one) and sent us both back to cantonments. Several Afgháns, with whom I fell in afterwards, protested to me that they had seen Muhammad Akbar shoot the envoy with his own hand; amongst them Mirza Bahá-ud-dín Khán, who, being an old acquaintance, always retained a sneaking kindness for the English.

I am, my dear Eyre, yours very truly,

C. Mackenzie.

Kábul, 29th July, 1842.

LETTER ADDRESSED BY CAPTAIN G. ST. P. LAWRENCE, LATE MILITARY SECRETARY TO THE ENVOY, TO MAJOR POTTINGER, C.B., LATE IN CHARGE OF THE KÁBUL MISSION.

Sir,

In compliance with your request, I have the honour to detail the particulars of my capture, and of the death of my ever-to-be-lamented chief.

On the morning of the 23rd December, at 11 a.m., I received a note from the late Sir W. H. Macnaghten, warning me to attend, with Captains Trevor and Mackenzie, an interview he was about to have with Sirdár Muhammad Akbar Khán. Accordingly, with the above-named officers, at about 12, I accompanied Sir William, having previously heard him tell Major-General Elphinstone to have two regiments of infantry and two guns ready for secret service. In passing through cantonments, on my observing that there were more Afgháns in cantonments than usual, or than I deemed safe, the envoy directed one of his Afghán attendants to proceed and cause them all to leave, at the same time remarking how strange it was that, although the general was fully acquainted with the then very critical state of affairs, no preparations appeared to have been made, adding, "However, it is all of a piece with the military arrangements throughout the siege."

He then said, "There is not enough of the escort with us," to which I replied, that he had only ordered eight or ten, but that I had brought sixteen, and that I would send for the remainder, which I accordingly did, asking Lieutenant Le Geyt to bring them, and to tell Brigadier Shelton, who had expressed a wish to attend the next interview, that he might accompany them. On passing the gate, we observed some hundreds of armed Afgháns within a few yards of it, on which I called to the officer on duty to get the reserve under arms, and brought outside to disperse them, and to send to the General to have the garrison on the alert. Towards Mahmud Khán's fort were a number of armed Afgháns, but we observed none nearer.

The envoy now told us that he, on the night previous, had received a proposal from Sirdár Muhammad Akbar Khán to which he had agreed, and that he had every reason to hope it would bring our present difficulties to an early and happy termination; that Muhammad Akbar Khán was to give up Naib Amín-ullah Khán as a prisoner to us, for which purpose a regiment was to proceed to Mahmúd Khán's fort, and another corps was to occupy the Bálá Hisár. Sir William then warned, me to be ready to gallop to the king with the intelligence of the approach of the regiment, and to acquaint him with Akbar's proposal.

On one of us remarking that the scheme seemed a dangerous one, and asking if he did not apprehend any treachery, he replied: "Dangerous it is, but, if it succeeds, it is worth all risks; the rebels have not fulfilled even one article of the treaty, and I have no confidence in them, and if by it we can only save our honour, all will be well; at any rate, I would rather suffer a hundred deaths than live the last six weeks over again." We proceeded to near the usual spot, and met Sirdár Muhammad Akbar Khán, who was accompanied by several Ghalzí chiefs, Muhammad Shah Khán, Dost Muhammad Khán, Khudá Baksh Khán, Azad Khán, &c.

After the usual salutations, the envoy presented a valuable horse which Akbar had asked for, and which had been that morning purchased from Captain Grant for three thousand *rupees*. The *Sirdár* acknowledged the attention, and expressed his thanks for a handsome brace of double barrelled pistols which the envoy had purchased from me, and sent to him, with his carriage and pair of horses, the day before.

The party dismounted, and horse-cloths were spread on a small hillock which partially concealed us from cantonments, and which was chosen, they said, as being free from snow. The envoy threw himself on the bank with Muhammad Akbar and

Captains Trevor and Mackenzie beside him; I stood behind Sir William till, pressed by Dost Muhammad Khán, I knelt on one knee, having first called the envoy's attention to the number of Afgháns around us, saying that if the subject of the conference was of that secret nature I believed it to be, they had better be removed. He spoke to Muhammad Akbar, who replied, "No, they are all in the secret."

Hardly had he so said, when I found my arms locked, my pistols and sword wrenched from my belt, and myself forcibly raised from the ground and pushed along, Muhammad Sháh Khán who held me, calling out, "Come along, if you value your life." I turned, and saw the envoy lying, his head where his heels had been, and his hands locked in Muhammad Akbar's, consternation and horror depicted in his countenance. Seeing I could do nothing, I let myself be pulled on by Muhammad Sháh Khán. Some shots were fired, and I was hurried to his horse, on which he jumped, telling me to get up behind, which I did, and we proceeded, escorted by several armed men who kept off a crowd of Ghazís, who sprang up on every side shouting for me to be given up for them to slay, cutting at me with their swords and knives, and poking me in the ribs with their guns: they were afraid to fire, lest they should injure their chief.

The horsemen kept them pretty well off, but not sufficiently so to prevent my being much bruised. In this manner we hurried towards Muhammad Khán's fort, near which we met some hundreds of horsemen who were keeping off the Ghazís, who here were in greater numbers, and more vociferous for my blood. We, however, reached the fort in safety, and I was pushed into a small room, Muhammad Sháh Khán returning to the gate of the fort and bringing in Captain Mackenzie, whose horse had there fallen. This he did, receiving a cut through his *nímcha* (Scother coat) on his arm, which was aimed at that officer, who was ushered into the room with me, much exhausted and bruised from blows on his head and body.

We sat down with some soldiers who were put over us with a view to protect us from the mob, who now surrounded the house, and who till dark continued execrating and spitting at us, calling on the men to give us up to be slaughtered.

One produced a hand (European) which appeared to have been recently cut off; another presented a blunderbuss, and was about to fire it, when it was knocked aside by one of our guard. Several of the *sirdárs* came in during the day, and told us to be assured that no harm should befall us; that the envoy and Trevor were safe in the city (a falsehood, as will be afterwards seen). Naib Amín-ullah Khán and his sons came also. The former, in great wrath, said that we either should be, or deserved to be, blown away from a gun. Muhammad Sháh Khán and Dost Muhammad Khán begged he would not so talk, and took him out of the room.

Towards night food was given to us, and *postíns* to sleep on: our watches, rings, and silk handkerchiefs were taken from us; but in all other respects we were unmolested. The followers of Muhammad Sháh Khán repeatedly congratulated him on the events of the day, with one exception, *viz.* an old *Mullá*, who loudly exclaimed that "the name of the faithful was tarnished, and that in future no belief could be placed in them; that the deed was foul and could never be of advantage to the authors."

At midnight we were taken through the city to the house of Muhammad Akbar Khán, who received us courteously, lamenting the occurrences of the day: here we found Captain Skinner, and for the first time heard the dreadful and astounding intelligence of the murder of the envoy and Captain Trevor, and that our lamented chief's head had been paraded through the city in triumph, and his trunk, after being dragged through the streets, stuck up in the Chár Chauk, the most conspicuous part of the town. Captain Skinner told us, that the report was, that on Muhammad Akbar Khán's telling Sir William to accompany him, he refused, resisted, and pushed the *sirdár* from him; that in consequence he was immediately shot and his body cut to pieces by the Gházís; that Captain Trevor had been conveyed behind Dost Muhammad Khán as far as Muhammad Khán's fort, where he was cut down, but that his body was not mangled, though carried in triumph through the city.

On the following morning (24th) we (Captain Skinner, Mackenzie, and self) were taken to Nawáb Zamán Khán's house, escorted by Sultán Ján and other chiefs, to protect us from the Gházís; there we met Captains Conolly and Airey (hostages) and all the rebel *sirdárs* assembled in council. The envoy's death was lamented, but his conduct severely censured, and it was said that now no faith could be placed in our words. A new treaty, however, was discussed, and sent to the, general and Major Pottinger, and towards evening we returned as we came to Muhammad Akbar's, where I remained a prisoner, but well and courteously treated till the morning of the 26th, when I was sent to Naib Amín-ullah Khán.

On reaching his house I was ushered into his private apartment. The *Naib* received me kindly, showed me the envoy's original letter in reply to Muhammad Akbar's proposition, touching his being made Sháh Shujá's Wazír, receiving a *lakh* of *rupees* on giving the *Naib* a prisoner to us, thirty *lakhs* on the final settlement of the insurrection, &c. To this the *Naib* added that the envoy had told Muhammad Akbar's cousin that a *lakh* of *rupees* would be given for his (Amín-ullah Khán's) head. I promptly replied, "'Tis false," that Sir William had never done so, that it was utterly foreign and repugnant to his nature, and to British usage. The *Naib* expressed himself in strong terms against the envoy, contrasting his own fair and open conduct with that of Sir William. He told me that General Elphinstone and Major Pottinger had begged I might be released, as my presence was necessary to enable them to prepare bills on India, which it had been arranged the *sirdárs* were to get.

After some delay, consequent on my asking for Captain Mackenzie to be released with me, and Muhammad Akbar's stoutly refusing the release of either of us, I was sent into cantonments on the morning of the 29th, escorted by the *Naib's* eldest son and a strong party of horse and foot, being disguised as an Afghán for my greater protection. I must here record that nothing could exceed the *Naib's* kindness and attention to me while under his roof.

     I have, &c, &c.,
  (Signed)   G. St. P. Lawrence,
         Military Secretary,
         Late Envoy and Minister.

Camp Zúdáh,
Ten miles south of Tizín,
10th May, 1842.

CHAPTER 12

Suspense in Cantonment

But what were our troops about all this time? Were no steps taken to rescue the envoy and his friends from their perilous position? Where was the bodyguard which followed them from cantonments? These questions will naturally occur to all who read the foregoing pages, and I wish it were in my power to render satisfactory answers.

The Native bodyguard had only got a few hundred yards from the gate in their progress to the scene of conference, when they suddenly faced about and came galloping back, several shots being fired at them in their retreat. Lieutenant Le Geyt, in passing through the gate, exclaimed that the envoy had been carried off, and it was understood that, finding his men would not advance to the rescue, he came back for assistance.

Intense was the anxiety and wretched the suspense felt by all during the rest of the day. A number of Afgháns, who were trafficking in cantonments at the time of the conference, on hearing the report of firearms in that direction, endeavoured to escape, but were detained by the officer at the gate. No certain tidings regarding the envoy could be obtained: many confidently affirmed that he was alive and unharmed in Muhammad's fort; but Lieutenant Warren stoutly maintained that he had kept his eye upon Sir William from the moment of his leaving the gate, and had distinctly seen him fall to the ground, and the Afgháns hacking at his body. The agony of his poor wife during this dread interval of suspense may be imagined.

December 24th.—The fate of the envoy and his three companions remained a mystery, until the arrival of a note from Captain Conolly notifying his death and that of Captain Trevor, and the safety of Captains Lawrence and Mackenzie.

The two latter officers had been that morning escorted to a conference of chiefs at the house of Nawáb Zamán Khán, where the late envoy's conduct was severely commented on; but his death was nevertheless lamented. The treaty was again discussed; and, after a few alterations and additions had been made, it was sent to General Elphinstone, with an explanation of the breach of faith which had cost the envoy his life.

General Elphinstone now requested Major Pottinger to assume the office of political agent and adviser, which, though still suffering greatly from his wound, and incapacitated from active bodily exertion, that gallant officer's strict sense of public duty forbade him to decline, although he plainly perceived our affairs to be so irretrievably ruined as to render the distinction anything but enviable, or likely to improve his hardly-earned fame.

The additional clauses in the treaty now proposed for our renewed acceptance were—

1st. That we should leave behind all our guns excepting six.

2nd. That we should immediately give up all our treasures.

3rd. That the hostages should be all exchanged for married men, with their wives and families. The difficulties of Major Pottinger's position will be readily perceived when it is borne in mind that he had before him the most conclusive evidence of the late envoy's ill-advised intrigue with Muhammad Akbar Khán, in direct violation of that very treaty which was now once more tendered for consideration.

December 25th.—A more cheerless Christmas-day perhaps never dawned upon British soldiers in a strange land; and the few whom the force of habit urged to exchange the customary greetings of the season, did so with countenances and in tones indicative of anything but merriment. At night there was an alarm, and the drum beat to arms, but nothing occurred of any consequence.

December 26th.—Letters were received from Captain Mackeson, political agent at Pesháwar, announcing the march of strong reinforcements from India. An offer was made by Muhammad Usmán Khán to escort us all safe to Pesháwar for five *lakhs* of *rupees*; and shortly after this the *Naib Amír* arrived, with a verbal agreement to certain amendments which had been proposed in the treaty by Major Pottinger. He was accompanied by a Káshmír merchant and several Hindú *sharofs*, for the purpose of negotiating bills to the amount of fourteen *lakhs* of *rupees*, payable to the several chiefs on the promise of the late envoy.

Major Pottinger being altogether averse from the payment of this money, and indeed strongly opposed to any treaty binding the Indian Government to a course of policy which it might find inconvenient to adopt, a council-of-war was convened by the general, consisting of himself, Brigadiers Shelton and Anquetil, Colonel Chambers, Captain Bellew, assistant quartermaster-general, and Captain Grant, assistant adjutant-general. In the presence of this council, Major Pottinger declared his conviction that no confidence could be placed in any treaty formed with the Afghán chiefs; that, under such circumstances, to bind the hands of Government, by promising to evacuate the country, and to restore the deposed *Amír*, and to waste moreover so much public money, merely to save our own lives and property, would be inconsistent with the duty we owed our country and the Government we served; and that the only honourable course would be either to hold out to the last at Kábul, or to force our immediate retreat to Jallálábád.

This, however, the officers composing the council, one and all, declared to be impracticable, owing to the want of provisions, the surrender of the surrounding forts, and the insuperable difficulties of the road at the present season; they therefore deemed it preferable to pay any sum of money rather than sacrifice the whole force in a hopeless prolongation of hostilities. It was accordingly determined, *nem. con.*, that Major Pottinger should at once renew the negotiations which had been commenced by Sir William Macnaghten, and that the sums promised to the chiefs by that functionary previous to his murder should be paid.

Major Pottinger's objections being thus over-ruled, the tendered treaty was forthwith accepted, and a requisition was made for the release of Captain Lawrence, whose presence was necessary to prepare the bills on India. Pour married hostages, with their wives and children, being required by the chiefs, a circular was sent round, to ascertain if that number would volunteer to remain, a salary of two thousand *rúpís* per month being guaranteed to each as an inducement.

Such, however, was the horror entertained of Afghán treachery since the late tragical occurrence, that some officers went so far as to say they would sooner shoot their wives at once, than commit them to the charge of men who had proved themselves devoid of common honour and humanity. There were, in fact, but one or two who consented to stay, if the general considered that by so doing they would benefit the public service.

[The following are the replies, as given by Lady Sale:—
Lieutenant Eyre said, *if it was to be productive of great good he would stay with his wife and child.* The others all refused to risk the safety of their families. Captain Anderson said he would rather put a pistol to his wife's head and shoot her; and Sturt, that his wife and mother should only be taken at the point of the bayonet: for himself, he was ready to perform any duty imposed upon him.'

The simple fact is, that on the question being put officially, Lieutenant Eyre replied that he was ready to do whatever the general might think *most conducive to the public good* under the circumstances.]

December 27th.—The chiefs were informed that it was contrary to the usages of war to give up ladies as hostages, and that the general could not consent to an arrangement which would brand him with perpetual disgrace in his own country.

December 29th.—The *Naib Amír* came in from the city with Captain Lawrence and the *sharofs*, when the bills were prepared without farther delay. Captains Drummond, Walsh, Warburton, and Webb, having been accepted as hostages, were sent to join Captains Conolly and Airey at the house of Nawáb Zamán Khán. A portion of the sick and wounded, amongst whom was Lieutenant Haughton of the Gúrkah regiment, were likewise conveyed to the city, and placed under the protection of the chiefs. Three of the *Sháh's* guns, with the greater portion of our treasure, were made over during the day, much to the evident disgust of the soldiery.

December 30th.—The remainder of the sick went into the city. Lieutenant Evans, Her Majesty's 44th Foot, being placed in command; Dr. Campbell, 54th Native Infantry, with Dr. Berwick, of the Mission, in medical charge of the whole., Two more of the *Sháh's* guns were given up. It snowed hard the whole day. A crowd of armed Ghalzís and Gházís took up a threatening position close to the eastern gate, and even attempted to force an entrance into cantonments. Much annoyance was daily experienced from these people, who were in the habit of plundering the peaceable dealers, who flocked in from the city with grain and forage, the moment they issued from the cantonments; they even committed frequent assaults on our *sepoys*, and orders to fire on them on such occasions where repeatedly solicited in vain, although it was well known that the chiefs themselves advised us to do so, and the general had given Brigadier Shelton positive instructions to that effect, whenever circumstances might render it advisable.

The consequence was that our soldiers were daily constrained to endure the most insulting and contemptuous taunts and treatment, from fellows whom a single charge of bayonets would have scattered like chaff, but who were emboldened by the apparent tameness of our troops, which they doubtless attributed to the want of common pluck rather than to the restraints of discipline. Captains Mackenzie and Skinner obtained their release this evening, the latter officer having, since the outbreak of the rebellion, passed through some curious adventures in the disguise of an Afghán female.

January 5th.—Affairs continued in the same unsettled state until this date. The chiefs postponed our departure from day to day on divers pretexts. It had been agreed that Nawáb Jabár Khán should escort us to Jallálábád with about two thousand followers, who were to be entertained for that purpose.

It is supposed that, up to the very last, the majority of chiefs doubted the reality of our intention to depart: and many, fearful of the civil discords for which our retreat would be the signal, would have gladly detained us at Kábul. Attempts were made continually by Akbar Khán. to wean the Hindústánís from their allegiance, and to induce them to desert. Numerous cautions were received from various well-wishers, to place no confidence in the professions of the chiefs, who had sworn together to accomplish our entire destruction. Sháh Shujá himself sent more than one solemn warning, and, finding we were bent on taking our own course, used his utmost endeavours to persuade Lady Macnaghten to take advantage of his protection in the Bálá Hisár. He also appealed to Brigadier Anquetil, who commanded the *Shah's* force, "if it were well to forsake him in the hour of need, and to deprive him of the aid of that force, which he had hitherto been taught to consider as his own?" All was, however, unavailing. The general and his council-of-war had determined that go we must, and go we accordingly did.

★★★★★★

In the foregoing chapters I have offered what I honestly believe to be a faithful narration of the dismal train of events which preceded the evacuation of Kábul, and the abandonment of Sháh Shujá, by the British army. In taking a retrospective view of those unprecedented occurrences, it is evident that our reverses may be mainly attributed to a lack of ordinary foresight and penetration on the part of the chief military and civil authorities, on their first entering on the occupation of this country; a country whose innumerable fortified strongholds and difficult mountain passes, in the hands of a proud and warlike population, never really subdued nor reconciled to our rule, though unable to oppose the march of a disciplined army through their land, ought to have induced a more than common degree of vigilance and circumspection in making adequate provision against any such popular outbreak as might have been anticipated, and did actually occur.

But, instead of applying his undeniable talents to the completion of that conquest which gained him an illustrious title and a wide renown, Lord Keane contented himself with the superficial success which attended his progress through a country hitherto untraversed by an European army since the classic days of Alexander the Great; he hurried off, with too great eagerness to enjoy the applause which awaited him in England, and left to his successors the far more arduous task of securing in their grasp the unwieldy prize of which he had obtained the nominal possession.

On his return to India, Lord Keane took with him a large portion of the Bengal force with which he had arrived at Kábul; the *whole* of the Bombay troops made a simultaneous homeward movement; and the army, with which he had entered Afghánistán, was thus reduced to a miserable moiety, before any steps had been taken to guard against surprise by the erection of a stronghold on the approved principles of modern warfare, or the establishment of a line of military posts to keep open our communications with India, on which country the army must necessarily for a long time have been entirely dependent for the munitions of war. The distance from Kábul to Firozpur, our nearest Indian station, is about six hundred miles. Between Kabul and Pesháwar occur the stupendous and dangerous defiles of Khurd-Kábul, Tizín, Parídaral, Jagdallak, and Khaibar, throughout whose whole extent food and forage are procurable only at long intervals and even then with much difficulty.

From Pesháwar to Firozpur is the Panjáb, or country of the Sikhs, traversed by five great rivers, and occupied by a powerful nation, on whose pacific professions no reliance could be placed. Along this extended line of communication Lord Keane established but one small solitary post, in the fort of Ali Masjid, in the heart of the Khaibar pass. He left behind him, in fact, an army whose isolated position and reduced strength offered the strongest possible temptation to a proud and restless race to rally their scattered tribes in one grand effort to regain their lost independence.

In Lord Keane's successors may be seen the same disposition to be too easily satisfied with the outward semblance of tranquillity. Another brigade was ere long withdrawn from a force already insufficient for any great emergency; nor was their position for holding in subjection a vanquished people much improved by their establishment in an ill-situated and ill-constructed cantonment, with their commissariat stores separated from their lines of defence. To the latter-mentioned error may be mainly attributed the evacuation of Kábul and the destruction of the army; for there can be no doubt that, notwithstanding all the difficulties of our position, had the cantonments been well supplied *with* provisions, the troops could have easily held out until the arrival of reinforcements from India.

The real cause of our defeat was, beyond all question, famine. We were not *driven*, but *starved*,[1] out of Kábul; and every allowance ought in common justice to be made for men who, from the very commencement of the conflict, saw the combined horrors of starvation and a rigorous winter frowning in their face,—no succours within reach,—their retreat cut off,—and all their sanguinary efforts either altogether fruitless, or at best deferring for a few short days the ruin which on every side threatened to overwhelm them.

In connection with this subject, I may be excused for quoting, in conclusion, the powerful reasoning of a recent writer in the *Bombay Times*:—

> When a soldier finds that his every movement is directed by a master mind; that, when he is apparently thrust into the greatest danger, he finds, in truth, his greatest security; that his march to engage an apparently superior force is not a wild sacrifice, but the result of a well-calculated plan; when he knows that, however appearances may be, he is sure to come off with honour, for his brethren in arms are already in progress to assist him, und will not fail to be forthcoming at the hour appointed; when he sees that there is a watchful eye over him, providing for all his

---

1. The envoy, in a report to the Government of India, written just afterwards, but which did not reach India in due course, states, paragraph 12, there is " not one day's provisions left;" and, paragraph 17, "We had been fighting forty days against very superior numbers, under great disadvantages; in a day or two we must have perished from hunger, to say nothing of the advanced season of the year, and the extreme cold, from which our Native troops were suffering severely."

wants, assisting him to overcome all his difficulties, and enabling him to reap the fruit of all his successes; when he finds that even retreat is but a preparation for victory, and, as if guided by Providence, all his movements, though to him incomprehensible, are sure to prove steps to some great end;—when the soldier finds this, he rises and lies down in security, and there is no danger which he will not brave. But when, in everything they undertake, they find the reverse of the picture I have drawn; when they are marched, as they imagine, to glory, but find it is only to slaughter; when even victory brings no fruit, and retreat they discover to be flight; when the support they hope for comes not, and they find their labours to be without end or purpose; when the provisions they look for daily are issued to them no more, and they see all their efforts paralysed; the stoutest heart will fail, the bravest sink; for the soldier knows that, do what he will, his efforts can only end in ruin and dishonour.

[An intercepted letter from one of the Kábul chiefs to a friend at Kandahár throws some light on the losses sustained by the Afgháns up to the time of the envoy's murder. He writes as follows:—

Abd-ulah Khán and his two sons are dead; also Táz Muhammad Khán, the son of Amír Muhammad Khán. *Great numbers of the chiefs of the Kábulis and Kazilbáshís have been killed in the various actions, and above two thousand men have been killed and wounded of the Mussulmáns.*]

CHAPTER 13

The Retreat of the Army, and its Annihilation

January 6th.—At last the fatal morning dawned, which was to witness the departure of the Kábul force from the cantonments, in which it had sustained a two-months' siege, to encounter the miseries of a winter march through a country of perhaps unparalleled difficulty, where every mountain defile, if obstinately defended by a determined enemy, must inevitably prove the grave of hundreds.

Dreary indeed was the scene, over which, with drooping spirits and dismal forebodings, we had to bend our unwilling steps. Deep snow covered every inch of mountain and plain with one unspotted sheet of dazzling white, and so intensely bitter was the cold, as to penetrate and defy the defences of the warmest clothing.

No signs of the promised escort appeared: but at an early hour the preparations commenced for our march. A cut was made through the eastern rampart, to open an additional passage for the troops and baggage, a sufficient number of gun-waggons and platform planks were taken down to the river for the formation of a temporary bridge, and every available camel and *yábú* (the whole amounting to two thousand) was laden with military stores, commissariat supplies, and such small proportion of camp-equipage as was indispensably necessary to shelter the troops in a climate of extraordinary rigour.

The strength of the whole force at this time was, so far as can now be ascertained, very nearly as follows:—

1 troop of Horse Artillery	90	} 690 Europeans.
H.M.'s 44th Foot	600	
5th Regt. Light Cavalry, 2 squad.	260	
5th Shah's Irreg. do. (Anderson's)	500	
Skinner's Horse, 1 rissála	70	} 970 Cavalry.
4th Irreg. do. 1 do.	70	
Mission escort, or body-guard	70	
5th Native Infantry	700	
37th do.	600	
54th do.	650	
6th Shah's Infantry	600	} 2,840.
Sappers and Miners	20	
Shah's do.	240	
Half the Mountain Train	30	
Total	4,500 fighting-men.	

6 Horse Artillery guns.
3 Mountain Train do.

Besides the above, the camp-followers amounted, at a very moderate computation, to about twelve thousand men, besides women and children. These proved from the very first mile a serious clog upon our movements, and were, indeed, the main cause of our subsequent misfortunes. It is to be devoutly hoped that every future commander-in-chief of the Indian army will adopt decisive measures to prevent a force employed on field service from being ever again afflicted with such a curse.

The order of march was as follows:—

H.M.'s 44th Foot	} The advance, under Brigadier Anquetil.
Sappers and Miners	
Irreg. Horse, 1 squad.	
3 Mountain Train guns	
The escort, with the ladies	} Main column, under Brigadier Shelton.
The invalids and sick	
2 Horse Artillery guns	
Anderson's Irreg. Horse	
37th Native Infantry, with treasure	
5th Native Infantry, with baggage	
54th Native Infantry	} Rear-guard, under Colonel Chambers.
6th Shah's Infantry	
5th Light Cavalry	
4 Horse Artillery guns	

All being ready at 9 a.m., the advance commenced moving out. At this time not a single Afghán was to be seen in any direction, and the peaceable aspect of affairs gave rise to strong hopes that the chiefs intended to remain true to their engagements.

At 10 a.m. a message was brought from Nawáb Jabár Khán, requesting us to defer our departure another day, as his escort was not yet ready to accompany us. By this time, however, the greater part of the force was in motion, and a crowd of Afgháns, who had issued from the village of Bemárú, impatient for plunder, had forced their way into the northern cantonment, or Mission Compound (which, owing to some mistake, had been evacuated too soon by the Sháh's 6th Infantry), and were busily engaged in the work of pillage and destruction. The advance was delayed for upwards of an hour at the river, having found the temporary bridge incomplete; and it was noon ere the whole had crossed over, leaving a clear road for the main column to follow.

The order of march in which the troops started was, however, soon lost, and the camp-followers with the public and private baggage, once out of cantonments, could not be prevented from mixing themselves up with the troops, to the utter confusion of the whole column.

The main body, with its long train of laden camels, continued to pour out of the gate until the evening, by which time thousands of Afgháns, the majority of whom were fanatical Gházís, thronged the whole area of cantonments, rending the air with their exulting cries, and committing every kind of atrocity. The rearguard, being unable to restrain them, was obliged to provide for its own safety by taking up a position outside, on the plain, where a great quantity of the baggage had been brought to a stand-still at the canal (within one hundred and fifty yards of the gate), whose slippery sides afforded no safe footing for the beasts of burden. The bridge across the river, being by this time impracticable, occasioned additional delay.

The Afgháns, who had hitherto been too busily engaged in the work of plunder and destruction to take much notice of the troops, now began to line the ramparts, and annoy them with a mischievous fire of *jazails*, under which many fell; and it became necessary, for the preservation of those who remained, to spike and abandon two of the Horse Artillery guns.

Night had now closed around; but the Gházís, having fired the residency and almost every other building in the cantonment, the conflagration illuminated the surrounding country for several miles, presenting a spectacle of fearful sublimity. In the mad fervour of their religious zeal, these ignorant fanatics even set fire to the gun-carriages belonging to the various pieces of ordnance, which we had left in position round the works, of whose use the Afghán chiefs were thus luckily deprived. The general had been often urged to destroy these guns, rather than suffer them to fall into the enemy's hands, but he considered that it would have been a breach of the treaty to do so. Before the rearguard commenced its march, Lieutenant Hardyman of the 5th Light Cavalry, with fifty rank and file, were stretched lifeless on the snow.

Much baggage was abandoned at starting, and much was plundered on the road. Scores of worn-out *sepoys* and camp-followers lined the way, having sat down in despair to perish in the snow. It was 2 a.m. ere the rearguard reached camp at Baigrám, a distance of only five miles. Here all was confusion. The tents had been pitched without the slightest regard to regularity, those of different regiments being huddled together in one intricate mass, mixed up with baggage, camp-followers, camels, and horses, in a way which beggars description. The flimsy canvas of the soldiers' tents was but a poor protection from the cold, which towards morning became more and more intense; and thousands of poor wretched creatures were obliged to lie down on the bare snow, without either shelter, fire, or food. Several died during the night; amongst whom was an European conductor of ordnance.

About twenty *jazailchís*, who still held faithfully by Captain Mackenzie, suffered less than the rest, owing to their systematic mode of proceeding. Their first step on reaching the ground was to clear a small space from the snow, where they then laid themselves down in a circle, closely packed together, with their feet meeting in the centre; all the warm clothing they could muster among them being spread equally over the whole. By these simple means sufficient animal warmth was generated to preserve them from being frost-bitten; and Captain Mackenzie, who himself shared their homely bed, declared that he had felt scarcely any inconvenience from the cold. It was different with our *sepoys* and camp-followers, who, having had no former experience of such hardships, were ignorant how they might best provide against them, and the proportion of those who escaped, without suffering in some degree from frost-bites, was very small. Yet this was but the beginning of sorrows!

January 7th,—At 8 a.m. the force moved off in the reverse order of yesterday—if that could be called order which consisted of a mingled mob of soldiers, camp-followers, and baggage-cattle, preserving not even the faintest semblance of that regularity and discipline on which depended our only chance of escape from the dangers which threatened us. Even at this early stage of the retreat scarcely one-half of the *sepoys* were fit for duty; hundreds had, from sheer inability to keep their ranks, joined the non-combatants, and thus increased the confusion. As for the Sháh's 6th Infantry, it was nowhere to be found; only a few straggling files were perceptible here and there; and it was generally believed that the majority of the regiment had absconded during the night to Kábul.

At starting, large clods of hardened snow adhered so firmly to the hoofs of our horses, that a chisel and hammer would have been requisite to dislodge them. The very air we breathed froze in its passage out of the mouth and nostrils, forming a coating of small icicles on our moustaches and beards.

The advance proceeded onward without molestation, though numerous small bodies of Afghán horse and foot were observed hanging about our flanks, and moving in a parallel direction with ourselves. These were at first supposed to form a part of our escort, hut the mistake was soon discovered by their attacking the reargaurd, commanded by Brigadier Anquetil, consisting of Her Majesty's 44th, Lieutenant Green's Mountain Train guns, and a squadron of Irregular Horse. Much baggage fell into the enemy's hands, who, though in some degree kept in check by the guns, exhibited a bold fronts and maintained a harassing fire on our troops, whose movements were terribly crippled by the disorderly multitude that thronged the road in front.

The latter being for several minutes brought to a stand-still by a deep water-cut which intersected the road, the Mountain Train guns endeavoured to pass clear of them by making a short detour, in doing which they got separated from the infantry, and—one happening at this unlucky moment to upset—the enemy seized the opportunity to rush forward and capture them, before Her Majesty's 44th, who saw too late their awkward predicament, could render effectual assistance.

A gallant example was, however, shown by Lieutenant Green and his few artillerymen, who made a sudden charge upon the foe, and spiked the guns, but, not being supported, they were obliged a second time to abandon them. Lieutenant White, the Adjutant of Her Majesty's 44th, received a severe wound through the face on this occasion.

Brigadier Anquetil now sent to the front for reinforcements, which, however, it was found impracticable to furnish, from the crowded state of the road. The Afghán horse shortly after this charged into the very midst of the column of baggage, and carried off large quantities of plunder, creating the greatest confusion and dismay. Numbers fell from wounds, and still greater numbers from mere bodily weakness produced by cold, fasting, and fatigue. It was found necessary to spike and abandon two more Horse Artillery guns, which the horses were found perfectly incapable of dragging any further through the deep snow.

On the arrival of the advance at Búta-i-khák, the general, having been informed that the rear was in danger of being entirely cut. off, ordered a halt, and sent back all the troops that could be spared, together with the two remaining guns, to drive off the enemy, who had now assembled in great numbers in the rear, and were proceeding to crown some heights on the right commanding the road. This was, however, prevented by our troops under Brigadier Shelton, who took possession of the nearer heights, and kept the enemy in check for upwards of an hour. On this occasion. Lieutenant Shaw, of the 54th Native Infantry, was wounded severely in the thigh. Meanwhile Captain Skinner had fallen in with a follower of Muhammad Akbar Khán, from whom having learned that the chief was encamped near at hand, he accompanied the man to his master's presence.

Muhammad Akbar now informed Captain Skinner that he had been sent by the chief to escort us to Jallálábád, and declared that we had been attacked in consequence of having marched contrary to their wishes. He insisted on our halting at Búta-i-khák till the following mornings in which case he would provide food, forage, and firewood for the troops; but he said that he should expect six hostages to insure our not marching beyond Tizín before tidings should be received of General Sale's evacuation of Jallálábád, for which an order had been already despatched to that officer, in compliance with the stipulations of the treaty.

These terms having been agreed to, the firing ceased for the present, and the force came to a halt on some high ground near the entrance of the Khurd-Kábul pass, having in two days accomplished a distance of only ten miles from Kabul.

Here, again, the confusion soon became indescribable. Suffice it to say that an immense multitude of from fourteen thousand to sixteen thousand men, with several hundred cavalry horses and baggage cattle, were closely jammed together in one monstrous, unmanageable mass. Night again closed over us, with its attendant train of horrors,—starvation, cold, exhaustion, death; and of all deaths I can imagine none more agonising than that where a nipping frost tortures every sensitive limb, until the tenacious spirit itself sinks under the extreme of human suffering.

January 8th.—At an early hour the treacherous Afgháns again commenced to molest us with their fire, and several hundreds having assembled in hostile array to the south of the camp, the troops were drawn up in expectation of an attack. Major Thain, putting himself at the head of the 44th Foot, and exhorting the men to follow him, led them boldly on to the attack; but the enemy did not think proper to await the shock of bayonets, and effected a hasty retreat. In this business Her Majesty's 44th Foot behaved with a resolution and gallantry worthy of British soldiers.

Captain Skinner again went to communicate with Muhammad Akbar Khán, who demanded that Major Pottinger and Captains Lawrence and Mackenzie should immediately be made over to him, which was accordingly done, and hostilities again ceased; the *sirdár* promising to send forward some influential men to clear the pass from the Ghalzís, who occupied it, and were lying in wait for our approach. Once more the living mass of men and animals was in motion. At the entrance of the pass an attempt was made to separate the troops from the non-combatants, which was but partially successful, and created considerable delay. The rapid effects of two nights, exposure to the frost in disorganizing the force can hardly be conceived. It had so nipped the hands and feet of even the strongest men, as to completely prostrate their powers and incapacitate them for service; even the cavalry, who suffered less than the rest, were obliged to be lifted on their horses. In fact only a few hundred serviceable fighting-men remained.

The idea of threading the stupendous pass before us, in the face of an armed tribe of blood-thirsty barbarians, with such a dense irregular multitude, was frightful, and the spectacle then presented by that waving sea of animated beings, the majority of whom a few fleeting hours would transform into a line of lifeless carcasses to guide the future traveller on his way, can never be forgotten by those who witnessed it. (See written extracts in note following). We had so often been deceived by Afghán professions, that little or no confidence was placed in the present trace; and we commenced our passage through

The Khurd-Kabul Pass

the dreaded pass in no very sanguine temper of mind. This truly formidable defile is about five miles from end to end, and is shut in on either hand by a line of lofty hills, between whose precipitous sides the sun at this season could dart but a momentary ray. Down the centre dashed a mountain torrent, whose impetuous course the frost in vain attempted to arrest, though it succeeded in lining the edges with thick layers of ice, over which the snow lay consolidated in slippery masses, affording no very easy footing for our jaded animals. This stream we had to cross and recross about eight-and-twenty times.

> *Note:*—When the avenging army under General Pollock was in progress to Kábul in the September following, Lieutenant Greenwood, of Her Majesty's 31st Regiment, writes:—
>> On entering the Khurd-Kábul pass we were all struck with the utmost astonishment. The other passes are as nothing in comparison with this almost impregnable defile. The dead of General Elphinstone's army lay in heaps; in some places they seemed to be mowed down in whole battalions. Although eight months had elapsed, they had been preserved in the snow, and their ghastly faces seemed to call upon us for revenge.
>
> Major Smith, of Her Majesty's 9th Foot, thus describes the same scene:—
>> Next morning we marched through the Khurd-Kábul pass to Búda-i-khák. The scene we witnessed was full of the most painful interest. At this fatal spot not less than three thousand individuals of the Kábul army were massacred by the Afgháns. Nine English ladies, with eighteen or twenty young children, witnessed the frightful spectacle, and shared its dangers. There is a grandeur in the scenery of this pass which seemed to accord with the hideous aspect of the road along which we travelled, strewed for two miles like a charnel house with mouldering skeletons. What feeling was excited in our troops by such objects may readily be conceived.
>
> The Rev. J. N. Allen, Chaplain to the army under General Nott, writes on the 14th October 1842:—
>> Marched at 6 a.m. through the Khurd-Kábul—a stupendous pass. It is closed in by hills and overhanging rocks, which, if defended, would be exceedingly dangerous, al-

most impossible to crown, and a cause of immense loss even to the most intrepid and well-organized force with favourable weather. It will easily be conceived, therefore, what it must have been to the troops under General Elphinstone, starved, dispirited, and disorganized, in the month of January; the ground deep in snow, and exposed to the fire of crowds of Afgháns.

The entrance to the pass would have formed a fine subject for Salvator Rosa. The gorge looked dark, gloomy, and threatening. The craggy and fantastic rocks towered almost perpendicularly on both sides, many of them quite so, to an enormous height. The foreground was occupied by the skeletons of the ill-fated troops, and with the larger forms of camels and horses. . . . All around was horror. A *valley of the shadow of death* it was indeed; and everyone felt sensibly relieved when we emerged from it.

As we proceeded onwards, the defile gradually narrowed, and the Ghalzís were observed hastening to crown the heights in considerable force. A hot fire was opened on the advance, with whom were several ladies, who, seeing their only chance was to keep themselves in rapid motion, galloped forward at the head of all, running the gauntlet of the enemy's bullets, which *whizzed* in hundreds about their ears, until they were fairly out of the pass. Providentially the whole escaped, with the exception of Lady Sale, who received a slight wound in the arm.[1] It ought, however, to be mentioned, that several of Muhammad Akbar's chief adherents, who had preceded the advance, exerted themselves strenuously to keep down the fire; but nothing could restrain the Ghalzís, who seemed fully determined that nobody should interfere to disappoint them of their prey. Onward moved the crowd into the thickest of the fire, and fearful was the slaughter that ensued. An universal panic speedily prevailed, and thousands, seeking refuge in flight, hurried forward to the front, abandoning baggage, arms, ammunition, women, and children, regardless for the moment of everything but their own lives.

The rearguard, consisting of Her Majesty's 44th and 54th Native Infantry, suffered severely; and at last, finding that delay was only destruction, they followed the general example, and made the best of

---

1. She was recovered on the 10th of May following, having been meanwhile most kindly treated in the family of Nawáb Zimán Khán at Kábul.

their way to the front. Another Horse Artillery gun was abandoned, and the whole of its artillerymen slain. Captain Anderson's eldest girl,[2] and Captain Boyd's youngest boy, fell into the hands of the Afgháns. It is supposed that three thousand souls perished in the pass, amongst whom were Captain *Paton*, Assistant-Quartermaster-General; and Lieutenant *St. George*, 37th Native Infantry; Majors *Griffiths*, 37th Native Infantry, and *Scott*, Her Majesty's 44th; Captains *Bott*, 5th Cavalry, and *Troup*, Brigadier-Major Sháh's force. Dr. *Cardew* and Lieutenant *Sturt*, engineers, were wounded, the latter mortally.

This fine young officer had nearly cleared the defile when he received his wound, and would have been left on the ground to be hacked to pieces by the Gházís who followed in the rear to complete the work of slaughter, but for the generous intrepidity of Lieutenant Mein of Her Majesty's 13th Light Infantry, who, on learning what had befallen him, went back to his succour, and stood by him for several minutes, at the imminent risk of his own life, vainly entreating aid from the passersby. He was at length joined by Sergeant Dean of the Sappers, with whose assistance he dragged his friend on a quilt through the remainder of the pass, when he succeeded in mounting him on a miserable pony, and conducted him in safety to camp, where the unfortunate officer lingered till the following morning, and was the only man of the whole force who received Christian burial. Lieutenant Mein was himself at this very time suffering from a dangerous wound in the head, received in the previous October, and his heroic disregard of self, and fidelity to his friend in the hour of danger, are well deserving of a record in the annals of British valour and virtue.[3]

On the force reaching Khurd-Kábul, snow began to fall, and continued till morning. Only four small tents were saved, of which one belonged to the general: two were devoted to the ladies and children, and one was given up to the sick; but an immense number of poor wounded wretches wandered about the camp destitute of shelter, and perished during the night. Groans of misery and distress assailed the ear from all quarters. We had ascended to a still colder climate than we had left behind, and were without tents, fuel, or food: the snow was

---

2. The author's little boy (now a Major of Artillery in Bengal, [as at time of first publication]), who was strapped on the back of a faithful Afghán servant, had a very narrow escape, owing to the animal falling and throwing them off in the middle of the pass."

3. The above passage was quoted by Sir Robert Peel, then Prime Minister of England, in the House of Commons. Lieutenant, now Colonel, Mein still survives on the active list, (as at time of first publication).

the only bed for all, and of many, ere morning, it proved the *winding-sheet*. It is only marvellous that any should have survived that fearful night!

January 9th.—Another morning dawned, awakening thousands to increased misery; and many a wretched survivor cast looks of envy at his comrades who lay stretched beside him in the quiet sleep of death. Daylight was the signal for a renewal of that confusion which attended every movement of the force. The general had intended us to march at 10 a.m., but a large portion of the troops, with nearly all the camp-followers, moved off without orders at 8 a.m., and had advanced about a mile from the camp, when they were recalled by the general, in consequence of a communication from Muhammad Akbar Khán, who promised to use every endeavour to furnish us with supplies, but strongly recommended us to halt until he could make some proper arrangements for escorting us down safely.

There can be no doubt that the general feeling in camp was adverse to a halt, there being scarcely even a native soldier who did not plainly perceive that our only chance of escape consisted in moving on as fast as possible. This additional delay, therefore, and prolongation of their sufferings in the snow, of which one more march would have carried them clear, made a very unfavourable impression on the minds of the native soldiery, who now for the first time began very generally to entertain the idea of deserting; nor is it at all astonishing that these symptoms should have first developed themselves amongst the *Sháh's* native cavalry, who were, for the most part, exceedingly young soldiers, and foresaw full well the fatal result of all these useless and pernicious delays. The love of life is strong in every breast.

These men had hitherto behaved remarkably well, notwithstanding the numerous efforts that had been made to detach them from their duty; and, if their fealty at last gave place to the instinct of self-preservation, be it remembered in their favour, that it was not until the position of the force, of which they formed a part, had become altogether desperate beyond the reach of cure.

Towards noon Captain Skinner arrived in camp with a proposition from Muhammad Akbar Khán that all the widowed ladies and married families, whose destitute situation in camp rendered them objects of universal pity and sympathy, should at once be made over to his protection, to preserve them from further hardships and dangers; in this case he promised to escort them down safely, keeping them one day's march in rear of the army. The general, though not himself disposed to place much confidence in Muhammad Akbar's friendly professions, was strongly recommended by Captain Skinner to trust him on the present occasion, as he felt assured that such a mark of confidence would be attended with happy results to the whole force.

Anxious at all events to save the ladies and children from further suffering, the general gave his consent to the arrangement, and told Captain Skinner to prepare all the married officers and ladies to depart immediately with a party of Afghán horse, who were in waiting to receive them. His intention also was that all the wounded officers in camp should have had the option of availing themselves of the same opportunity to seek Muhammad Akbar's protection; but the others were hurried off by the Afgháns before this had become generally known, and only two were in time to join them.[4]

Up to this time scarcely one of the ladies had tasted a meal since leaving Kábul. Some had infants a few days old at the breast, and were unable to stand without assistance. Others were so far advanced in pregnancy, that, under ordinary circumstances, a walk across a drawing-room would have been an exertion; yet these helpless women, with their young families, had already been obliged to rough it on the backs of camels, and on the tops of the baggage *yábús*: those who had a horse to ride, or were capable of sitting on one, were considered fortunate indeed. Most had been without shelter since quitting the cantonment—their servants had nearly all deserted or been killed—and, with the exception of Lady Macnaghten and Mrs. Trevor, they had lost all their baggage, having nothing in the world left but the clothes on their backs; those, in the case of some of the invalids, consisted of *nightdresses* in which they had started from Kábul in their litters.

Under such circumstances a few more hours would probably have seen some of them stiffening corses. The offer of Muhammad Akbar was consequently their only chance of preservation. The husbands, better clothed and hardy, would have infinitely preferred taking their chance with the troops; but where is the man who would prefer his own safety, when he thought he could by his presence assist and console those near and dear to him?

It is not therefore wonderful that, from persons so circumstanced,

---

4. Captain Troup, Brigadier-Major, *Sháh's* force, and Lieutenant Mein, Her Majesty's 13th Light Infantry, who went as Lady Sale's protector.
Lieutenants Waller and Eyre were likewise suffering from severe and painful wounds received in action at Kábul, which totally disabled them from active service.

the general's proposal should have met with little opposition, although it was a matter of serious doubt whether the whole were not rushing into the very jaws of death, by placing themselves at the mercy of a man who had so lately imbrued his hands in the blood of a British Envoy, whom he had lured to destruction by similar professions of peace and goodwill.

But whatever may have been the secret intent of Akbar's heart, he was at this time our professed friend and ally, having undertaken to escort the whole force to Jallálábád, in safety. Whatever suspicions, therefore, have been entertained of his hypocrisy, it was not in the character of an *enemy* that he gained possession of the married families; on the contrary, he stood pledged for their safe escort to Jallálábád, no less than for that of the army to which they belonged; and by their unwarrantable detention as prisoners, no less than by the treacherous massacre of the force, he broke the universal law of nations, and was guilty of an unpardonable breach of faith. Shortly after the departure of the married families, it was discovered that the troopers of the Sháh's Irregular Cavalry and of the Mission Escort were deserting in great numbers, having been enticed away, as was supposed, by Muhammad Akbar, to whom a message of remonstrance was in consequence sent. He assured the general, in reply, that not only would he refrain from enticing the men away, but that every future deserter from our camp should be shot.

Meanwhile a large body of Afghán horse had been observed in the vicinity of camp, in company with the cavalry deserters; and, fears being entertained that it was their design to attack the camp, a general parade of the troops was ordered for the purpose of repelling them. The 44th Foot at this time was found to muster one hundred files, and the native infantry regiments, on an average, about sixty files each. Of the Irregular Horse not above one hundred effective troopers remained, and the 5th Light Cavalry, though more faithful to their salt, had been reduced by casualties to about seventy fighting-men. On the arrival of Muhammad Akbar's answer to the general's message, the opportunity was taken of the troops being paraded, to explain to them its purport, and to warn them that every man who might be discovered deserting would be shot.

At this very time, a *chupraasí* of the Mission, being caught in the act, was instantly shot, as an example to the rest, by order of the general, and the crime thus received a salutary check. Captain Mackay, having been chosen to convey to General Sale a fresh order for the evacuation of Jallálábád, was sent over in the evening to the *sirdár* with that view. The promises of Muhammad Akbar to provide food and fuel were unfulfilled, and another night of starvation and cold consigned more victims to a miserable death.

January 10th,—At break of day all was again confusion, the troops and camp-followers crowding promiscuously to the front so soon as the orders for a march were given, every one dreading, above all things, to be left in the rear. The European soldiers were now almost the only efficient men left, the Hindústánís having all suffered more or less from the effects of frost in their hands and feet; few were able even to hold a musket, much less to pull a trigger; in fact, the prolonged delay in the snow had paralysed the mental and bodily powers of the strongest men, rendering them incapable of any useful exertion. Hope seemed to have died in every breast.

The advanced guard (consisting of Her Majesty's 44th Foot, the sole remaining Horse Artillery gun, and about fifty troopers of the 5th Cavalry) having managed with much difficulty to push their way to the front, proceeded a couple of miles without molestation, as far as a narrow gorge between the precipitous spurs of two hills, through which flowed a small stream. Towards this point numbers of Afghán foot had been observed hurrying, with the evident intention of opposing the passage of the troops, and were now found to occupy the height on the right in considerable force. No sooner did the advance approach within shot, than the enemy, securely perched on their post of vantage, commenced the attack, pouring a destructive fire upon the crowded *column*, as it slowly drew nigh to the fatal spot.

Fresh numbers fell at every volley, and the gorge was soon choked with the dead and dying: the unfortunate *sepoys*, seeing no means of escape, and driven to utter desperation, cast away their arms and accoutrements, which only dogged their movements without contributing to their defence, and along with the camp-followers fled for their lives. The Afgháns now rushed down upon their helpless and unresisting victims, sword in hand, and a general massacre took place. The last small remnant of the Native Infantry regiments were here scattered and destroyed; and the public treasure, with all the remaining baggage, fell into the hands of the enemy. Meanwhile, the advance, after pushing through the Tangí with great loss, had reached Kabar-i-Jabár, about five miles ahead, without more opposition.

Here they halted to enable the rear to join, but, from the few stragglers who from time to time came up, the astounding truth was brought to light, that, of all who had that morning marched from Khurd-Kábul, they were almost the sole survivors, nearly the whole of the main and rear columns having been cut off and destroyed. About fifty Horse Artillery men, with one 12-pounder howitzer, seventy files Her Majesty's 44th, and one hundred and fifty cavalry troopers, now composed the whole Kábul force; but, notwithstanding the slaughter and dispersion that had taken place, the camp-followers still formed a considerable body.

The approach of a party of Afghán horse induced the general to draw up his little force in line, preparatory to an expected attack; but on its being ascertained to be Muhammad Akbar Khán and his followers, Captain Skinner was despatched to remonstrate with him on the attack on our troops after a treaty had been entered into and their safety guaranteed.

In reply, he expressed his regret at what had occurred, but said that, notwithstanding all his endeavours, he found it impossible to restrain the Ghalzís, who were in such a state of excitement as to be beyond the control even of their own chiefs. As a last resource, he recommended that the few remaining troops should lay down their arms, and place themselves entirely under his safeguard, in which case he could ensure their safe escort to Jallálábád; but that as the camp-followers still amounted to some thousands, and far outnumbered his own people, there was no alternative but to leave them to their fate. To these terms the general could not bring himself to consent, and the desperate march was resumed. Here Captain Mackay rejoined the troops, as the *sirdár* considered it impossible for him at present to make his way safe to Jallálábád.

About five more miles led down the steep descents of the Haft Kotal, into a narrow defile, or confined bed of a mountain stream.

A ghastly sight here met the eye, the ground being strewn with the bodies of a number of camp-followers, with whom were several wounded officers and soldiers, who, having gone on ahead of the column, were attacked on reaching the foot of the hill, and massacred. The heights commanding the defile (which was about three miles long) were found crowned with the enemy. Muhammad Akbar and his train had taken a short cut over the hills to Tizín, and were followed by the few remaining troopers of the Irregular Cavalry. Dr. Magrath, seeing them take, as he thought, a wrong direction, hastened to recall them, and was taken prisoner by a Ghalzí chief. In their passage down the defile, a destructive fire was maintained on the troops from the heights on either side, and fresh numbers of dead and wounded lined the course of the stream. Brigadier Shelton commanded the rear with a few Europeans, and but for his persevering energy and unflinching fortitude in repelling the assailants, it is probable the whole would have been there sacrificed.

The diminished remnant reached the encamping-ground in the Tizín valley at about 4 p.m., having lost since starting from Kábul, inclusive of camp-followers, about twelve thousand men; no less than fifteen officers were killed and wounded in this day's disastrous march.

Although it was now sufficiently plain that Muhammad Akbar either could not or would not act up to his friendly professions, the general endeavoured to renew his worse than useless negotiation with that chief, in the faint hope that something might still be done to better the situation of the troops; but Captain Skinner, who was deputed on the occasion, returned with precisely the same answer as before; and as the general could not in honour accede to his proposal, all hope of aid from that quarter was at an end.

It was now determined to make an effort, under cover of darkness, to reach Jagdalak, a distance of twenty-two miles, by an early hour on the following morning, the principal object being to get through the strong and dangerous pass of that place before the enemy should have sufficient notice of their intention, to occupy it in any force. As there existed a short cut from Tizín to Jagdalak over the hills, the success of the attempt was very doubtful; but the lives of all depended on the issue; and at 7 p.m. the little band renewed its forlorn and dismal march, word having been previously sent to Muhammad Akbar that it was the general's intention to move only as far as Seh Bábá, distant seven miles. On moving off, the last gun was abandoned, and with it Dr. Cardew, who had been lashed to it in the hope of saving him.

This gentleman had rendered himself conspicuous from the commencement of the siege for his zeal and gallantry, and had become a great favourite with the soldiery in consequence, by whom his hapless fate was sincerely lamented. Dr. Duff, the superintending surgeon of the force, experienced no better fortune, being left in a state of utter exhaustion on the road midway to Seh Bábá. Little or no molestation was experienced by the force until reaching Seh Bábá, when a few shots being fired at the rear, there was an immediate rush of camp-followers to the front, and the main body of the 44th European soldiers, who had hitherto been well in advance, getting mixed up in the crowd, could not be extricated by withdrawing them to the rear, owing to the narrowness of the road, which now traversed the hills to Barik-áb.

Bodies of the neighbouring tribes were by this time on the alert, and fired at random from the heights, it being fortunately too dark for them to aim with precision; but the panic-stricken camp-followers now resembled a herd of startled deer, and fluctuated backwards and forwards, *en masse*, at every shot, blocking up the entire road, and fatally retarding the progress of the little body of soldiers who, under Brigadier Shelton, brought up the rear.

At Barik-áb a heavy fire was encountered by the hindmost from some caves near the roadside, occasioning fresh disorder, which continued all the way to Kattar-Sang, where the advance arrived at dawn of day, and awaited the junction of the rear, which did not take place till 8 a.m.

January 11th.—The distance from Jagdalak was still ten miles; the enemy already began to crowd the surrounding heights, and it was now evident that the delay occasioned by the camp-followers had cut off the last chance of escape.

From Kattar-Sang to Jagdalak it was one continued conflict; Brigadier Shelton with his brave little band, in the rear, holding overwhelming numbers in check, and literally performing wonders. But no efforts could avail to ward off the withering fire of *jazails*, which from all sides assailed the crowded column, lining the road with bleeding carcasses. About 3 p.m. the advance reached Jagdalak, and took up its position behind some ruined walls that crowned a height by the roadside. To show an imposing front, the officers extended themselves in line, and Captain Grant, assistant adjutant-general, at the same moment received a wound in the face. From this eminence they cheered their comrades under Brigadier Shelton in the rear, as they still straggled their way gallantly along every foot of ground, perseveringly followed up by their merciless enemy, until they arrived at their ground. But even here rest was denied them; for the Afgháns, immediately occupying two hills which commanded the position, kept up a fire from which the walls of the inclosure afforded but a partial shelter.

[It may interest the reader to peruse the following utterance of General Shelton himself, at Gosport, in January 1844, on the presentation of new colours to the 44th Regiment:—
[When the Europeans were left to their own resources, the men

of the 44th showed their sterling worth;—from that moment I assumed the command of the rearguard, and in going through the Tizín pass, annoyed by a galling and destructive fire from the heights on both flanks, and when crowds of savage Ghalzís rushed like a torrent upon the rear, this brave little band, obedient to my voice, halted, faced about, and repelled the appalling numbers of the enemy under a tremendous fire, with a boldness and determined courage that might have extracted admiration from the very stones under their feet; and though they had been now four days and four nights on the snow, these noble fellows performed a forced march of two days and one night, without halting—repelling the incessant attacks of the enemy, under a destructive fire that strewed the whole line of road with the dead bodies of their comrades, with a constancy and unyielding courage that will command my admiration and respect so long as I live; and what I now state, was under my own personal observation. No man ever thought of surrender, but all fell gloriously with their arms in their hands, fighting to the last, and only sixteen remained of the number that marched from Kábul.]

The exhausted troops and followers now began to suffer greatly from thirsty which they were unable to satisfy. A tempting stream trickled near the foot of the hill, but to venture down to it was certain death. Some snow that covered the ground was eagerly devoured, but increased, instead of alleviating, their sufferings. The raw flesh of three bullocks, which had fortunately been saved, was served out to the soldiers, and ravenously swallowed. At about half-past 3 a message having been brought from Muhammad Akbar to Captain Skinner requesting his presence, that officer promptly obeyed the call, hoping thereby, even at the eleventh hour, to effect some arrangement for the preservation of those who survived. The harassed and worn-out troops, in the expectation of a temporary truce during his absence, threw themselves down to snatch a brief repose; but even, this much-needed luxury was denied them by their vigilant foes, who now, from their commanding position, poured into the crowded inclosure death-dealing volleys in rapid succession, causing the utmost consternation among the terrified followers who rushed wildly out in the vain hope of finding shelter from the fire.

At this perilous juncture Captain Bygrave, with about fifteen brave

Europeans, sallied forth in the full determination to drive the enemy from the heights, or perish in the attempt. Unflinchingly they charged up the hill, the enemy retreating before them in the greatest trepidation. The respite, however, thus signally gained was of but short duration, for the heroic little band had no sooner returned than the enemy re-occupied their posts of vantage, and resumed their fatal fire. Thus passed the time until 5 p.m., when Captain Skinner returned from his interview with Muhammad Akbar, bringing a message to the general from that chiefs who requested his presence at a conference, and demanded Brigadier Shelton and Captain Johnson as hostages for the evacuation of Jallálábád.

The general, seeing no alternative, made over temporary command to Brigadier Anquetil, and departed with the two above-named officers under the escort of Muhammad Sháh Khán. The troops witnessed their departure with despair, having seen enough of Afghán treachery to convince them that these repeated negotiations were mere hollow artifices designed to engender confidence in their victims, preparatory to a fresh sacrifice of blood. The general and his companions were received by the *sirdár* with every outward token of kindness, and no time was lost in supplying them with the bodily sustenance they so greatly needed; they were likewise assured that immediate arrangements should be made for the supply of food to the famishing troops, and for their safe escort to Jallálábád, after which they were shown into a small tent, to enjoy, for the first time since leaving Khurd-Kábul, a quiet and refreshing sleep.

January 12th.—Numerous Ghalzí chiefs, with their attendant clansmen, flocked in from the neighbouring parts to pay their homage to Muhammad Akbar; and about 9 a.m. a conference was held, at which the three British officers and all the influential chiefs were present. All the latter were loud and profuse in their expressions of bitter hatred against the English, and for a long time the *sirdár's* efforts to conciliate them seemed to be unsuccessful; but the offer of two *lakhs* of *rúpís* appeared at last in some measure to appease them, of which sum Muhammad Akbar promised to advance one *lakh* himself, and to be security for the other. The day nevertheless wore on without anything decisive having been agreed upon. The general became impatient to rejoin his force, and repeatedly urged the *sirdár* to furnish him with the necessary escort, informing him at the same time that it was contrary to British notions of military honour that a general should be separated from his troops in the hour of danger; and that he would infinitely prefer death to such a disgrace.

The *sirdár* put him off with promises, and at 7 p.m., firing being heard in the direction of the pass, it was ascertained that the troops, impatient of farther delay, had actually moved off. From the time of the general's departure the situation of the troops had been in truth one of dark and cruel suspense, unenlightened by one solitary ray of hope. At an early hour in the morning, before the enemy had yet made their appearance on the hills, Major Thain, accompanied by Captain Skinner, rode out a few hundred paces in the direction of Muhammad Akbar's camp, in expectation of meeting a messenger from the *sirdár* to the last-named officer; a Ghalzí soldier suddenly made his appearance, and, passing Major Thain, who was several yards in advance, went close up to Captain Skinner, and shot him with a pistol through the face.

Major Thain instantly returned to camp, and announced this act of treachery. The unfortunate officer was carried inside the inclosure, and lingered in great pain till 3 p.m. In him the State lost an officer of whose varied merits as a soldier and a man it is difficult to speak too highly. A deep feeling of anguish and despair now pervaded the whole assemblage. The extremes of hunger, thirst, and fatigue were suffered alike by all; added to which, the Afgháns again crowned the heights and recommenced hostilities, keeping up a galling fire the whole day with scarcely half an hour's intermission. Sally after sally was made by the Europeans, bravely led on by Major Thain, Captain Bygrave, and Lieutenants Wade and Macartney; but again and again the enemy returned to worry and destroy. Night came, and all farther delay in such a place, being useless, the whole sallied forth, determined to pursue the route to Jallálábád at all risks.

The sick and wounded were necessarily abandoned to their fate. Descending into the valley of Jagdalak, they pursued their way along the bed of the stream for about a mile and a half, encountering a desultory fire from the Ghalzís encamped in the vicinity, who were evidently not quite prepared to see them at such an hour, but were soon fully on the alert, some following up the rear, others pressing forward to occupy the pass. This formidable defile is about two miles long, exceedingly narrow, and closed in by lofty precipitous heights. The road has a considerable slope upwards, and, on nearing the summit, further progress was found to be obstructed by two strong barriers formed of branches of the prickly holly-oak, stretching completely across the defile. Immense delay and confusion took place in the general struggle to force a passage through these unexpected obstacles, which gave ample time for the Ghalzís to collect in force.

A terrible fire was now poured in from all quarters, and a massacre even worse than that of Tangá Táríkí commenced, the Afgháns rushing in furiously upon the pent-up crowd of troops and followers, and committing wholesale slaughter. A miserably small remnant managed to clear the barriers. Twelve officers,[5] amongst whom was Brigadier Anquetil, were killed. Upwards of forty[6] others succeeded in pushing through, about twelve[7] of whom, being pretty well mounted, rode on ahead of the rest with the few remaining cavalry, intending to make the best of their way to Jallálábád. Small straggling parties of the Europeans marched on under different officers; the country became more open, and they suffered little molestation for several miles, most of the Ghalzís being too busily engaged in the plundering of the dead to pursue the living. But much delay was occasioned by the anxiety of the men to bring on their wounded comrades, and the rear was much harassed by sudden onsets from parties stationed on the heights, under which the road occasionally wound. On reaching the Súrkáb River, they found the enemy in possession of the bridge, and a hot fire was encountered in crossing the ford below it, by which Lieutenant Cadet, Her Majesty's 44th, was killed, together with several privates.

January 13th.—The morning dawned as they approached Gandámak, revealing to the enemy, who had by this time increased considerably in their front and rear, the insignificance of their numerical strength. To avoid the vigorous assaults that were now made by their confident foe, they were compelled to leave the road, and take up a defensive position on a height to the left of it, where they made a resolute stand, determined to sell their lives at the dearest possible price. At this time they could only muster about twenty muskets.

Some Afghán horsemen, approaching from the direction of Gandámak, were now beckoned to, and an attempt was made by Lieutenant Hay to enter upon some pacific arrangement. Hostilities were for a few minutes suspended, and, at the invitation of a chief. Major Griffiths, the senior officer, accompanied by Mr. Blewitt to act as interpreter, descended the hill to a conference. Several Afgháns now ascended the height, and assumed a friendly tone towards the little party there stationed; but the calm was of short duration, for the sol-

---

5, 6, 7. Appendix.

diers, getting provoked at several attempts being made to snatch away their arms, resumed a hostile attitude, and drove the intruders fiercely down. The die was now cast, and their fate sealed; for the enemy, taking up their post on an opposite hill, marked off man after man, officer after officer, with unerring aim. Parties of Afgháns rushed up at intervals to complete the work of extermination, but were as often driven back by the still dauntless handful of invincibles.

At length, nearly all being wounded more or less, a final onset of the enemy, sword in hand, terminated the unequal struggle, and completed the dismal tragedy. Major Griffiths and Mr. Blewitt had been previously led off to a neighbouring fort, and were thus saved. Of those whom they left behind. Captain Souter alone, with three or four privates, was spared, and carried off captive, having received a severe wound in the shoulder; he had tied round his waist before leaving Jagdalak the colours of his regiment, which were thus miraculously preserved.

It only remains to relate the fate of those few officers and men, who rode on ahead of the rest after passing the barriers. Six of the twelve officers, Captains Bellew, Collier, Hopkins, Lieutenant Bird, Drs. Harpur and Brydon, reached Futhábád in safety, the other six having dropped gradually off by the way and been destroyed. Deceived by the friendly professions of some peasants near the above-named town, who brought them bread to eat, they unwisely delayed a few moments to satisfy the cravings of hunger; the inhabitants meanwhile armed themselves, and, suddenly sallying forth, cut down Captain Bellew and Lieutenant Bird; Captains Collyer and Hopkins, and Drs. Harpur and Brydon, rode off, and were pursued; the three former were overtaken and slain within four miles of Jallálábád; Dr. Brydon by a miracle escaped, and was the only officer of the whole Kábul force who reached that garrison in safety.

Such was the memorable retreat of the British army from Kábul, which, viewed in all its circumstances,—in the political and military conduct which preceded and brought about such a consummation, the treachery, disaster, and suffering which accompanied it,—is, perhaps, without a parallel in modern history.[8]

---

8. A most remarkable historical parallel may, however, be found in Book V, of Caesar's *Commentaries*, in the description there given of the insurrection of the Gauls under Ambiorix, wherein the Roman general, Sabinus, figures as an exact prototype of Elphinstone, with an almost identical result in the details of unavailing valour, ending in a hollow treaty with treacherous chieftains, a disorderly retreat of the Roman army, and its final annihilation.

CHAPTER 14

Captivity of the Hostages

[In the early editions of this work the account of the military operations which ended in the retreat and destruction of the British army was followed by rough notes made by the author[1], descriptive of the life in captivity of himself and his comrades. After the lapse of so many years it has not appeared advisable to the author to encumber the work with details, many of them trivial, the interest attaching to which has long since passed away. The chief incidents of a public nature which followed the captivity of the ladies and soldiers referred to in the foregoing narrative will be found related in the following pages extracted from a memoir of the career of Sir Vincent Eyre, published by the editor in the *Calcutta Review* some twelve years ago. The reader will observe that the extract begins with the incidents immediately preceding the surrender of Eyre, his wife, and thirty-seven others as hostages to Muhammad Akbar.]

Then came the retreat, with its attendant horrors, rivalling those experienced by the French in their winter march from Moscow. Eyre's wound was still intensely painful, and incapacitated him from mounting a horse without assistance. To quote his own words:

> Deep snow covered every inch of mountain and plain with one unspotted sheet of dazzling white, and so intensely bitter was the cold as to penetrate and defy the defences of the warmest clothing.
>
> The thermometer stood at several degrees below zero; and men's beards were coated with icicles. There was a mingled multitude of four thousand five hundred fighting men (including seven hundred

---

1. These are republished by Leonaur in full in the second part of this book.

European soldiers) and twelve thousand native camp-followers, with their women and children. Their route lay through the Khurd-Kábul pass:

> .... a truly formidable defile, about five miles from end to end, shut in by lofty hills, between whose precipitous sides the sun, at this season, could dart but a momentary ray.'

There, half concealed behind rocks and bushes, eager hordes of armed Ghalzís lay in ambush for their prey. The scene that ensued may be more easily imagined than described. The treachery of the chiefs was but too evident. Perched securely on high, the foe defied all attempts to silence or dislodge them. It was necessary to run the gauntlet of their fire; and not less than three thousand souls perished in the attempt.

Eyre and his family, consisting of wife and a little boy, emerged safely from the gorge; the latter, being strapped to the back of a faithful Afghán servant on horseback, had a very narrow escape, owing to the horse falling and throwing them both off when in the very middle of the pass. To crown the misfortunes of the day, snow began to fall, and thousands had to pass the night without shelter, food, or fire. Only four small tents were saved, under which some of the women, children, and wounded found refuge. Eyre and Lieutenant Mein sat up all night in attendance on their dying friend Sturt, of the Engineers, who had been mortally wounded in the pass. At her husband's side his youthful bride also kept watch with them. She was the daughter of the gallant Sale, and well worthy of such a sire.

To assuage Sturt's burning thirsty Eyre and Mein were obliged to wander, alternately, through the camp in search of fire to melt a cupful of snow; and often before they could regain the tent the contents had frozen again into a hard mass. Sturt did not survive the night, and was buried at early dawn. Mein's disinterested devotion to his wounded friend in hurrying back to save him at the risk of his own life, and dragging him through the pass under the enemy's fire, was justly extolled by Sir Robert Peel in Parliament, who quoted the scene *verbatim* from Eyre's book.

Meanwhile, Muhammad Akbar, like a vulture watching his prey, scanned every movement of the force from the neighbouring heights. Shortly after the retreat commenced, he had demanded that Pottinger and two other officers should be given up as hostages, and prompt compliance had been yielded. But still he was not satisfied. The ladies, married families, and wounded officers were next required to be made over to his care, an assurance being given to the general that by such a mark of confidence alone could the chiefs be induced to provide for the wants of the force, and to restrain their followers from acts of hostility. The general himself, in a memorandum which he subsequently drew up, thus explains his own motives:

> I complied with his wish, hoping that, as from the very commencement of negotiations the *sirdar* had shown the greatest anxiety to have the married people as hostages, this mark of trust might elicit a corresponding feeling in him.

Eyre, on receiving a verbal order to prepare for the departure of himself and family, sought the general, in order to hear it from his own lips. The poor general was greatly distressed, but, warmly pressing his hand, urged him to mount and be off, as the escort sent by Muhammad Akbar, was impatient to start; so there seemed to be no alternative. Muhammad Akbar, although suspected of treachery, was then professedly our ally, with whom a treaty existed. Hostilities were therefore at an end, so far as he was concerned. It was pretended, on his behalf, that the Ghalzí chiefs on the previous day exerted themselves in vain to restrain their followers.

Captain Nicholl now commanded the artillery in person, and Eyre felt that his own presence could no longer be of any service to the force. His obvious duty was to obey the general's wishes at all hazards; he therefore departed with the new batch of hostages, consisting of seven officers, ten ladies, and twenty-two children. Among them were Ladies Macnaghten and Sale. Counting, then, seven officers left behind at Kábul, and three made over on the march, the chiefs had now gained possession of seventeen British officers, nominally as hostages for the fulfilment of the treaty.

Eyre and his associates in misfortune remained as captives in the hands of Muhammad Akbar during eight and a half months, Eyre occupying his leisure in recordings on such scraps of paper as he could collect, the strange and stirring incidents which he had witnessed, while yet they were fresh in his own memory and in the minds of his fellow-captives, from whom, as well as from such public and private documents as had been saved and were within his reach, he industriously gleaned many important and interesting particulars. His chief object in these labours was to place, as far as in him lay, the whole unvarnished truth before the British public at the earliest practicable opportunity. He thus wrote to a friend:

> I feel well assured that the more my statements are sifted, the more clearly will their truth be established in all essential points. Heaven knows I would give my right hand that such events as I have described had never occurred; but, having occurred, why should I conceal them? Is the loss of an army nothing? Can our national interests be advanced by glossing over such unheard-of calamities and disgrace?

In another letter he thus expresses himself:

> I wrote my narrative because it was at the time very doubtful whether any of the chief actors would survive, and I felt an anxious desire that, should we perish in captivity, the public might be able to judge properly of the respective merits of all concerned. I can boldly assert that there is not a sentence which I do not believe to be strictly true.

Perhaps few narratives written under such circumstances have so well stood the test of time,[2] or have met more general and lasting approval. We have little doubt that honest old Gascoignes the poet, who underwent some similar experiences in his youth during the wars in the Low Countries in the sixteenth century, very accurately expresses Eyre's feelings in regard to his volume on Kábul in the following *stanza* from the poem entitled *The Fruites of War*:

> *Go, little booke! God graunt thou none offende,*
> *For so meant he who sought to set thee forth,*
> *And when then commest where soldiers seem to wend,*
> *Submit thyselfe as writte but little worth.*
>
> *Confesse withal that thou hast bene too bolde*
> *To speak so plaine of haughtie hartes in place,*
> *And say that he which wrote thee coulde have tolde*
> *Full many a tale of blouds that were not base.*

The story of the captivity was appended to Eyre's narrative in the form of a journal, and may still be read with interest. We must content

---

2. On one occasion, during his visit to Europe in 1855-56, Eyre happened to be looking over the book-shelves of a bookseller's shop in Paris, when he suddenly came upon his own work, translated into French. It is impossible to imagine a more pleasing surprise to an author than such a discovery.

ourselves with a few of the more prominent episodes. On the fourth day after their surrender to Muhammad Akbar they were joined by the general himself, with Brigadier Shelton and Captain Hugh Johnson, and learned with profound dismay and grief that the remainder of the force had been gradually shot down in the passes, the chiefs having played them false even to the end, notwithstanding all the concessions that had been made.

It was evidently Muhammad Akbar's game to hold his captives as trump cards wherewith to extort from the British Government better terms for himself and country than he could well hope to obtain by any other means at his disposal. Hence they found themselves, on. the whole, well treated, although their anxieties were kept alive by the fact that a small, though influential, section existed among the Ghalzí chiefs who made no secret of their inclination to put the whole party to death; and whose debates on this momentous subject were often carried on in tones sufficiently loud to be overheard by their intended victims.

Their first place of confinement was the fort of Badíábád, in the district of Lughmán, a stronghold of one of these same Ghalzí chieftains, haying walls twenty-five feet high, and lofty flanking towers, surrounded by a *faussebraye* and deep ditch. Here they remained three months, during which they were allowed to exchange letters with their friends in Jallálábád, where Sale still maintained his defensive position. On February 19th they were alarmed by a violent rocking of the earth, accompanied by a loud subterranean rumbling sound; the lofty parapets around them fell in with a thundering crash; the dwelling-house waved and tottered like a ship at sea, and all within it simultaneously rushed out into the central court-yard, to find their terror-stricken Afghán keepers upon their knees, ejaculating loud prayers to *Allah* for protection. It seemed as though the last day had arrived. Eyre had a narrow escape from being crushed to death by a mass of the wall, under which he chanced to be standing while tending his horse, which he had been permitted to retain.

The same earthquake levelled in a few seconds the walls of defence which Sale's force had, with continuous labour, repaired and. strengthened at Jallálábád. But the Afgháns were unprepared to take advantage of the chance thus offered. On April 9th tidings reached the captives that Muhammad Akbar's camp had been surprised by Sale, and his force completely routed, and on the following day they were hurried off towards the mountains, after a sharp debate among the chiefs on the expediency of destroying them at once.

Poor General Elphinstone, in his already shattered state of health, could ill bear up under the fatigues and privations he had to undergo, and died at Tizín on April 23rd, "a happy release for him", says Eyre, "from suffering of mind and body. Deeply he felt his humiliation, and bitterly regretted the day when he resigned the home-borne pleasures of his native land to hazard the reputation of a proud name in a climate and station for which he was physically unfit."

The body was forthwith forwarded by Muhammad Akbar to General Pollock (by that time at Jallálábád) for honourable interment—a tribute of respect to a fallen foe highly creditable to the Afghán chief.

On the following day Captain Colin Mackenzie was despatched on a mission to General Pollock, taking with him the first portion of Eyre's narrative. After perusal by General Pollock, it was forwarded by the latter to Lord Ellenborough's private secretary, and eventually to England for publication. Colin Mackenzie's journeys to and fro proved full of peril, for, although disguised as an Afghán and escorted by a well-known and popular sort of Rob Roy, or freebooter, named Buttí, in the pay of 'Muhammad Akbar, whose knowledge of that wild mountainous country and its still wilder inhabitants stood him in good stead, he was in frequent and imminent danger of discovery and consequent death from parties of wandering Ghalzís, whom they unexpectedly encountered, and who persisted in being unpleasantly inquisitive regarding the suspicious-looking traveller, with his face and form so closely muffled up in the folds of his turban and large sheepskin cloak, leaving his eyes scarcely as visible as those of the roughest Skye terrier, and whom it was necessary to palm off as a sick chief of Pesháwar sent by Muhammad Akbar under Butti's escort to his native place. One glimpse of the white skin beneath his wide Afghán trousers (which he found it next to impossible to prevent from rising above his knee) would have been his death-warrant. But Heaven protected him.

The propositions whereof he was the bearer were, that the British general should treat with Muhammad Akbar as the acknowledged head of the Afghán nation; that there should be an exchange of prisoners, including all on each side; that the British should retire from Afghánistán; and that General Pollock should pay down a handsome *douceur* in money. In case of these arrangements being effected, Muhammad Akbar would be glad to enter into an alliance, offensive and defensive, with the British. This, however, was only his public message, but, in secret, Mackenzie had been desired to ascertain if a private arrangement could not be made, to the effect that General Pollock should ensure an amnesty to Muhammad Akbar and his followers for the past, and that the British Govern ment should bestow on him a large *jagír*. In this case he would willingly assist Pollock in reconquering Afghánistán.

Mackenzie returned from his mission on May 3rd without having opened any prospect of release for the captives, although the negotiation, as far as it went, had been of a friendly nature. He was immediately despatched a second time with more moderate proposals, but again returned with an equally ineffectual result. On May 23rd Muhammad Akbar removed all his captives from the Zaudak valley to a fort in the vicinity of Kábul. Here Mackenzie had nearly died of typhus fever, the result of his recent fatigues and exposure. Muhammad Akbar selected Major Colin Troup as his next envoy, and he was absent in that capacity from the 10th to the 27th of July, but brought back no definite reply. Pollock was, in fact, busy in preparing for an advance on Kábul, with stringent instructions from Lord Ellenborough to proceed with his military preparations without reference to any negotiations. Meanwhile, typhus fever and dysentery spread alarmingly among the captives, and, on August 7th, Captain John Conolly breathed his last. His brother, the celebrated Arthur Conolly, had but recently been decapitated at Bukhára, after having been confined at the bottom of a dry well, in company with Colonel Stoddart, for eighty days, without change of raiment.

On August 23rd nine officers of the Ghazní garrison joined the Kábul captives. Among them was the brave young Nicholson, destined to a brilliant career in the Panjáb, and a heroes death sixteen years later in the moment of victory at Delhi. He now became Eyre's messmate, and beguiled the hours with animated details of the scenes he had witnessed during the ineffectual defence of that fortress; with him, too, was Dr. Thomas Thomson, since risen to eminence as a botanist and a traveller. On August 25th all were hurried off towards Bámíán, *en route* to Kulum in Usbeg Tátary, with a threat held out that they would be sold into bondage on arrival. Eyre and Mackenzie were both at this time to ill to travel on horseback, and were packed into a pair of panniers to balance each other on each side of a camel, a mode of travelling for invalids which their miserable experience on that memorable journey did not enable them to recommend for general adoption, except in cases where the penalty of torture has been incurred.

They had a strong escort, consisting of some four hundred Afghán soldiers, deserters from the British service, under one Sálah Muhammad, their former *subadar*. Their route lay over the steep mountain-passes of Sufaid Kúh, Unai, Hájígak and Kálu, the latter attaining an altitude of thirteen thousand four hundred feet, whence Eyre describes the view as "presenting a boundless chaos of barren mountains, probably unequalled in wild terrific grandeur." The valley of Bámíán, beyond the Indian Caucasus, was reached on September 3rd.

And now, at the very time when hope began to yield to despair in all their breasts, and a life of wretched slavery seemed their inevitable lot, aid came from an unexpected quarter, and their speedy deliverance was at hand. Eyre thus tells the story in a letter to a friend in Calcutta:—

> On Sunday, September 11th, Sálah Muhammad, having received a positive order from Muhammad Akbar for our immediate march to Kulum, our desperate condition induced Pottinger to tempt him with the offer of a bribe for our release. Captain Johnson volunteered to be agent in the matter, and found him more accessible than was expected. This man had hitherto kept aloof from any attempt at friendly intercourse with the prisoners, towards whom his manner had been invariably haughty and his language harsh. Great, therefore, was our astonishment to learn that he had been seduced from his allegiance to Muhammad Akbar and bought over to our side.
>
> Meanwhile, the rapid advance of the two English armies upon Kábul, and the probable defeat of Muhammad Akbar, led us to expect that chief's arrival among us as likely to happen at any moment. It was, therefore, necessary to be prepared against any sudden surprise. The Hazarah chiefs in the Valley were sounded and found favourable to our scheme. The men composing our guard were gained over by a promise of four months, pay. A new governor was set up over the Hazarah province by Major Pottinger, the existing governor being too much in Muhammad Akbar's interests to be trusted.
>
> On September 16th the country was considered sufficiently safe to admit of our setting out on our return towards Kábul. We had only proceeded a few miles when a messenger met us

with the news of General Pollock's victory over Akbar, which cheering intelligence was shortly afterwards confirmed by a note from Sir Richmond Shakespear, who was hastening to our assistance with six hundred Kazilbásh horsemen. On the 17th we recrossed the Kálu pass, and encamped about three miles from its base. We had been here about two hours, when horsemen were descried descending the pass of Hájígak. Instantly Sálah Muhammad's men were on the alert and formed up in line. Judge of our joy when the banner of the Kazilbásh was distinguished streaming in the air, and imagine, if you can, with what emotions of delight and gratitude we eagerly pressed forward to greet our gallant countryman, Sir Richmond Shakespear, who soon came galloping up to where we stood. For the first time after nine miserable months of thraldom we felt the blessedness of freedom. To God be all the glory, for He alone could bring it to pass!

There was still some danger that Muhammad Akbar might intercept their flight, but at Shakespear's suggestion Pollock despatched Sale's brigade to meet them at Kot-Ashrú. All doubt was then at an end; they were once more under the safe-guard of British troops, who lined the heights of Sufaid Khák and who raised hearty cheers of welcome as the procession threaded the pass; among them most conspicuous rode the gallant Sale, with his long-lost wife and daughter by his side.

On the 21st Pollock's camp at Kábul was reached, where the Horse Artillery guns fired a salute in honour of the event, and thus happily terminated the tragedy of the Kábul insurrection.

The events of those days have still such a thrilling interest for British readers that we have been tempted to linger perhaps too long over that portion of Eyre's career in connection with which his name first became familiarly known. It was his strange destiny to witness the *Alpha* and *Omega* of the downfall of the old *Sepoy* army; for it is now generally admitted that the first seeds of the mutiny of 1857 were sown in the Kábul campaign. In allusion to this, Kaye, in his *Sepoy War*, declares:

> The charm of a century of conquest was then broken. The *Sepoy* regiments, no longer assured and fortified by the sight of that ascendant star of fortune which once had shone with so bright and steady a light, shrunk from entering the passes

which had been the grave of so many of their comrades. It was too true; the Sikhs were tampering with their fidelity. Bráhman emissaries were endeavouring to swear them with holy water not to advance at the word of the English commander. Nightly meetings of delegates from the different regiments were held, and perhaps we do not even now know how great was the danger.

Before leaving Kábul, Eyre, through a strange accident, recovered his friend Maule's Bible, on the fly-leaf of which the owner had thus written, as if prophetically, two days before his murder:

In case of my death I wish this book to be sent to my mother, or nearest living relative.

No Muhammadan will knowingly destroy the Word of God, and it is remarkable that Arthur Conolly's prayer-book, wherein he had entered a touching record of his sufferings and aspirations in the well at Bukhára, was, after the lapse of many years, left at the door of his sister's house in London by a mysterious foreigner, who simply left word that he came from Russia, but of whom no trace could be discovered after a most diligent search.

Returning with Pollock's force to India, Eyre was posted to the new troop of Horse Artillery, raised to replace the old first troop, first brigade, which had perished in the Afghán passes, and with whose services at Kábul he had been so intimately associated. In his public report to the commandant of the Artillery regiment, Eyre, speaking of the siege, thus writes:

The gunners, from first to last, never once partook of a full meal or obtained their natural rest: of the hardships and privations undergone it would be difficult to convey an adequate idea. Throughout the last struggle all eye-witnesses concur in testifying to their stubborn valour.

[The original editor may be pardoned for concluding this brief sketch of the captivity, by here extracting from the regimental orders of the commandant of the artillery the opinion expressed by that officer of the conduct of the men of that corps employed in Kábul.]

Extract From Regimental Orders by Brigadier W. H. L. Frith, Commandant of Artillery, dated 10th March 1843.

The total absence of official details on the subject has hitherto prevented the Commandant from noticing the conduct of the late 1st Troop, 1st Brigade, Horse Artillery during the insurrection at and disastrous retreat from Kábul; he now publishes extracts from a letter received yesterday from Lieutenant V. Eyre, late Commissary of Ordnance. as a public record of the high state of discipline and determined bravery exhibited by this gallant and devoted troop on all occasions.

It will always be a subject of sincere gratification to reflect on the noble manner in which they sustained the character of the corps under the severest trials, and in a climate that multiplied an hundred-fold the difficulties with which they had to contend, whilst their fate in the unequal struggle demands the deepest sympathy.

Extract from a letter from Lieutenant V. Eyre, late Commissary of Ordnance in Kábul, to Captain E. Buckle, Assistant Adjutant-General, Artillery:—

It is necessary to premise, that at the commencement of the rebellion on the 2nd November 1841, a portion of General Elphinstone's force was sent to occupy the Bala Hissar, and the remainder was concentrated in the cantonment; to the former. Captain Nichol and Lieutenant Stewart were attached with four guns, and to the latter Brevet-Captain Waller, with two guns. On the 9th of November, Captain Nichol, by order of the General, strengthened Captain Waller's detachment with an additional gun, and the troop thus became equally divided.

The first active service performed in the field by the Horse Artillery was on the afternoon of the 3rd of November, when a sally was made under Major Swayne, 5th Native Infantry, and a body of the enemy was defeated principally by the fire of the guns. On this occasion Captain Waller was severely wounded, and from that date up to the 22nd of November, when I was myself disabled, the virtual command of the Horse Artillery detachment in the cantonment devolved upon me; during this period several severe actions took place with the enemy, in all of which our arms were more or less successful.

One fort was breached and taken by assault, another was taken by a *coup de main*, and, besides several sorties of minor importance, two great actions were fought on the 10th and 13th of November against the collective forces of the enemy, amounting on each occasion to several thousands of horse and foot, in which our side was completely triumphant, and two of their guns were captured.

Provisions, of which there had been from the beginning an alarming scarcity, soon began entirely to fail. The cold of winter set in with unusual rigour, the defence of our long line of low ramparts grievously harassed the troops, the guns placed in battery at the several angles of the cantonment required the constant attendance of the Artillerymen by day and night.

The gunners, from first to last, never once partook of a full meal, or obtained their natural rest; of the hardships and privations undergone it would be difficult to convey an adequate idea.

During the whole of this most trying period, the behaviour of the Horse Artillerymen was distinguished by a degree of patience, cheerfulness, zeal, and fortitude, that excited the unbounded admiration of every eye-witness, and filled the heart of every artillery officer with pride and delight.

On the 23rd November, Brigadier Shelton sallied forth with about seven hundred bayonets and one gun, which (there being no artillery officer available) was commanded by Sergeant Mulhall. An immense army of Afghans poured forth to battle, and a terrible conflict ensued. Sergeant Mulhall and his brave gun's crew committed great havoc amid the dense masses of the enemy, exhibiting a very high degree of professional skill; but their efforts, though partially successful, were ineffectual to repel the overwhelming hosts of assailants. Galled by the fatal fire of Afghan rifles, the infantry lost heart and fled, abandoning our gun to its fate; staunch to the last, the Artillerymen stood by their charge until they were nearly all exterminated. Sergeant Mulhall himself escaping by a miracle, with his clothes perforated with bullets in divers places.

In the public report of this day's operations in the field. Brigadier Shelton did ample justice to the Artillery Sergeant and his devoted little detachment, but the document has, I fear, been lost.

On the 14th December, a treaty having been entered upon, our troops were withdrawn from the Bala Hissar, and Captain

Nichol, on arriving in cantonments, requested me to send in a report of the conduct of his men, which I did, but that also was subsequently lost on the retreat.

That the Horse Artillery sustained their high fame to the last is well known. On the retreat of the army from Kábul, owing to the starved condition of the horses, which disabled them from pulling the guns through the deep snow and rugged mountain-passes, the guns were, one by one, spiked and abandoned. In the Khurd-Kábul pass a whole gun's crew perished rather than desert their charge. On nearing Jagdallak some Horse Artillery-men, headed by Captain Nichol, acting as Dragoons, charged and routed a party of the enemy's cavalry.

Throughout the last struggle up to Gandámak all eye-witnesses concur in testifying to their stubborn valour. They died like true soldiers, selling their lives dearly.

Only three men escaped with life, being taken prisoners. Two others, who were left behind with the detachment of wounded at Kábul, also survived.

(True Copy.)   E. Buckle, A.A.G.A.

A handsome Monument has been erected by the Artillery Corps at Dum Dum to the memory of all those of the Service who fell in Afghanistan, with the inscription following:—

Sacred to the Memory
of
Captain Thomas Nichol,
Lieutenant Charles Stewart,
Sergeant Mulhall,
and the
Non-commissioned Officers and Men of the
1st Troop, 1st Brigade, Bengal Horse Artillery,
who fell in the performance of their duty
during the insurrection at, and retreat from, Cabul,
in the Months of
November and December 1841,
and
January 1842,
on which occasion of unprecedented trial
22 Officers and Men

upheld
in the most noble manner
the character of the Regiment to which they belonged.
This gallant band formed the oldest Troop in the
Bengal Artillery.
It had previously been distinguished
on numerous occasions,
having served
in Egypt, in the Maratta and Nepaul Wars,
and in Ava.
Sacred also to the Memory of
Lieut. Charles Alexander Green, B.A.,
who perished
in command of a detail of Shah Shooja's mountain train,
and whose gallant conduct emulated that
of his comrades.
Also to the Memory of
Lieutenant Richard Maule,
Artillery,
who was killed at the outbreak of the
Afghán insurrection,
November 1841,
and likewise of
Lieutenant A. Christie, of the same Regiment,
killed in the Kyber Pass,
on the return of the victorious army
under the command of
Major-General Sir George Pollock, G.C.B., &c.
of the
Bengal Artillery.
As a Tribute of
Admiration, Regard, and Respect,
This Monument
is erected by the
Artillery Regiment.
Fortis cadere cedere non potest.

Appendix A

LETTER FROM CAPTAIN COLIN MACKENZIE
TO LIEUTENANT V. EYRE.
(Referred to at page 69.)

My Dear Eyre,
As you wish for an account of the manner in which I was besieged in the Kela-i-Nishan Khan, in the breaking out of the Cabul insurrection, I comply, although unwilling to appear so often in the first person, as I necessarily must, in order to give you a clear idea of the fatal nature of the blunder committed, in not sending me assistance from cantonments. I have by me a copy of some notes, which I made at the request of the late Major Thain, then *aide-de-camp* to our lamented chief, General Elphinstone. You are aware that the fort, in which I chanced to be living, contained the *godowns* of the *Shah's* commissariat; and that in one part the quarters of Brigadier Anquetil were situated. For the defence of these, a guard of one *havildar*, two *naick,*, and eighteen *sepoys* had been assigned. The fort itself lies between that quarter of Cabul called the Moorad Khánah and its most western suburb, the Deh-i-Affghan.

The Cabul River flows between the fort and the Kuzzilbash quarter (the Chundoul), to the south. Close to it, to the north, divided by a narrow road and a high wall, is a large grove of mulberry trees, known by the name of the Yahoo Khanah, in which the *Yaboos* of the Shah's commissariat used to be kept; but from which towards the end of October, 1841, they had fortunately been removed into camp at Seeah Sung. In this Yaboo Khánah was a guard of six *suwars*; and, by chance, a detachment of a *jemadar* and ninety-five men of Captain Ferris's

Juzailchees; as also another of the *Shah's* sappers, consisting of one *jemadar* and fifty-nine men, including *havildars* and *naicks*. These last were encumbered with a host of women and children, brought up from their native country with them by the express orders of the Supreme Government. The house of Captain Troup, late Brigade-Major of the Shah's force, built so as to be capable of a tolerable defence, is about forty yards to the east of the fort, across a narrow canal; and the large tower, occupied by the late Captain Trevor and his family, lies across the river to the south-east, distant about seven hundred yards. This also, at the time, was perfectly defensible.

You will easily perceive that, with these posts in our possession, and commanding, as we did, the open space between us, it was a point of importance to maintain our ground until the arrival of what we hourly expected, a regiment from the cantonment, whose presence would have immediately decided the wavering Kuzzilbashes in our favour, and would have cut off all communication between the insurgent population of Deh-i-Affghan and their rascally brethren in the Moorad Khánah. Spreading far beyond the Yaboo Khánah, in the direction of cantonments, and circling round the west of the fort down to the river's edge, are walled gardens and groves, which afford excellent cover to a lurking enemy, who were enabled to come, without much danger, to within a few yards of my defences.

Early on the morning of the 2nd of November, 1841, as I was preparing to go into cantonments with my baggage, intending to accompany the Envoy on the following day down to Peshawar, it was reported to me that an alarming riot had taken place in the town. Brigadier Anquetil and Captain Troup had gone out on their usual morning ride, not supposing the disturbance was of the importance it has since proved to be. I waited for the return of the above two officers for about an hour, previous to adopting decided measures, either for defence or retreat,—at the same time causing all the guards to stand to their arms. Suddenly a naked man stood before me, covered with blood, from two deep sabre-cuts in the head, and five musket-shots in the arm and body. He proved to be a *suwar* of Sir W. Macnaghten, who had been sent with a message to Captain Trevor, but who had been intercepted by the insurgents.

This being rather a strong hint as to how matters were going on, I immediately gave orders for all the gates to be secured, and personally superintended the removal of the detachments in the Yaboo Khánah, with their wives and families, into the fort. At the same time I caused loop-holes to be bored in the upper walls of Captain Troup's house, in which were a *naick* and ten *sepoys*. Whilst so employed, the armed population of Deh-i-Affghan came pouring down through the gardens, and commenced firing on us. I threw out skirmishers; but, in order to save the helpless followers, we were obliged to abandon the tents and baggage. In covering the retreat, one of my men was killed, and one badly wounded; while about five of the enemy were killed.

The whole of the gardens were then occupied by the Affghans, from which, in spite of repeated sallies made during the day, we were unable to dislodge them; on the contrary, whenever we returned into the fort, they approached so near as to be able, themselves unseen, to kill and wound my men through the loop-holes of my own defences. The canal was during the day cut off, and so closely watched, that one of my followers was shot, while trying to fetch some water; but we fortunately found an old well in Brigadier Anquetil's quarters, the water of which was drinkable. Towards the afternoon, having no ammunition but what was contained in the soldiers' pouches, I communicated with Captain Trevor, who still held his tower, apparently unmolested. Even *then*, Khán Shereen Khán, the chief of the Kuzzilbashes, and four or five other *Kháns* of consequence, among them the leaders of the Hazirbash regiments, were with poor Trevor, *earnestly expecting that some decided measures on the part of the British would justify them in openly taking our part.*[1]

Trevor despatched my requisition, for ammunition *at least*, if

---

1. During the expedition into Kohistan, under General M'Caskill I accompanied it, having been placed by General Pollock in charge of Shahzadee Shapoor and the Kuzzilbash camp. In my frequent communications with Khán Shereen Khán, some of the late Kuzzilbash leaders, and with other chiefs of the Kuzzilbash faction, all the circumstances of the late insurrection were over and over again recapitulated, one and all declaring positively that the slightest exhibition of energy on our part in the first instance, more especially in reinforcing my post and that of Trevor, would at once have decided the Kuzzilbashes, and all over whom they possessed any influence, in our favour. Khán Shereen also confirmed the idea that an offensive movement on the opposite side of the town by Brigadier Shelton, had it been made in the early part of the fatal 2nd of November, would at once have crushed the insurrection.

not for more effectual assistance, into cantonments, where it arrived safely, the distance not being more than one mile and a half. Shortly after, our spirits were raised by the apparent approach of a heavy cannonade, and volleys of musketry from the direction of the Moorad Khánah, and by the flight through the gardens of the multitudes who were assailing me, towards Dehi-Affghan, from which quarter crowds of women and children began to ascend the hill, evidently in expectation of an assault from our soldiery. But these cheering sounds died away, and it was in vain that we strained our eyes, looking for the glittering bayonets through the trees, and round the corners of the principal street leading from cantonments.

My besiegers swarmed back with shouts, and it required much exertion on my part to prevent despondency amongst my people, which feeling had been strongly excited by the confirmation of the rumour of the murder of Sir Alexander Burnes, his brother, and Captain Broadfoot; by the sight of the smoke from his burning house; and by the intelligence that the treasury of Captain Johnson, also in the town, had been sacked, and the guard slain. In the evening I served out provisions from the Government stores. The attacks continued at intervals during the night, and we had most disagreeable suspicions that the enemy were undermining our north-west tower, or bastion. At early dawn we sallied out to ascertain this, but were driven in again, after finding our apprehensions too well verified. There is much dead ground about all Affghan forts, on which it is impossible to bring musketry to bear; and the towers can always be undermined, in the absence of hand-grenades on the part of the besieged.

To meet this attempt, we sunk a shaft inside the ground-floor of the tower, and I placed four resolute men on the brink, ready to shoot the first man who should enter. The extent of the fort required all my men to be on duty at the same time, and some now began to wax weary. The cheerfulness of the remainder was not improved by the incessant howling of the women over the dead and dying. As a trait indicative of the character of the Affghan *juzailchees*, I must mention, that whenever they could snatch five minutes to refresh themselves with a pipe, one or other of them would twang a sort of rude guitar, as an accompaniment to some martial song, which, mingling with the above notes of war, sounded very strangely.

In the middle of this day (3rd November), to my great grief, I saw the enemy enter Captain Trevor's tower; and a report was brought to us by two of his servants, who escaped across the river, that he and his family had all been killed, which, though it afterwards proved to be untrue, had a bad effect on my men, whose ammunition had now become very scarce, in spite of my having husbanded it with the greatest care.

The scene of plunder now going on in Trevor's house was evident from our ramparts; and the enemy, taking possession of the top, which overlooked my defences, pitched their balls from their large *juzails* with such accuracy, as to clear my western face of defenders; and it was only by crawling on my hands and knees up a small flight of steps, and whisking suddenly through the door, that I could ever visit the tower that had been undermined. The guard from Captain Troup's house now clamoured for admittance into the fort; and as Mr. Fallon, that gentleman's writer, called out to me that they were ready to abandon their post, I let them in, barricading my own door with sacks of flour. Against the door and small wicket, on Brigadier Anquetil's side, I had already piled heaps of stones and large timbers.

In the afternoon the enemy brought down a large wall-piece against us, the balls from which shook the upper walls of one of our towers, alarming the *juzailchees* much, who dread the effect of any species of ordnance. This disposition to despair was increased by the utter failure of ammunition, and by the Affghans bringing down quantities of firewood and long poles with combustible matter at the ends, which they deposited under the walls of the Yaboo Khánah, in readiness to burn down my door. Some *suwars* who were stationed on Brigadier Anquetil's side of the fort, now broke into a sort of half-mutiny, and began pulling down the barricade against his gate, to endeavour to save themselves by the speed of their horses. This I quelled, by going down amongst them with a double-barrelled gun, and threatening to shoot the first man who should disobey my orders.

In the evening I was quite exhausted, as were my people; having by that time been fighting and working for nearly forty hours without rest. Indeed, on my part, it had been without refreshment, as eating was impossible from excitement and weariness; and my absence for five minutes at a time from any part of the works disheartened the fighting men. Added to this, my wounded were dying for want of medical aid. I therefore yielded to the representations of my *juzailchee jemadar*, and of Mr. Fallon, from both of whom I received valuable assistance during the whole affair, and prepared for a retreat to cantonments. This we determined should take place during the early part of the night, at which time, it being then the fast of the *Ramazan*, we calculated the enemy would be at their principal meal. I ordered the *juzailchees* to lead, and to answer all questions in case of encountering a post of the enemy. The wounded were placed on what *yaboos* I possessed, abandoning everything in the shape of baggage; these, with the women and children, followed next in order; and I myself proposed to bring up the rear with my few regulars, who, I fondly imagined, would stick by me in case of a hot pursuit.

We were to avoid the town, and to follow the course of the small canal above mentioned, and afterwards to strike off by lanes, and through some fields, in the direction of cantonments. A night retreat is generally disastrous, and this proved no exception to the general rule; but, notwithstanding my strict order that all baggage should be left behind, it being very dark, many of the poor women contrived to slip out with loads of their little property on their shoulders, making their children walk, whose cries added to the confusion and to the danger of discovery.

On going among the women to see that my orders for leaving all their property were obeyed, a young Ghoorka girl of 16 or 18, who had girded up her loins and stuck a sword into her *kummerbund*, came to me, and throwing all that she possessed at my feet, said, "*Sahib!* you are right; life is better than property." She was a beautiful creature, with fair complexion and large dark eyes, and, as she stood there with her garments swathed around her, leaving her limbs free, she was a picture full of life, spirit, and energy. I never saw her afterwards; and fear she was either killed or taken prisoner on the night march.

Before we had proceeded half a mile, the rear missed the advance, upon whom a post of the enemy had begun to fire. All my regulars had crept ahead with the *juzailchees*, and I found myself alone with a *chuprassee* and two *suwars*, in the midst of a helpless and wailing crowd of women and children. Riding on by myself along a narrow lane, to try and pick out the road, I found myself suddenly surrounded by a party of Affghans, whom at first I took to be my own *juzailchees*, and spoke to them as such. They quickly undeceived me, however, by crying out, "*Feringhee hust*," " Here is an European," and attacking me with swords and knives. Spurring my horse violently, I wheeled round, cutting from right to left, for I, fortunately, had my own sword drawn previous to the surprise.

My blows, by God's mercy, parried the greater part of theirs, and I was lucky enough to cut off the hand of my most outrageous assailant. In short, after a desperate struggle, during which I received two slight sabre-cuts, and a blow on the back of my head from a fellow, whose sword turned in his hand, which knocked me half off my horse, I escaped out of the crush, passing unhurt through two volleys of musketry from the whole picket, which, by that time, had become alarmed and had turned out. They pursued me; but I soon distanced them, crossing several fields at speed, and gaining a road which I perceived led round the western end of the *Shah's* garden. Proceeding cautiously along, to my horror, I perceived my path again blocked up by a dense body of Afgháns. Retreat was impossible; so, putting my trust in God, I charged into the midst of them, hoping that the weight of my horse would clear my way for me, and reserving my sword-cut for the last struggle. It was well that I did so, for by the time I had knocked over some twenty fellows, I found that they were my own *juzailchees*.

If you ever experienced sudden relief from a hideous nightmare, you may imagine my feelings for the moment. With these worthies, after wandering about for some time, and passing unchallenged by a sleepy post of the enemy, I reached the cantonments. During the night ,any stragglers of my party, principally followers, dropped in. During the whole business, from first to last, including the retreat, I had under a dozen killed, and about half that amount wounded, nearly half the former being followers; whereas about thirty of the enemy had bitten the dust, and gone to their place.

I cannot close this letter to you without remarking that, amongst other lamentable errors which led to our heavy downfall, that of omitting in the first instance to strengthen my post was, next to Shelton's refusal to pour his brigade into the town, while the rioters yet amounted to barely two hundred men, the greatest. But the whole blame cannot, in this particular instance, be attributed to our poor friend General Elphinstone. He had not been sufficiently informed as to the importance of my position, nor as to the facility with which a strong reinforcement could have reached me. That he was specially anxious personally as to my safety there could be no doubt, as was shown by the warmth of his reception of me.

I need not remind you of the devoted heroism displayed throughout the siege by Hussain Khán, the *juzailchee jemadar*, and the handful of brave men who accompanied him, and who personally attaching themselves to me remained under my command to the last. Numbers of them fell; others were disabled; a few departed to their own homes on the day when I was taken prisoner and Sir W. Macnaghten was murdered; and, I believe, nearly the sole survivors are some ten or fifteen men, who, with their brave leader, Hussain Khán, are now with us in camp. These proceed with the rest of the *juzailchee* corps under Captain Ferris to Ferozepore, where, we hear, they are to be disbanded, and sent back to their own country, to be destroyed by their blood-thirsty countrymen as a reward for their fidelity to us; and yet these were the men who, during the period I was beleaguered in the fort of Nishan Khán, at a time when I was quite unknown to them, not only refused to listen to the repeated propositions of the Affghans outside to deliver me up to their vengeance, their own safety being thereby insured, but who, during the siege of cantonments, laughed to scorn the most tempting offers on the part of Ameenoolah Khán, Mahomed Akbar, and other Affghan chiefs, to induce them to join the general cause of Islam against the Kaffirs, invariably bringing the letters, in which they were conveyed, for my inspection and perusal.[2]

Yours very sincerely,
C. Mackenzie.

Camp, Rawul Pindee,
En route to Ferozepore, Nov. 19, 1842.

---

2. They were disbanded at Jhelum, in the Punjab, each of the old soldiers receiving a donation of twelve months' pay, and the rest a gratuity in proportion to the length of their services, with which they all seemed very well satisfied.—V. E.

Appendix B

No. 1.

DESPATCH FROM MAJOR-GENERAL ELPHINSTONE, ADDRESSED TO THE SECRETARY TO THE GOVERNMENT.

Buddeeabad.

Sir,—With the deepest regret, I have the honour to forward, for the information of the Right Honourable the Governor-General in Council, the annexed memorandum of occurrences preceding and during the insurrection at Cabul, up to this date.

The state of my health and mental sufferings previous to, and consequent on, the unfortunate occurrences, render me little competent to furnish such complete information as I might have done, had it not been for the total destruction of my entire staff and all official documents and memoranda; and I have only been able to remedy the deficiency through the kind assistance of Major Pottinger and Captain Lawrence, who having aided me with facts and dates, I trust, however meagre the account may be, that its tenor is, upon the whole, perfectly correct.

I beg to be allowed to express my sense of the gallant manner in which the various detachments sent out were led by Brigadier Shelton, and of the invariably noble conduct of the officers on those occasions, particularly of those who fell leading their men; *viz.* Colonel Mackrell, Captains Swayne, Robinson, M'Crea, and Lieutenant Raban, Her Majesty's 44th Foot; Colonel Oliver and Captain Macintosh, 5th Native Infantry; Captain Westmacott and Lieutenant Gordon, 37th Native Infantry; Captain Walker, 4th Local Horse, and Lieutenant Laing, 27th Native Infantry.

I hope I may also be permitted to record my sense of the zeal and exertions of my lamented *Aide-de-Camp* Major Thain, and my acting Quartermaster-General Captain Paton, both of whom were severely wounded, as also Captain Grant, assistant adjutant-general, and my *Aide-de-Camp* Captain Airey. I had inadvertently omitted Captain Bellew, assistant quartermaster-general, who, at the storm of the Rika-bashee and Mahomed Sherreef's fort, evinced the greatest gallantry and volunteered to carry the powder-bags.

From Brigadier Anquetil, commanding the *Shah's* force, and Colonel Chambers, commanding the cavalry, I on all occasions received the most cordial assistance; and I take this opportunity to record the ever-ready zeal and gallant conduct of Captain Troup, Major of Brigade, Shah Shooja's force.

Throughout the whole siege the utmost zeal was manifested by Lieutenant Sturt, Engineers, and by Lieutenant V. Eyre, Commissary of Ordnance, who, in consequence of the paucity of artillery officers, on all occasions volunteered his services, and was unfortunately wounded.

Captain Colin Mackenzie, Assistant Political Agent, Peshawar, volunteered to take charge of a body of *Juzailchees*, and was engaged in every affair, his and their conduct being most conspicuous.

The manner in which the soldiers, European and Native, bore up without a murmur against all privations and very harassing duty, at a most inclement season, was highly creditable to them, and more particularly the Horse Artillery, who on all occasions upheld the character of that distinguished corps.

Among the many valuable and promising officers who have fallen in the recent retreat, I would especially mention Captains Skinner and Hay, 61st and 35th Native Infantry; Lieutenant Le Geyt, Shah's 2nd Cavalry; and Lieutenant Bird, Shah's 6th Infantry; the latter officer distinguished himself in the assault and capture of the Rika-bashee Fort.

Of the surviving officers, my thanks are due to Major Eldred Pottinger, C.B., Political Agent, and Captain George St. P. Lawrence, Military Secretary to the late Envoy and Minister, for their cordial assistance and co-operation till the death of their lamented chief; and to Captain Anderson, Shah's 2nd Cavalry, and Captain Bygrave, Paymaster, for their zeal and alacrity in the performance of their duty, amid trials and difficulties almost unprecedented.

> I have the honour, &c.
> W. K. Elphinstone.

To the Secretary to Government.

No. 2.

The following extracts from a memorandum of Major-General Elphinstone deserve attention, both as supporting some of the Author's statements, and exhibiting in some degree the unfortunate General's disadvantages, as enumerated by himself.—original Editor.

******

I was unlucky in the state of my health; as, during the whole siege, I was not able to move without difficulty, except on horseback, and then not easily. On the evening of the 2nd, going round the guards, I had a very severe fall, the horse falling on me. I was obliged to return home therefore. I then asked Captains Paton and Grant if they thought all had been done, and told them to see that Brigadier Anquetil made the arrangements in the Mission Compound; and it was a great loss to me that, shortly after his coming into cantonments, he was taken ill, by which I was deprived of his assistance, which he would cordially have afforded me. *The extent of the cantonment—the unfinished state of everything in it—its indefensible position, commanded as it was on every side—particularly the facilities afforded for the approach of matchlocks,—added much to our difficulties.* The troops were on half rations, and the whole of them on duty every night, and often all day, from threatened attacks. The want of artillery officers, notwithstanding Captain (Lieutenant) Eyre's volunteering. Captain Waller being wounded early in the business.—On the 9th, not finding myself equal to the duties, particularly at night, when I could not get about on horseback, I recalled Brigadier Shelton from the Bala Hissar

I was unlucky, also, in not understanding the state of things, and being wholly dependent on the Envoy and others for information.

No. 3

The passage next quoted clearly shows that it was in obedience to the General's order that the married officers, as well as their wives and children, resigned themselves to Mahomed Akbar. This is, of course, a point of peculiar interest to those officers, especially as misrepresentation upon it has gone forth.—Original Editor.

******

EXTRACT FROM A MEMORANDUM BY MAJOR-GENERAL W, K, ELPHINSTONE, C.B., OF THE EVENTS PRECEDING AND DURING THE INSURRECTION AT CABUL.

On the 9th (January) the march was ordered at 10 a.m., but, consequent on a message from the Sirdar, requesting us to halt till he could organize an escort for us, and promising supplies and firewood, it was countermanded. But a similar scene of confusion to that of the day before had taken place, and it was past midday before anything like order was restored.

Captain Skinner returned to the *Sirdar*, by whom he was again sent back with a proposal that the married people and their families should be made over to him, promising honourable treatment to the ladies. *I complied with his wish*, being desirous to remove the ladies and children, after the horrors they had already witnessed, from the further dangers of a camp, and hoping that, as from the very commencement of negotiations the *Sirdar* had shown the greatest anxiety to have the married people as hostages, this mark of trust might elicit a corresponding feeling in him.

(Signed)   W. K. Elphinstone,
           Major-General.

Appendix C

MEMORANDUM OF RELEASED CAPTIVES WHO JOINED GENERAL POLLOCK'S CAMP AT KÁBUL IN SEPTEMBER 1842.

Officers	35
Soldiers	51
Civilians	2
Officers' Wives	10
Soldiers' Wives	2
Children	22
Total	122

Among the present survivors (besides the author, as at time of first publication) are Lieutenant-General Sir George Lawrence, K.C.S.I., C.B., Lieutenant-General Colin Mackenzie, C.B., Lieutenant-General Sir I. Talbot Airey, K.C.B., Major-General J. Haughton, C.S.I., Colonel G. Mein.

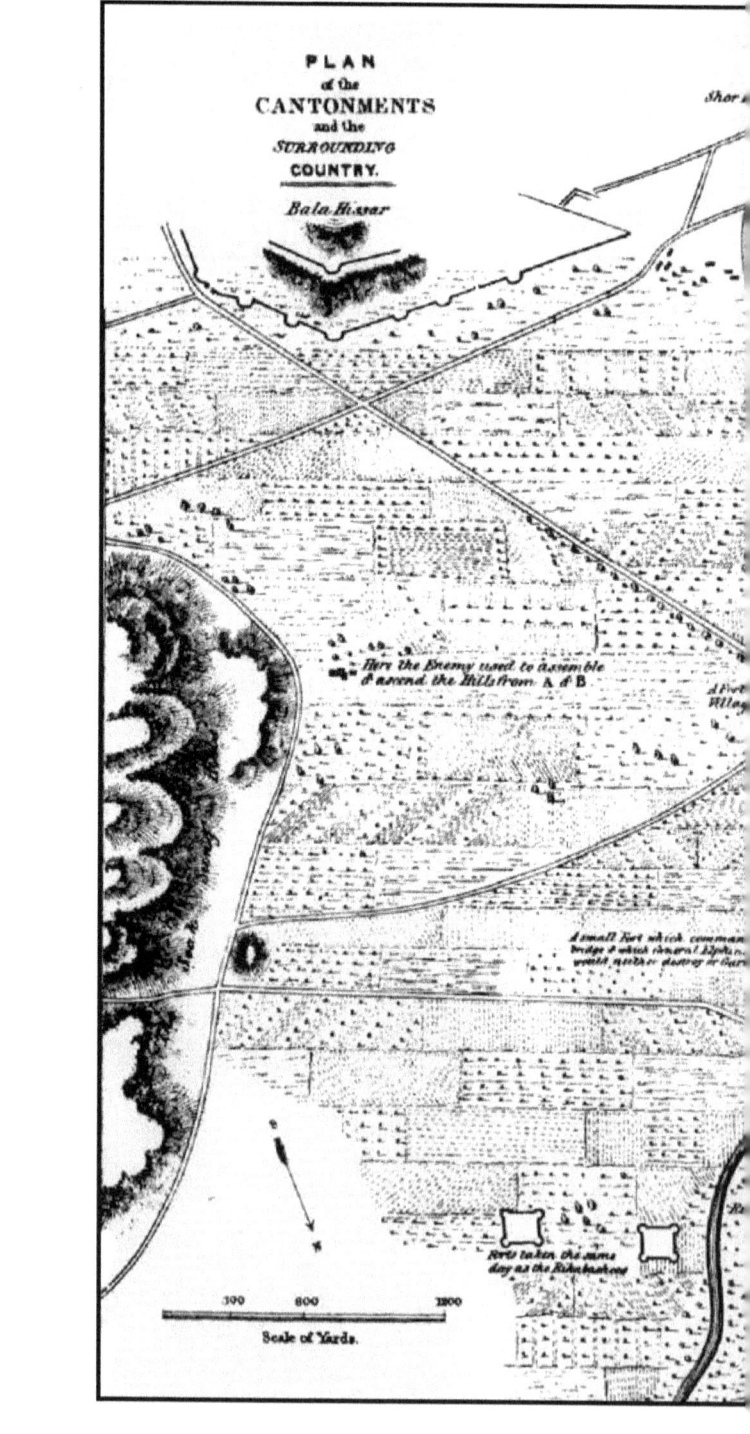

Rough Notes During Imprisonment in Affghanistan, 1843

Contents

The Notes 217
Appendix 261

The Notes

ORIGINAL EDITOR'S NOTICE

The following "rough notes" will be found a very interesting sequel to the foregoing narrative. They are strictly what they profess to be—penned in haste, to be despatched when opportunity should serve, as perhaps the last proof of his existence, which the writer might give his friends for many a day. How narrowly the Cabul prisoners did at last escape an indefinitely prolonged captivity, is known to all. And now that a gracious Providence has so restored them, it is hoped that the Author will, at a future opportunity, be enabled to add *more particulars* of an every-day life with such a party in an Afghan prison, and to fill up the gap which necessarily now remains between the 29th of June, when these Notes break off, and the 21st of September, on which happy day they again breathed the air of freedom.

January 9th.—In my notes on the retreat of the British force from Cabul, I have already mentioned the departure, from Gen. Elphinstone's camp at Khoord-Cabul, of the ladies, with their husbands and other officers, to the proffered protection of Mahomed Akber Khan; but it may be expedient briefly to remind the reader of the mode in which this event was brought about. I have been assured by Major Pottinger that, on the night of the 8th, the *Sirdar*, having spontaneously entered on the subject, expressed to that officer his serious apprehensions of the peril to which the ladies and children would be exposed by remaining in camp (it being impossible to restrain the Giljyes from a continuance of hostilities), and that, with a view to prevent further misery and suffering to the individuals in question, he should lose no time in proposing to the General that all the ladies and married families might be made over to his care for safe escort to Jellalabad, keeping one march in rear of the army.

Major Pottinger having declared his entire approval of the *Sirdar's* humane intentions, advantage was taken of Capt. Skinner's return to camp on the following morning, to make known the proposal to Gen. Elphinstone; and a small party of Affghan horse was sent with him, to escort all such as might be able to avail themselves of the offer. The General, hoping that so signal a mark of confidence in Mahomed Akber's good faith, might be attended with beneficial results to the army, and anxious at all events to save the ladies from a prolongation of the hardships they had already endured, readily consented to the arrangement; and, under the peculiar circumstances of the case, deemed it incumbent on him to send their husbands also, more especially as some were helpless from severe wounds.

The whole[1] were accordingly ordered to depart immediately with the Affghan escort, by whom we were impatiently hurried off, before the majority had been made clearly to comprehend the reason of their being so suddenly separated from their companions in trouble. At that time so little confidence was placed by any of us in Mahomed Akber's plausible professions, that it seemed as though we were but too probably rushing from a state of comparative safety into the very jaws of destruction; but, placing our dependence on a watchful Providence, we bade a hasty, and as it proved to many, an eternal, farewell to our friends, and mournfully followed our conductors to the place allotted for our reception, about two miles distant from camp.

The road lay through ravines and wilds of the most savage description, one universal garb of snow clothing the dreary and uninviting scene. On the way we passed several hundred Giljye horse drawn up in line, as if in readiness for an attack on the camp. Half an hour's ride brought us to a small fort perched on the edge of a precipitous bank, which we ascended by a slanting slippery path, and entered the gate with a mistrust by no means diminished by the ferocious looks of the garrison, amidst a circle of whom some of us were kept standing for several minutes, during which our sensations were far from agreeable.

At last, however, we were shown into a small inner court, where, to our great relief, we found our three countrymen. Major Pottinger, and Capts. Mackenzie and Lawrence, who had been made over as

---

1. Lady Macnaghten, Lady Sale,★ Mrs. Sturt, her daughter, Capt. Boyd, wife, and child, Capt. Anderson, *ditto, ditto,* Lieut. Waller,★ *ditto, ditto,* Lieut. Eyre,★ *ditto, ditto,* Mr. Ryley, *ditto, ditto,* Mrs. Trevor and seven children, Mrs. Mainwaring and child, Capt. Troup,★ Lieut. Mein,★ Serjt. Wade and family. N.B. Those marked thus ★ were wounded.

hostages at Bootkhak, and in the midst of whom sat, to the inexpressible joy of his parents, the youngest boy of Capt. and Mrs. Boyd, who, having been picked up in the Khoord-Cabul pass on the previous day by one of Mahomed Akber's followers, had been committed by that chief to Major Pottinger's protection. The accommodation provided for us, though the best the place afforded, was of the most humble description, consisting of three small dark hovels, into which ladies and gentlemen were promiscuously crowded together, the bachelors being, however, separate from the married families. But even this state of things was heaven itself compared with the cold and misery we had been suffering in camp on the bare snow, and we felt most thankful for the change. The court-yard was all day crowded with the friends and relations of Mahomed Akber, whose bearing towards us was exceedingly kind and courteous; but their presence obliged the ladies to remain closely immured in their dark cells.

In the course of the afternoon the chief himself made his appearance, and, having requested an interview with Lady Macnaghten, expressed to that lady his sorrow at having been instrumental to her present misfortunes, and his desire to contribute to her comfort as long as she remained his guest. But an Affghan nobleman's ideas of comfort fall very far short of an English peasant's; and we soon learned to consider spoons, forks, and other table gear as effeminate luxuries, and plunged our fingers unhesitatingly into the depths of a greasy *pilao*, for which several of us scrambled out of one common dish. The warmth of a wood[2] fire, though essential to protect us from the severe extremes of cold, could only be enjoyed at the expense of being blinded and half-stifled by the smoke; the bare ground was our only bed, and *postheens* (or sheepskin cloaks) our only covering; but these and various other inconveniences were indeed of small moment, when weighed in the balance against the combination of horrors we had escaped, and which still encompassed our unhappy countrymen and fellow-soldiers in camp.

January 11th.—At about 11 a. m. we started, under an escort of about 50 horse, for Tezeen, having been previously cautioned to use our swords and pistols in case of need, as an attack might be expected from the blood-thirsty Ghazees who thronged the road. The retreating army had marched over the same ground on the previous day, and ter-

---

2. The Affghans are in many parts of the country almost entirely dependent for fuel on a species of Artemisia, or southernwood, which grows everywhere in the greatest profusion, and scents the whole atmosphere with its powerful fragrance.

rible was the spectacle presented to our eyes along the whole line of road: the snow was absolutely dyed with streaks and patches of blood for whole miles, and at every step we encountered the mangled bodies of British and Hindoostanee soldiers, and helpless camp-followers, lying side by side, victims of one treacherous undistinguishing fate, the red stream of life still trickling from many a gaping wound inflicted by the merciless Affghan knife. Here and there small groups of miserable, starving, and frost-bitten wretches, among whom were many Women and children, were still permitted to cling to life, perhaps only because death would in their case have been a mercy. The bodies of Major Scott and Ewart, and of Dr. Bryce, were recognised.

Numerous parties of truculent Ghazees, the chief perpetrators of these horrors, passed us laden with booty, their naked swords still reeking with the blood of their victims. They uttered deep curses and sanguinary threats at our party, and seemed disappointed that so many of the hated *Feringhees* should have been suffered to survive. We reached Tezeen, a distance of sixteen miles, at close of day, where the fort of Mahomed Khan received us for the night. Here we found Lieut. Melville of the 54th N. I., who had delivered himself up to Mahomed Akber on the previous day, having received some slight sword cuts in defending the colours of his regiment. We were also sorry to see no less than 400 of our irregular Hindoostanee horse encamped outside the fort, having deserted to the enemy on the 9th and 10th. They belonged chiefly to Anderson's horse and the body-guard.

January 12th.—At 10 a.m. we again proceeded on our journey down the Tezeen valley preceded by the cavalry deserters. At Seh Baba, striking off from the high road, which here crosses some hills to the right, we kept bur course along the stream,[3] to the fort of Surroobee, a distance of sixteen miles. Between Tezeen and Seh Baba we encountered the same horrifying sights as yesterday; we passed the last abandoned horse-artillery gun, the carriage of which had been set on fire by the Ghazees, and was still burning; the corpse of poor Cardew lay stretched beside it, with several of the artillery-men. A little further on we passed the body of Dr. Duff, the superintending surgeon to the force, whose left hand had suffered previous amputation with a *penknife* by Dr. Harcourt! Numbers of worn-out and famished camp-followers were lying under cover of the rocks, within whose crevices

---

3. I have not particularised the features of such portions of the high road as we traversed, because they were already well known.

they vainly sought a shelter from the cold.

By many of these poor wretches we were recognised, and vainly invoked for the food and raiment we were unable to supply. The fate of these unfortunates was a sad subject of reflection to us,—death in its most horrid and protracted form stared them in the face; and the agonies of despair were depicted in every countenance. The fort of Surroobee belongs to Abdoolah Khan, Giljye. Near Seh Baba we were overtaken by Dr. Macgrath of the 37th N. I., who had been taken prisoner on the 10th, and was now sent to join our party; we were thus unexpectedly furnished with medical assistance, of which the sick and wounded had sorely felt the want.

January 13th.—Resuming our march at 10 a. m., we crossed the hills in a southeast direction towards Jugdulluk. The road in many places was very steep, and for several miles traversed a high tableland, presenting no signs of cultivation or human propinquity. Within about five miles of Jugdulluk, we again entered the high road, along which our army had recently passed; and the first sight that presented itself was the body of a fine European soldier:—Again our path was strewed with the mangled victims of war.—We reached Jugdulluk late in the evening; and, passing by the ruined inclosure within which the remnant of the force had so hopelessly sought shelter, we beheld a spectacle more terrible than any we had previously witnessed, the whole interior space being one crowded mass of bloody corpses. The carnage here must have been frightful.

The body of Capt. Skinner was recognised, and an Affghan was persuaded by Capt. Lawrence to inter it during the night, Mahomed Akber's consent having been previously procured. About two hundred yards below this fatal spot we found three ragged tents pitched for our reception, Mahomed Akber Khan being encamped hard by; and we now learned for the first time that Gen. Elphinstone, Brigadier Shelton, and Capt. Johnson, were *hostages* in his hands, the rest of the force having been annihilated. Mr. Fallon, an assistant in one of the public offices, had also been taken prisoner at the same time.

January 14th.—Shortly after sunrise we pursued our journey, accompanied by Akber Khan, with his hostages, or rather *prisoners*, and about 600 horse, of whom the Hindoostanee deserters formed a part. The road took a northerly direction up a gorge in the hills, and thence proceeded for five or six miles up a narrow defile, through which runs a small stream whose upper surface was covered with ice. Throughout these regions of snow the cold was intense, and we passed several springs whose waters, arrested by the frost, hung suspended in long glittering icicles from the rocks, exhibiting a spectacle whose brilliancy would, under less depressing circumstances, have called forth exclamations of wonder and admiration, which we had not now the heart to utter. After clearing this defile, our course became somewhat easterly, through a more open country, and over a tolerably good road, for four or five miles, when we entered another short defile leading over a rocky *ghat*, after surmounting which the road again improved, until we reached the steep and difficult pass of Udruk-budruck.

The ascent was about 1000 feet, up a narrow winding path, which, from the sharp and jagged nature of the rocks, scarcely afforded a practicable footing for our horses and camels. From the summit we had an extensive view of the country to the north, bounded by lofty snow-clad hills, the intervening space being broken up into innumerable ravines, whose barren surface was unrelieved by a single tree, the only signs of vegetable life being confined to the banks of the Cabul River, which partially fertilized the narrow valley immediately below us. The descent into this plain, down the rugged mountain side, was infinitely more tedious, and attended with greater peril, than the previous ascent, our jaded beasts threatening to cast their riders with violence on the rocks at every step. It was dark ere we reached the fort of Kutz, after a fatiguing journey of twenty-four miles, which had occupied no less than ten hours.

This place belongs to Mahomed Ali Khan, Giljye, and is situated near the right bank of the Punjsheer River. Although the clouds threatened rain, we were refused admittance within the walls, and were consequently obliged to repose in the open air, exposed the whole night to a high cutting wind. Fortunately we had now descended into a milder climate, or the poor ladies and children must have suffered severely. At midnight we were roused up by the arrival of our daily meals, consisting of half-baked cakes of unleavened bread, and untempting lumps of tough mutton; but our servants had by this time prepared us some hot tea, which was far more satisfactory to wearied travellers than the solid fare of Affghan cooks.

January 15th.—At an early hour we were again on the move, and a few hundred yards brought us to the Cabul River, which at the ford was divided into two branches, the last extremely rapid, and the water reaching up to our saddle-girths; many of the ladies, being mounted on ponies, were obliged to dismount, and ride astride on the chargers of their Affghan acquaintance, to avoid getting wet. Nothing could exceed the politeness and attention of Mahomed Akber on this occasion, who manifested the greatest anxiety until all had crossed over in safety. Several men and ponies were swept down by the violence of the current and drowned; a whole host of camp dogs, whose masters had been slain, and who had attached themselves to us, remaining on the other side, to our great relief.—Our course was now north-easterly, over a barren undulating country, for about ten miles, until we reached the fertile valley of Lughmanee, at the border of which we crossed a wide and rapid stream; the whole plain beyond was thickly studded with small high-walled forts and villages, by whose inhabitants we were greeted, *en passant*, in no measured terms of abuse, in which exercise of speech the fair sex, I am sorry to say, bore a conspicuous part, pronouncing the English ladies not only immoral in character, but downright "scarecrows" in appearance, and the gentlemen, "dogs," "base born," "*infidels*," "devils," with many other unpronounceable titles equally complimentary, the whole being wound up with an assurance of certain death to our whole party ere many hours should elapse.

We also passed within a mile of a plain white building on our left, which was pointed out as the tomb of Lamech the father of Noah, and a favourite place of pilgrimage with the Affghans. At about 3 p. m. we reached the walled town of Turghurree, within which we found lodging, after a march of about sixteen miles. We found the Affghan gentry most agreeable travelling companions, possessing a ready fund of easy conversation and pleasantry, with a certain rough polish and artless independence of manner, which, compared with the studied servility and smooth-tongued address of the Hindoostanee nobles, seldom fails to impress our countrymen in their favour.

January 16th.—We were well pleased to find that a day's halt had been determined upon, which was no less acceptable for the needful rest it secured for man and beast, than for the opportunity it afforded us of performing our Sabbath devotions, which, under present circumstances, could not fail to be a source of more than ordinary comfort. Some disturbance was occasioned during the day by a party of Giljyes threatening to attack the town, and a few shots were exchanged from both sides, by which two or three men were said to have been killed. The affray was believed to have originated in discontent at the division of the spoil of our army. This place has a small *bazar*, and many poor wanderers from our camp were permitted to take refuge within the walls, where a meal was dealt out to them daily by some charitable Hindoo residents.

January 17th.—The *Sirdar's* intention had been to keep us at Turghurree for several days; but, owing to the hostile spirit evinced towards us by the populace, he was obliged to hurry us away. At 11 a. m. we accordingly resumed our journey, under a guard of about 200 *Juzailchees*, whom it had been necessary to collect or our protection. Crowds of Affghans lined the walls to witness oaf departure, and some of our small remains of baggage fell a prey to the insatiable love of plunder, for which the Giljyea are notorious. Many of our Hindoostanee servants, who had hitherto followed our fortunes, now left us, under the idea that the *Sirdar* had decided upon our destruction. We pursued a northeasterly course along the valley, passing numerous forts, and at 2 a.m. reached Buddeeabad, a distance of eight miles, where one of the chief strongholds of Mahomed Shah Khan, Giljye, had been vacated for our reception.

The accommodation provided for us here was better than we had hitherto experienced. The fort was of a square form, each face about 80 yards long, with walls 25 feet high, and a flanking tower at each corner. It was further defended by a *faussebray* and deep ditch all round, the front gate being on the southwest face, and the postern on the northeast, each defended by a tower or bastion. The Zuna-Khaneh, or private dwelling, occupied two sides of a large square space in the centre, shut in by a high wall, each wing containing three apartments raised about eight feet from the ground, and the outer side of the principal room, consisting entirely of a wooden framework, divided into five compartments, with ornamented panels in each, made to slide up and down at pleasure. All the better sort of houses in the country have the chief rooms constructed in this manner, which is better adapted for the summer than the winter season, as it admits of a free circulation of air, but is an insufficient barrier against the cold.

There was no supply of water inside the fort, but a small river ran past, at the distance of half a mile on the southeast side, and a little stream or canal about 100 yards outside the walls. It is singular that few Affghan forts have wells, notwithstanding the general abundance of water near the surface in all the cultivated valleys; and it would, generally speaking, be very easy to cut off the external supply of that necessary element, thus forcing the garrison to surrender without expending a shot. This fort is quite new, having been built since our occupation of the country. The owner, Mahomed Shah Khan, is father-in-law of Mahomed Akber Khan, and is one of the few chiefs who never deigned to acknowledge Shah Shooja. Insatiable avarice and ambition are his ruling passions, and, as our conquest put an end to his promising schemes of aggrandizement, his hatred towards us is intense.

Unhappily he exercised great influence over his son-in-law, of whose cause in fact he was the chief supporter; and he was generally admitted to have been the principal instigator to the treacherous seizure of our envoy, for whose murder, however, which was committed in the heat and impulse of the moment, he is not answerable. Mahomed Akber and his cousin Sultan Mahomed Khan, familiarly called Sultan Jan, accompanied us to Buddeeabab, where they endeavoured to arrange matters for our comfort to the utmost of their power. Sultan Jan is eminently handsome, proportionately vain, and much given to boasting. Both he and the *Sirdar* were equally kind and courteous; but the latter is in manner a more perfect gentleman, and never, like his cousin, indulges in comparisons to the disadvantage of the English, of whom he invariably speaks with candour and respect.

The *Sirdar* has been completely baulked in his plans by the refusal of Gen. Sale to vacate Jellalabad, on which he had by no means calculated; even now he could not be persuaded that an order from Major Pottinger would not be obeyed by Captain Macgregor, the political authority there, although the Major constantly assured him that with us a prisoner, however exalted his rank, not being considered a free agent, has no power or control over any public officers of government, however much his inferiors in rank and station. I have no doubt his hope was that General Sale, yielding to the apparent necessities of the case, would have vacated the town and forthwith retreated to Peshawur, in which case he made pretty sure of the assistance of the Khyberries, in completing the annihilation of the British force.

January 18th.—Mahomed Akber and Sultan Jan departed, with the professed object of attempting the reduction of Jellalabad, and apparently very confident of success. As we remained immured in the fort of Buddeeabab until the 11th of April, I can scarcely expect that a minute detail of daily occurrences during that period would interest the reader. It would be equally idle to note down the various reports that reached us from time to time of passing events. The Affghans excel all the world in the ready fabrication of falsehoods, and those about us were interested in keeping us in the dark as much as possible. Nevertheless the truth could not always be concealed, and we managed, notwithstanding all their vigilance, to obtain pretty accurate intelligence of what was passing in the world without, though of course it was difficult entirely to separate the wheat from the chaff.

On our first arrival we suffered some inconvenience from the want of clean linen, having in our transit from fort to fort been much pestered by vermin, of which, after they had once established a footing, it was by no means an easy matter to rid ourselves. The first discovery of a real living l-o-u-s-e was a severe shock to our fine sense of delicacy; but custom reconciles folk to anything, and even the ladies eventually mustered up resolution to look one of these intruders in the face without a scream. The management of our household matters, as well as the duty of general surveillance, was committed to a *Mehmandar*, who generally took advantage of his temporary authority to feather his own nest, by defrauding us in respect to the quality and quantity of our needful supplies. Moossa Khan was the first agent of this kind with whom we had to deal; and he was so little restrained by scruples, as to pass for a most consummate rogue even among Affghans.

For mere ordinary civility the unfortunate widow of the murdered Envoy found it her interest to repay him with costly presents of Cashmere shawls, &c., and was twice induced to pay twenty *rupees* for the recovery of a favourite cat, which Moossa Khan had actually stolen from her himself, for the sake of the expected reward. This man was, nevertheless, much trusted by Mahomed Akber, who valued him no less for his capacity for intrigue, than for his unscrupulous zeal in the performance of the meanest or wickedest purposes. Such a coadjutor could not long be spared from his master's side in attendance upon us, and he was accordingly relieved on the 20th January, for the purpose of carrying on intrigues against the British with the leading chieftains of the Punjab. His successor was an old acquaintance of Capt. Troup, named Meerza Bawndeen Khan, who in peaceful times styled himself *Syud*, but now for a time sunk his religious distinction in the more warlike title of Khan.

This man had, at the outbreak of the rebellion, been imprisoned on suspicion of favouring the English, but was released immediately on the arrival of Mahomed Akber, whom he had befriended during that chief's confinement at Bokhara, and to whose fortune he now attached himself. His manners were exceedingly boorish, and he took little pains to render himself agreeable, though, from his previous conduct, there was reason to believe that, under all his roughness of exterior, there lurked a secret preference for our cause. In most respects we certainly benefited by the change. On the 21st we had rain, and on the 22nd snow fell on the neighbouring hills.

On the 23rd there was snow in the fort itself, a proof of the unusual severity of the winter, being quite a rare occurrence in this valley.

We had hitherto received our food at the hands of Affghan cooks, who little consulted the delicacy of the European palate. Our daily diet consisted of boiled rice, mutton boiled to rags, and thick cakes of unleavened dough; which, for ladies and children, was not the most enviable fare, whilst the irregular hours at which it was served up interfered greatly with our own comforts. It was now arranged, however, greatly to the satisfaction of all concerned, that our meals should be prepared by our own Hindoostanee servants, the Affghans furnishing materials.

We had a visit from the *Sirdar* and Sultan Jan on the 23rd, the chief having his headquarters at present at Trighurree, where he was making preparation for the siege of Jellalabad. Major Pottinger, at his request, wrote a letter to Capt. Macgregor, explaining all that had occurred since the army left Cabul.

On the 24th, the *Sirdar*, having heard that we were much in want of money, sent 1000 *rupees* to be distributed among us.

On the 27th, he paid us another visit, his principal object being to induce Major Pottinger to make some alterations in the letter for Capt. Macgregor.

January 29th.—This day was rendered a joyous and eventful one to us, by the arrival from Jellalabad of a budget of letters and newspapers from our brother officers there garrisoned, who had likewise generously subscribed a quantity of clothes and other comforts from their little store for our use. It was truly gratifying to receive these proofs of sympathy from our countrymen, and to have a door of communication opened once more with the civilized world. Some of our friends managed to inform us of all that was going on, by dotting off letters of the alphabet in the newspapers, which is an easy mode of carrying on secret correspondence, and not likely to be detected by an Asiatic. In this manner we became acquainted with Brigadier Wild's failure in the Khyber pass, and with General Pollock's march from India: we also heard now for the first time that Dr. Brydon had reached Jellalabad alive, being the only officer who escaped out of the whole army which had left Cabul.

Captains Collyer and Hopkins, with Dr. Harper, were found dead within four miles of the town of Jellalabad. It is said that, one of the ill-fated trio having been wounded, the remaining two went back to his assistance; but for which act of charity they would probably have been saved. It is singular that Dr. Brydon was mounted on a miserable pony, and seemed, humanly speaking, one of the most unlikely persons of the whole force to effect so wonderful an escape. Capt. Bellew, Lieut. Bird, and two or three other officers, with several European soldiers, were killed near Futtehabad, having imprudently delayed at a village to satisfy the cravings of hunger, and thus given the inhabitants time to arm themselves and overpower them.

February 15th.—The tedium of a prison life was again relieved to-day by the arrival of Abdool Guffoor Khan and Dost Mahomed Khan from the *Sirdar*, bringing with them Major Griffiths of 37th N. I. and Mr. Blewitt, a clerk of the pay office, both of whom, with the Sergt.-Major of the 37th N. I., were taken prisoners at Gundamuk, after witnessing the massacre of almost all the officers and men who reached that place. Capt. Souter, H. M. 44th regiment, was led off at the same time by another chief, having preserved the colours of his regiment by tying them round his waist. The Sergt.-Major was so fortunate as to be set at liberty on the payment of certain *rupees* as a ransom, and a similar arrangement was on the point of being made for the release of Major Griffiths and Mr. Blewitt, when they were demanded by Mahomed Akber, and unwillingly delivered up by their captor. Major Griffiths had received a severe wound in the arm from a bullet. We were also delighted to learn that Capt. Bygrave, paymaster to the force, was safe, and would soon join us.

By command of Mahomed Akber we were this day ordered to deliver up our arms, which we had hitherto been permitted to retain. The cause of this was declared to be the discovery of a clandestine correspondence, carried on between Major Pottinger and Capt. Macgregor, which had so much displeased the *Sirdar*, that he sent a solemn warning to the Major to desist from such practices in future, significantly reminding him of the tragical fate of Sir William Macnaghten. Major Pottinger boldly acknowledged the fact of his having written privately to Jellalabad, and justified it on the plea that he had given no promise to the *Sirdar* to refrain from so doing. By Abdool Guffoor Khan we again enjoyed the gratification of receiving letters from our friends at Jellalabad. This chief was supposed to be friendly to our interests, having materially assisted Gen. Sale with supplies for his force. He was evidently much suspected by the Affghans about us, who maintained a strict watch over every word he uttered during his visit.

February 16th.—Captain Souter joined us today, having been made over to the *Sirdar* by the chief who captured him.

February 19th.—On the 6th, we had a heavy fall of rain, since which the weather had become exceedingly close. This morning it was remarked that an unusual degree of heat and stillness pervaded the air.

Whether these were premonitory symptoms of what was shortly to happen it is impossible to determine; but at 11 a. m. we were suddenly alarmed by a violent rocking of the earth, which momentarily increased to such a degree that we could with difficulty maintain our balance. Large masses of the lofty walls that encompassed us fell in on all sides with a thundering crash; a loud subterraneous rumbling was heard, as of a boiling sea of liquid lava, and wave after wave seemed to lift up the ground on which we stood, causing every building to rock to and fro like a floating vessel. After the scenes of horror we had recently witnessed, it seemed as if the hour of retribution had arrived, and that Heaven designed to destroy the blood-stained earth at one fell swoop.

The dwelling in which we lodged was terribly shaken, and the room inhabited by Lady Sale fell in,—her ladyship, who happened to be standing on the roof just above it, having barely time to escape. Most providentially, all the ladies, with their children, made a timely rush into the open air at the commencement of the earthquake, and entirely escaped injury. Gen. Elphinstone, being bedridden, was for several moments in a precarious position, from which he was rescued by the intrepidity of his servant *Moore*, a private of H. M. 44th, who rushed into his room and carried him forth in his arms.—The poor General, notwithstanding all that had occurred to cloud his fame, was greatly beloved by the soldiery, of whom there were few who would not have acted in a similar manner to save his life.—The quaking continued for several minutes with unabated violence, and a slight tremor in the earth was perceptible throughout the remainder of the day.

The Affghans were, for the time being, overwhelmed with terror; for, though slight shocks of earthquake are of common occurrence every year during the cold season, none so fearful as this had visited the country within the memory of the present generation. We shortly learned that our fort had been singularly favoured, almost every other fort in the valley having been laid low, and many inhabitants destroyed in the ruins. The town of Turghurree especially seems to have suffered severely, scarcely a house being left standing, and several hundreds of people having been killed in the fall.

The first idea that struck the Affghans, after their fears had subsided, was, that the defences of Jellalabad must have been levelled to the ground, and a high road made for the *Sirdar* and his followers to walk in. Elevated by this hope, they confidently attributed the late phenomenon to a direct interposition of the Prophet in their favour.

We all passed the night in the open air, being afraid to trust the tottering walls of our habitation, especially as shocks of earthquake continued to occur almost every hour, some of which were rather severe.

February 21st.—The swords of Gen. Elphinstone and Brigadier Shelton were this day returned to them by order of the *Sirdar*.

February 23rd.—Capt. Bygrave joined us in a very weak state, having suffered much from frost in one foot, and having entirely lost the ends of his toes. His adventures, after leaving Jugdulluk, were perilous, and his ultimate escape wonderful. After starting from Jugdulluk on the night of the 12th January, he was one of the first to surmount the strong barriers of prickly holly-oak which choked the pass. Collecting a small party of the men, who were similarly fortunate, he harangued them on the absolute necessity of their holding firmly together in the bond of discipline, for the preservation of their lives, declaring his willingness to lead them, if they would only obey orders, and act with spirit adequate to the emergency. The men, thus addressed, set up a loud cheer, and protested their intention to be guided solely by his commands and wishes.

For three or four miles they steadily kept their ranks, and held the pursuing enemy at bay; but at length the repeated onsets of the Affghan horsemen, who every moment increased in number in their rear, threw the little band into confusion, which Capt. Bygrave exerted himself in vain to remedy. The men would neither hold together, nor pursue their march with that steadiness of purpose, on which hung their only chance of safety. Capt. Bygrave at length finding all his efforts to save them unavailing, and foreseeing the inevitable destruction of the whole party, determined, as a last resource, to strike off the high road and endeavour to make his way over the hills to Jellalabad. Mr. Baness, an enterprising merchant, who had become involved in the difficulties that beset our army, was induced to accompany him in this hazardous undertaking. Their course for the first few miles was altogether north, in order to get as far as possible from the track of the pursuing Giljyes: by day they sought close cover—now among long rushes in the low bed of a mountain stream, and now under the thick foliage of evergreen shrubs on the summit of some lofty snow-clad peak.

Their sole subsistence was a few dry grains of coffee, of which Mr. Baness had a small supply in his pocket, with an occasional bit of wild liquorice root, which they fortunately discovered growing in the bed of the Soorkab River. Travelling entirely at night, they experienced great difficulties in steering a direct course among the tortuosities of the innumerable ravines, which every where intersected their desultory track; on one occasion they found themselves suddenly upon the high road, where the first sight that offered itself was the mangled body of an European soldier; and, fearing to proceed along a path so lately beset with enemies, they were obliged to avoid the danger by retracing their steps for many miles. Thus passed four wearisome nights and days, during which time Capt. Bygrave, with frost-bitten feet, and worn-out shoes, had suffered so much from lameness, as to become more and more incapable of progressing; until at last, in the extreme of weakness and misery, having declared to Mr. Baness his inability to proceed further, he endeavoured to persuade that gentleman to seek with him the nearest village, and throw themselves on the protection of a chief.

Mr. Baness would not, however, consent to run such hazard, and declared his intention to pursue his course to Jellalabad, if possible. Loth, however, to forsake his companion, he urged him unavailingly to fresh exertion; and at length, declaring that for the sake of his large family he was bound to proceed onward without delay, he took a mournful leave of his fellow-traveller, and, after twice returning in the forlorn hope of prevailing on him to move, departed on his solitary way. Left to himself, under such helpless circumstances, Capt. Bygrave almost yielded to despair,—but, after a prolonged slumber, found himself strong enough to walk, or rather crawl, a few miles further. The second night after Mr. Baness's departure brought him to a

Giljye village,[4] where, lying concealed till morning under some straw in a cave, he gave himself up to the first person who came near, who, being easily conciliated by the offer of some gold, conducted him to a neighbouring hut;—hence, after partaking of some refreshment, he was led to the residence of the chief of the village, Nizam Khan, who received him hospitably, and treated him with the utmost kindness for several days, when he was delivered up to the *Sirdar*, then encamped at Charbagh, in the neighbourhood of Jellalabad. There he found the chief actively employed in preparing gun-ammunition for the proposed siege; several of our captured guns were there, from which the Affghan smiths managed to extract the spikes in a very few hours.

March 3rd.—Severe shocks of earthquake every day. The *Meerza*, professing to have received an order from the *Sirdar*, insisted on searching the boxes of Lady Macnaghten and Captain Lawrence. Unfortunately, the former had a great number of valuable Cashmere shawls, all of which were critically examined in order to ascertain their probable worth: but much disappointment was evinced that no jewels were forthcoming, as it was generally believed that her ladyship possessed a large assortment. Nothing was taken from her on this occasion; but it might easily be foreseen that such booty would ere long prove an irresistible temptation to our Giljye friends.

A cruel scene took place after this, in the expulsion from the fort of all the unfortunate Hindoostanees, whose feet had been crippled by the frost. The limbs of many of these poor wretches had completely withered, and had become as black as a coal; the feet of others had dropped off from the ankle; and all were suffering such excruciating torture as it is seldom the lot of man to witness. Yet the unmerciful Giljyes, regardless of their sufferings, dragged them forth along the rough ground, to perish miserably in the fields, without food or shelter, or the consolations of human sympathy. The real author of these atrocities was generally believed to be the owner of the fort, Mahomed Shah Khan. The *Meerza*, however, though compelled to carry the order into effect, readmitted several of the unfortunate victims at night.

March 10th.—In consequence of the repeated earthquakes, we deserted the house, and took up our abode in some small wooden huts constructed by our servants. Tonight our slumber was broken by loud cries of "Murder!" which were found to proceed from Lady Sale's

---

4. Kutch Soorkab, four miles north of Gundamuk.

Hindoostanee *ayah*, whom one of her admirers, in a fit of jealousy, had attempted to strangle in her sleep. The wretch failing in his purpose, jumped over the wall, which was about twenty feet high, and, being discovered in the morning, narrowly escaped a hanging by Lynch law at the hands of the *Meerza*, who was with difficulty persuaded to alter his sentence to banishment from the fort.

March 11th.—Dost Mahomed Khan, accompanied by Imam Verdi, arrived from the *Sirdar*, and held a long private conference with Major Pottinger. It was generally supposed that Mahomed Akber had made some overtures to the Indian government relative to the return of the *Ameer* his father. Reports were in circulation of the fall of Ghuznee, which afterwards proved too true. We also learned on good authority that Khoda Bux Khan, a powerful Giljye chief, had left the *Sirdar*, whose cause seemed on the decline.

March 12th.—Very heavy rain. Heard of Gen. Sale's sortie from Jellalabad in consequence of a supposed attempt on the part of the Affghans to mine the walls;—many of the enemy killed.

March 13th.—A report abroad, which turned out true, that the *Sirdar* was wounded in the left arm by one of his own followers, who had been bribed with a lack of *rupees* by Shah Shooja. The assassin was ripped open, according to Affghan custom in such cases.

March 18th.—The *Meerza* was this day recalled by the *Sirdar*, and his place filled by the *Nazir* of Mahomed Shah Khan, Saleh Mahomed. We heard of the murder of Shah Shooja by the hand of Shooja Dowla, eldest son of Nuwab Zeman Khan, who shot the unfortunate old king with a double-barrelled gun, as they were proceeding together to the royal camp at Seeah Sung. It is a curious fact that Shah Shooja was present at the birth of his murderer, to whom he gave his own name on the occasion.

March 21st.—The inhabitants of this valley are said to be removing their families and property to the hills for safety. The Safees, a mountain tribe in the neighbourhood, were said to have created much alarm, having been bought over by Capt. Macgregor.

March 24th.—The *Nazir* endeavoured to find out what amount of ransom was likely to be paid for us, and gave out that two *lacks* of *rupees* would be accepted. This, however, seemed to us all a mere *ruse* to fathom our purses, and he was referred to Capt. Macgregor for the information he required.

March 29th.—Sooltan Jan is said to have gone to oppose General Pollock with 1000 horse.

April 1st.—We received letters from Jellalabad, by which we learned that Gen. Pollock had authorized Capt. Macgregor to ransom us. A severe thunderstorm at night.

April 3rd.—Heard of the destruction of the 27th N. I. at Ghuznee, and of another successful sortie made by Gen. Sale at Jellalabad, by which he obtained a large supply of cattle.

April 9th.—Tidings brought of Mahomed Akber's camp at Char Bagh having been surprised by Gen. Sale, when his whole force was completely routed, three guns recaptured, and the *Sirdar* himself and friends barely managed to save themselves by flight. The arrival of Mahomed Shah Khan this evening confirmed this joyful intelligence. It had been reported to us this morning that at a council of chiefs held at Tirghurree on the previous night, much debate had taken place regarding the disposal of their prisoners, when it was proposed by some to destroy us at once: our anxiety was, therefore, intense all day, until the *Khan* by his friendly manner somewhat reassured us. He had a long interview with Major Pottinger, who endeavoured to propose terms for our release; to which, however, the Khan would not listen for a moment, but said we must follow the *Sirdar's* fortune, who would start for the hills early next morning.

April 10th.—We were all ready for a start at an early hour, but no camels came till 3 p. m.; meanwhile a scene of pillage went on, in which Mahomed Shah Khan acted the part of robber-chief. His first act was to select all our best horses for himself, after which he deliberately rummaged Lady Macnaghten's baggage, from which he took shawls to the value of 5000*l*. He next demanded her jewels, which she was obliged reluctantly to give up, their value being estimated at 10,000*l*., or a lack of *rupees*. Not satisfied even with this rich plunder, he helped himself freely out of Capt. Lawrence's boxes to everything that look his fancy; after which, being well aware of the poverty of the rest, he departed. Fortunately my own riding horse was spared, through the kind interference of the *Meerza* who accompanied the *Khan*. This characteristic little drama having been acted, the signal was given for our departure, the European soldiers being left behind, with a promise of release on the payment of a ransom.

It was a treat to get free of the dismal high walls, within which we had been so long immured; and as we had arrived in the depth of winter, when all was bleak and desolate to the eye, the universal verdure with which returning spring had now clothed the valley struck us with all the force of magic. We had proceeded about four miles on the road towards Alishung, when our progress was arrested by a few horsemen, who galloped up waving their hands joyfully, and crying out "*Shabash!*" "Bravo!" "All is over! the *Feringhee* army has been cut up in the Khyber Pass, and all their guns taken by Sultan Jan!" The mutual joy of the Affghans seemed so perfectly sincere, that, notwithstanding the improbability of the story, we felt almost compelled to believe it, especially when the order was given to return forthwith to our old quarters at Buddeeabad.

On the way back the newcomers entered into full-length particulars regarding the alleged defeat of our army. The Ensofzyes, they said, had agreed to take three *lacks* of *rupees* for the free passage of our troops through the Khyber, of which half was paid in advance. They had no sooner fingered the cash, than they laid a trap with Sultan Jan for the simultaneous attack of the front and rear of the army in the narrowest part of the pass, which had proved entirely successful. We found the poor soldiers delighted to see us again; for, having heard several shots fired after our departure, they imagined we had all been killed. We were not long in discovering that the story we had heard was all a hoax, the real cause of our sudden return being some dispute among the chiefs, in consequence of which an attack on our party was anticipated; but we were told to hold ourselves in readiness for a fresh start on the following morning.

The whole population of the valley are in the greatest consternation for fear of an attack from the English force, and are bundling their families up to the hills for safety.

April 11th.—We were off again at 12 a. m. The first three miles were along the Tirghurree road, after which we struck off to the hills to the right. Our course now became westerly, and skirting the base of the hills for four or five miles, we crossed a low ridge into the cultivated valley of Alishung; where, after crossing a rapid, we passed close by Mahomed Akber Khan on the opposite bank, seated in a *nalkee* on a knoll by the roadside. He looked ill and careworn, but returned our salutes politely. A little further on we found three tents pitched for our reception, in which we had scarcely time to take shelter ere the rain fell in torrents, and continued all night. A very indifferent dish of tough mutton constituted our meal for the day.

In the course of the evening Sultan Jan arrived in the camp, with only about thirty horsemen left of the thousand with whom he went forth to battle; the rest had all fled. He seemed grievously crestfallen, and, unlike the *Sirdar*, exhibited his malice and spleen by cutting our acquaintance. Mahomed Akber, with the liberality which always marks the really brave, invariably attributes his own defeat to the fortune of war, and loudly extols the bravery exhibited by our troops led on by the gallant Sale. The guard around our camp consisted entirely of *Seiks*, under a Mussulman Rajah, who, having been banished many years ago by Runjeet Sing, was befriended by Dost Mahomed Khan, the then ruler of Cabul, to whose family he has ever since attached himself. He was a splendid-looking fellow, with very prepossessing manners, and expressed himself much disgusted with the Affghans, who took advantage of his going out to fight at Char Bagh to plunder his camp. Altogether, he seemed well disposed towards us, which, under our present circumstances, was cheering.

April 12th.—At our first starting this morning the bachelors were separated from the married families and ladies, and we went off by different roads. This sudden separation being very disagreeable to us all, Capt. Lawrence besought the *Sirdar* to permit us to proceed together as before. He also remonstrated with him for dragging the ladies and children with him all over the country, when they were so ill able to bear up against fatigue and exposure, representing that it would redound more to his honour to release them at once. Mahomed Shah Khan, who was present, upon this flew into a rage, and declared that "wherever he went we must all follow; that if our horses failed, we must trudge on foot; and that if we lagged behind, he would drag us along by force."

He is the greatest enemy we have, and seems at present to govern the *Sirdar* completely. He was, however, taken to task by Mahomed Akber for his rudeness, and we were allowed to proceed all together, as heretofore. The road lay among low hills over a sandy soil, with several slight ascents and descents, one ascent being rather steep and long. About half way we crossed a small stream, and, after travel- ling about twelve miles, found the camp pitched in a narrow ravine, through which flowed a rivulet, the ground being covered with bunches of tall reeds, to which the Affghans set fire at night. Two old goats were sent us for dinner, which, not being fit to eat, we returned, and were afterwards supplied with an awfully tough old sheep in exchange.

April 13th.—The road again lay over steeps. On the left we saw the pass of Udruk-budruk in the distance. We gathered quantities of a curious herbaceous plant, the under surface of whose leaves was covered with a beautiful crimson dewy-looking substance, which the Affghan ladies use as rouge. About twelve miles brought us to a small scantily-cultivated valley, in which were two small forts partially ruined by the earthquake. The inhabitants enjoy the credit of being the greatest thieves in the whole country, so they must be bad indeed. Our whole march was about fourteen miles.

April 14th.—At starting we crossed the pass of Bad-push, the ascent up which was not less than 1600 feet over a very steep and rocky road. The descent was less abrupt and comparatively short. On these hills grew the holly-oak, wild almond, and a *terebinthaceous* tree called Khinjuck, yielding a fragrant medicinal gum, which I imagined might be the myrrh or balsam of commerce. It is, at all events, in great repute among the Affghans, who find it efficacious for sabre wounds. A species of mistletoe grew in great profusion on its branches; the flower somewhat resembled that of the mango, and the young leaves were oblong, lanceolate, opposite, and slightly serrate. An evergreen shrub, with a jasmine-like flower, was very abundant.

Following the course of a stream about six miles, we reached the left bank of the Cabul River, which here issued from between some precipitous hills with an exceedingly rapid current. About a hundred yards from the bank stood a small fort. We crossed on a raft of inflated bullock-hides, the motion of which we found exceedingly pleasant. The horses crossed by a ford some distance higher up and about four miles round. On the right bank we found Mahomed Akber in his *nalkee*, to whom we paid our respects. The stream is about a hundred yards broad, and a few Affghans swam their horses over, though with some difficulty. The river is not navigable from this to Jellalabad, owing to the number of rapids and whirlpools.

April 15th.—We were kept waiting until noon for our horses, and in the mean time were amused by seeing a herd of cattle swim over the river; in attempting which they were all carried violently down a rapid, and several, failing to effect a landing, were obliged to return along the bank and make a second effort. No camels were brought with *kujawurs* for the weak ladies and the sick, who were accordingly forced to ride on horseback. Poor Gen. Elphinstone, who left Buddeeabad in a most precarious state of health, was much shattered by the fatigues of travelling, and seemed to be gradually sinking to the grave. The road ran for a mile along the bank of the river, and then suddenly turned up a ravine to the right. Two miles more led to a valley communicating with that of Tezeen, about a mile up which we encamped outside the fort of Surroobee, where we had previously halted on the 12th of January. Here was one of the mountain-train guns which had been captured on the retreat. We found that our Hindoostanee servants, who remained behind here, had been well treated by Abdoolah Khan, but the majority had died from the effects of frost-bites.

April 16th.—Mahomed Akber fortunately found it convenient to halt here, which proved seasonable both to man and beast; but we were told to expect a long journey into the hills in the neighbourhood of Tezeen, where it is the *Sirdar's* intention to conceal us. An Affghan, lately arrived from Cabul, informed us that the city was divided into two great parties, of whom the Dooranees and Kuzzilbashes formed one, and the Barukzies and Giljyes the other.

April 17th.—Another halt enabled us to enjoy a quiet Sunday. The *Sirdar* and a portion of his followers paid a visit to some neighbouring chiefs, but his people were deserting him fast. The Giljyes have been trying hard to excite the fears of the peasantry against the English by tales of our cruelty and oppression.

April 18th.—Having been warned last night to be ready for a march at dawn of day, we were all on the alert; but, after waiting a long time for orders to mount, we received a message from Mahomed Akber that we should await his return.

April 19th.—It rained hard all night and continued to pour the whole day, but we were obliged, nevertheless, to march sixteen miles to Tezeen. The road was up a narrow valley the whole way, crossing a stream twice before reaching Seh Baba, which we passed halfway, after which we crossed the stream continually. At Seh Baba we encountered a putrid smell from the decomposed bodies of those who fell on the retreat, which lined the whole road. In some places we passed high piles of human bodies still fresh, the remains probably of those unfortunate beings who, having escaped the knives of the Ghazees, had struggled for existence until they sunk under the combined miseries of famine and exposure.

The Affghans informed us that many had been driven to the miserable expedient of supporting life by feeding off the flesh of their deceased comrades!—From Seh Baba to Tezeen is one continued rise, the valley being about half a mile broad and shut in by lofty heights on both sides. The stream is at this season a perfect torrent from the melting snow. We passed several encampments of the wandering Giljyes, whose flocks browsed on the neighbouring hills. We were all wet to the skin in spite of our *posteens*, or sheepskin cloaks, and, on arriving at Mahomed Khan's fort at Tezeen, we found it so much dilapidated by the earthquake as to afford only the most scanty accommodation. The poor ladies were at first crammed into a small dirty room, filled with Affghan women, where they sat in their dripping clothes until, after much delay and trouble, they were accommodated with a separate apartment. As for the gentlemen, they had to scramble for shelter in a dark confined hovel, Capt. Mackenzie and myself preferring to pass the night in a stable with our horses, the rain dripping over us until morning.

This day's exposure decided the fate of Gen. Elphinstone, who reached the fort in a dying state.

Captain Mackenzie received an intimation this night of the *Sirdar's* intention to send him on a mission to Gen. Pollock's camp at Jellalabad.

April 20th.—It rained the whole day, and, having nothing dry to put on, we were more uncomfortable than ever. Mrs. Waller was delivered of a daughter. This was the fourth addition to our number of captives; Mrs. Boyd, Mrs. Riley, and a soldier's wife named Byrne, having been confined during our sojourn at Buddeeabad. A peculiar Providence seemed on all occasions to watch over the ladies, and nothing surprised us more than the slight nature of their sufferings on these occasions.

There was a severe shock of earthquake again today. These shocks have always appeared to me to be in some way connected with heavy rain beforehand.

April 21st.—Some tents having been pitched outside the fort, the whole of our party removed into them, with exception of the Wallers, ourselves, Gen. Elphinstone, Major Pottinger, Capt. Mackenzie, and Dr. Magrath, to all of whom permission was given to remain for the present in the fort. Atta Mahomed Khan, the owner of the place, expressed to us much annoyance at the conduct of his kinsman Mahomed Shah Khan in stirring up the rebellion, and hinted at his own desire to be on friendly terms with our government. It seems he was promised remuneration by Capt. Macgregor tor the damage done to his property by Gen. Sale's force in October 1841, to the fulfilment of which pledge he still looked forward.

The *Sirdar* was holding a *levée* today, at which Major Pottinger was present, when he burst into a violent passion, and declared that his own countrymen had basely deserted and betrayed him, although he had all along acted entirely at the instigation of the chiefs at Cabul, especially in the murder of the Envoy and the destruction of our army; yet these very men now refused to support him; and he solemnly swore that, if ever he had the power, a severe example should be made of them.

A part of the outer wall fell today from the effects of yesterday's earthquake. At night the ladies of Mahomed Shah Khan, and other chiefs who were travelling in our company, invited Mrs. Eyre to dinner. She found them exceedingly kind in manner and prepossessing in outward appearance, being both well dressed and good looking. They asked her the old question as to the gender of the Company Sahib, and were greatly wonderstruck to learn that England was governed by a woman. They expressed the utmost dread of Capt. Macgregor, whom they regard in the same formidable light in which a child does the giant of a nursery tale.

April 22nd.—A great bustle was created at an early hour this morning by the arrival of a messenger from the *Sirdar* to Dost Mahomed Khan, who was awakened from his slumbers in the General's room and immediately hurried away. Our fellow-captives in camp marched shortly afterwards for the Zanduk valley, near the Aman Koh, about eight miles south of Tezeen. There was apparently some apprehension entertained of a surprise from Cabul, as we ourselves were hurried off at about 9 a. m. to a small fort two miles higher up the valley, whither the Sirdar had preceded us. This sudden movement was a deathstroke to the General, who, though so weak as to be unable to stand, was made to ride on horseback the whole way.

April 23rd.—Mahomed Akber received about 6000 *rupees* from Cabul, probably sent by his uncle, Nuwab Jubbar Khan. Futty Jung, the eldest son of the murdered monarch, retained possession of the Bala Hissar, and demanded from the *Sirdar* that all the European prisoners should be rendered up to him. The residents of Cabul, we learned, were deserting the city in great numbers, from dread of our army, and all efforts to induce the people to oppose Gen. Pollock's advance were fruitless. This information at once decided the *Sirdar* to send Capt. Mackenzie to treat with Gen. Pollock without further delay, and that officer was warned to be in readiness to start at a moment's notice.

Someone having told the *Sirdar* that I could draw faces, he sent for me on that pretence; but to my surprise pumped me for half an hour on artillery matters, being very inquisitive as to the manufacture of fuses and port-fires, the mode of throwing shells from mortars and howitzers, and the mode of regulating the length effuse for different distances, on all which subjects I enlightened him just enough to render his darkness visible. Before I went, he requested me to take the likeness of one of his followers, and of a favourite Arab horse, and, though my performance was very indifferent, he expressed himself pleased. I was afterwards called to examine a sextant which had been just brought to him: it was greatly damaged, but I explained its uses; after which, finding he could make no better use of it, he made me remove the coloured glasses, which he proposed to convert into spectacles to preserve his eyes from the glare.

About 7 p. m. Major-General Elphinstone breathed his last,—a happy release for him from suffering of mind and body. Deeply he felt his humiliation, and bitterly regretted the day when he resigned the home-born pleasures of his native land, to hazard the high reputation of a proud name in a climate and station, for which he was constitutionally unfit. Of his merits I have already spoken at large in another place; but it is due no less to the memory of the dead than to the large circle of living friends and relatives, who, I feel assured will mourn his loss, that I should record how, to the very last moment of his being, he exhibited a measure of Christian benevolence, patience, and high-souled fortitude, which gained him the affectionate regard and admiring esteem of all who witnessed his prolonged sufferings and his dying struggles, and who regarded him as the victim less of his own faults, than of the errors of others, and the unfathomable designs of a mysterious Providence, by whom the means are always adapted to the end.

The *Sirdar* seemed to have been unconscious of the General's extreme danger until this morning, when he offered, too late, to grant him his release. Had he listened to the advice of those who wished him well, he would have adopted this generous course at Buddeeabad; but his chief supporters were interested in keeping him in the dark, and in frustrating every scheme that tended to reconcile him to the British nation; so the timely counsel was unheeded. His eyes at last were opened to the truth; and he now endeavoured to make all the amends in his power by offering to send the remains for honourable interment at Jellalabad. At 8 a. m. Capt. Mackenzie departed on his mission, which related principally to the release of the ladies and children.

April 25th.—A rude framework having been constructed by an Affghan carpenter, the General's body, after being well covered up in felt blankets, was packed in it, and the vacant spaces filled with the highly-scented leaves of worm-wood. At 2 p. m., all being ready, it was slung across the back of a camel, and sent off under a small guard of Giljyes, accompanied by one of the European soldiers who attended the deceased, whom the *Sirdar* thought likely to pass unnoticed in the common costume of the country. The *Sirdar* afterwards invited us all to sit with him outside the fort. Whilst we were engaged in conversation, a messenger arrived with letters from Loodianah, informing him that his family had been starved for a whole week.

On being told the contents, we all immediately pronounced the whole a mischievous fabrication; upon which the *Sirdar* somewhat bombastically proclaimed his disregard whether it were true or false, for that the destruction of his whole family should not alter his resolutions. He then resumed the previous conversation as if nothing had occurred, in the course of which he told me that the daily loss of life, by the fire of the cantonment guns during the siege, was between thirty and forty, but he declared that the shells fired from the Bala Hissar into the city did little or no damage to life or property.

April 26th.—Sad to say, the poor General's body was interrupted on its journey near Jugdulluk. It seems that the party in charge, on approaching the camp of some wandering Giljyes, were challenged, and thought that the best way to avoid discovery would be to assume confidence, and to come to a halt there for the night. The European soldier was covered up with blankets, and warned to remain quiet until morning. About 10 p. m., however, he was roused by a tumult of angry voices, in which the words "*Feringhee*" and "*Kafir*" were frequently repeated. A rush was shortly after made to where he was lying, and the covering being snatched from off his head, he was immediately attacked, and wounded in the arm with a sword, nothing saving his life but the thick blanket of felt which covered his body, and the interposition of a chief, who hurried him off to his tent.

The bigoted savages next stripped the body of the General, which they pelted with stones, and would have burned, but for the remonstrances of the *Sirdar's* men, who threatened them with the vengeance of their master. Mahomed Akber's annoyance was great on receiving these awkward tidings, but ire lost no time in despatching as large a party as he could spare, to rescue the European and repack the body.

In the course of conversation with Major Pottinger, the *Sirdar* asked him whether he would take his oath that he had never written anything to Jellalabad, but what had come to his (the *Sirdar's*) knowledge. The Major maintained a significant silence, but shortly afterwards, having occasion to remark that, if the treaty had been fulfilled, not a British soldier would now have remained in Affghanistan, the *Sirdar* emphatically asked him if he would swear to the truth of what he uttered, to which the Major readily consenting, the *Sirdar* seemed now for the first time to believe what he had before utterly discredited, and looked around upon his followers with an expression of face which seemed to say, "What a miserable fool then have I been!"

April 27th.—The *Sirdar* started with Major Pottinger to visit our fellow-prisoners in the Zanduh valley. Lieut. Waller and myself, in the course of our evening stroll, amused ourselves in observing some *Juzailchees* firing at a mark about 100 yards distant: almost every shot was well directed, but they were all so dilatory in loading, that a British soldier could have fired four or five shots to their one.

The European soldier who accompanied the General's body returned this evening, having been rescued by the *Sirdar's* men from the savages who detained him, and who now professed great contrition for having offended the *Sirdar*. The body, after being repacked, had been forwarded on its way to Jellalabad.

April 28th.—A *cossid*, bearing a letter from Capt. Conolly to Gen. Pollock, was intercepted and severely beaten by the *Sirdar's* men, and detained a prisoner until his return.

April 29th.—A wild sheep was brought in, having been shot in the neighbouring hills. Its horns resembled those of a common ram, but its face and general outline were not unlike an antelope, though more coarse and clumsy.

April 30th.—The *Sirdar* and Major Pottinger returned from their excursion. Whilst at Zanduh, Ameenoolah Khan and other chiefs sent to demand that Major Pottinger should be delivered up to him, or twelve *lacks* of *rupees* in his stead. The bills given by the Major on the Indian Government, payable on the safe arrival of the Cabul force at Jellalabad, having been dishonoured, the chiefs have been endeavouring to extort the money from the Hindoo *shroffs*.

May 1st.—Tonight the *Sirdar* sent us a large supply of English letters and newspapers which had just come from Jellalabad, where Capt. Mackenzie had arrived safe. These were the first letters we had received for eight months, and we sat up the greater part of the night devouring their contents.

May 2nd.—I was sent for by the *Sirdar* to examine a cavalry saddle, as he was anxious to know whether it was made of hog's skin. I told him it was a difficult question to decide, as both hog and cow skins were used, and could not easily be distinguished. As he gave me some knowing winks, and was evidently most unwilling that a good saddle should be sacrificed to the religious scruples of his *moolah*, who was seated in the room, I voted in favour of the cow; and, as Lieut. Waller afterwards declared himself on the same side, the *Sirdar*, considering that two witnesses decided the point, determined to hold his own: and I believe in his heart he cared little about the natural history of the hide, so long as it suited his purposes.

Late at night I was roused from bed by a message from the *Sirdar*, who pressed me hard to go and tight for him at Cabul against Ameenoollah Khan and Futty Jung. He was perfectly aware, he said, that no Englishman would serve against his own countrymen, but that in this case his enemies were equally hostile to the British; so that, in fighting for him, I should be serving my own country. I replied that I was already badly wounded and tired of fighting for the present; that I was quite incompetent, from my ignorance of Affghan politics, to form an opinion as to the rights and merits of the case; and that, even were I ever so much disposed to embrace his cause, no English officer or soldier could legally take arms under a sovereign power, without having first obtained the consent of his own sovereign. My refusal apparently annoyed him a good deal, and I was obliged to repeat it several times before he would allow me to return to rest.

May 3rd.—The Wallers and ourselves started for the Zanduh valley after breakfast, and had just mounted our horses, when Capt. Mackenzie made his appearance on his return from Jellalabad. His mission had not opened any immediate prospect of release for us, though the negotiation was, on the whole, of a friendly nature. After the exchange of a few words he was hurried off to the *Sirdar*, and we pursued our way to Zanduh. The road ascended the hills in a southeasterly direction, and was very steep and undulating for about three miles, when it descended into the narrow bed of a stream, one of the ramifications of the Tezeen valley, up which our course was southerly for the rest of the march. Four or five miles further brought us to camp, where the valley was a little wider, with cultivated *steppes* of land, on which the tents were pitched. Snow was still lying on the neighbouring heights, and about four miles further south the lofty mountain peak of Aman Koh reared its pine-clad crest.

On our way we noticed the juniper, which universally prevails in these hills, attaining in some spots the size of a goodly tree. Here and there we passed a few stunted pines, which might be considered as mere stragglers from the neighbouring forests of Suffed Koh. The wild almond, a showy and fragrant species of Edwardsia; a shrubby *crataegus*-looking plant, covered with blossoms; the yellow dog-rose, the sweet-briar, the *artemisia*, the white tulip, and a very pretty iris, constituted the prominent botanical features of the road over which we travelled. We found our friends enjoying themselves during the heat of the day, in shady bowers formed of juniper: the climate seemed delightful.

May 4th.—The *Sirdar* sent for Capt. Troup to accompany him and Major Pottinger to Cabul. Capt. Mackenzie was to start immediately on a second mission to Jellalabad.

May 5th.—The English hostages at Cabul were said to be under the protection of a *Syud*, son of the chief *moolah*; and Ameenoollah Khan, having endeavoured to seize them, had been driven into the Bala Hissar by Nuwab Zeman Khan, and his house in Cabul burned to the ground.

May 7th.—A hard frost this morning! the shrubs and herbs within reach of the spray of the stream being covered with large icicles. Our keeper now was Mahomed Rufeek, whose family resides at Candahar. From his pleasing manners, and constant civility and kindness, he soon became a general favourite. I took a long walk with him to-day among the hills south of camp; we saw nothing but juniper trees, anemones, and wild geraniums, the spring having only just commenced in that elevated region. The rocks were chiefly of limestone, with vertical *strata*.

May 8th.—This morning I was agreeably surprised by an Affghan bringing some of my own books and sketches for sale, of which I immediately possessed myself. In the forenoon a few drops of snow fell! The last three days were bitterly cold, and we enjoyed a blazing fire at night.

May 9th.—Enjoyed another walk in the hills, with a fine bracing air, and a magnificent view in the direction of Hindoo Khoosh, whose everlasting snows and jagged peaks bounded the scene. On our return we heard the cheerful note of the cuckoo. I found a curious parasite on the juniper.

May 10th.—Capt. and Mrs. Anderson were agreeably surprised by the arrival of their eldest girl from Cabul. It will be remembered that she was lost in the Khoord-Cabul pass during the retreat on the 8th of January; since which she had been an inmate of Nuwab Zeman Khan's family, where she was treated with the greatest possible kindness. She had been taught to say "My father and mother are *infidels*, but I am a Mussulman." Capt. Troup, who had obtained her release, wrote word that he and Major Pottinger were in Nuwab Jubbar Khan's house at Cabul; that the city was in a most unquiet state, and the opposite parties fighting every day, the Cabulees siding alternately with whichever side paid them best. At night, a note was received from Major Pottinger, who had just witnessed an engagement between the Barukzyes and Dooranees, in which the former were victorious; but he described the affair as more ludicrous than tragical, having been a forcible representation of the "battle of spurs."

May 12th.—Capts. Boyd, Waller, and myself, accompanied by two Affghans, ascended some lofty hills to the west. Some Giljyes of the Jubbar Khail overtook us, and offered to escort us to Jellalabad. Our attendants, instantly taking alarm, hurried us away homewards. We had a fine view of Hindoo Khoosh to the north, and Suffeed Koh to the south. At the height of 2000 feet above our camp, the husbandmen were only now ploughing the ground, whilst in the Zanduh valley, immediately below, the crops were green. We descended by the bed of a stream, on whose steep sides a species of wild onion grew abundantly. A beautiful *fritillaria* was also common; and an *asphodelous* plant bearing a gigantic *spadix* of yellow flowers, which I took for an *ornithogalum*. On our return, Dost Mahomed Khan, who was encamped near us, rated Mahomed Rufeek severely for allowing us to stray so far. This chief is a thorough boor in his ideas and manners, and is always exhibiting some mean and silly suspicion of our intentions: had it depended on him, we should all have been shut up in dark cells or narrow cages long ago.

May 16th.—Capt. Mackenzie returned from his second trip to Jellalabad, where Gen. Elphinstone's body had arrived safe and had been interred with due military honour. It does not appear that much was done towards effecting our release. The terms the *Sirdar* proposed to Gen. Pollock for our release were,—that he should be made governor of the Lughman province, and be exempted from attendance at court, and uncontrolled by our political officers. Of this proposal Gen. Pollock very properly took not the smallest notice. It seems that a despatch from the *Sirdar*, in which an offer was made to release the ladies and children unconditionally, which was sent after Capt. Mackenzie, did not reach him, having been intercepted, as was supposed, by Mahomed Shah Khan. Gen. Nott was expected to march for Cabul from Candahar on the 17th instant.

May 17th.—Capt. Mackenzie left for Cabul, to communicate the result of his mission to the *Sirdar*.

May 18th,—Dost Mahomed Khan was much struck by hearing Mahomed Rufeek read a Persian translation of the *Sermon on the Mount* out of Gladwain's *Moonshee*. He was fervent in his admiration of the *Lord's Prayer*, as well as of several other passages; and the injunction to pray in private seemed to throw light on our apparent neglect of outward observances. Corporal Lewis of H. M. 44th, who had been kept a prisoner at Tezeen in the fort of Khooda Bux Khan, was allowed to visit our camp today. The poor fellow had been starved and ill-treated by his savage captors, until he made an outward profession of Mahomedanism, when he received the name of Deen Mahomed, and was made to attend prayers with the faithful.

May 20th.—A beacon-light was burning all night on the hill above us, and pickets were thrown out in all directions. It was supposed that a *chuppao*, or night surprise, was expected.

May 22nd.—Our horses arrived from Cabul, for which city we received notice to march next morning.

May 23rd.—Marched about 9 a. m. Three of us obliged to walk for want of horses. Ladies travelled in *kujawurs*, laden on mules. We retraced our former track down the bed of the stream, and across the hills, to the fort where Gen. Elphinstone died. A few miles of descent made a great difference in the climate and the progress of vegetation; the wild roses were everywhere in full bloom, and, with other gay flowers, scented the air and enlivened the scene. We crossed a branch of the Tezeen valley; a short cut over the hills led us to the foot of the Huft Kotul, or hill of seven ascents. Here we once more encountered the putrid bodies of our soldiery, which thenceforward strewed the road as far as Khoord Cabul, poisoning the whole atmosphere.

A little beyond Kubbur-i-jubbar we passed two caves, on opposite sides of the road, full as they could hold of rotten carcasses. Thence to Tungee Tureekee the sight became worse and worse. Mahomed Rufeek asked me whether all this would not excite the fury of Gen. Pollock's army; I told him he need not be surprised if every house in Cabul were levelled to the ground. From the last-mentioned spot we turned off the high road to the left, and, passing a large ruined village, arrived at the fort of Khoord Cabul,—where we had previously lodged on the 9th of January,—after a fatiguing march of twenty-two miles. The contrast between the summer and winter aspect of the valley immediately below the fort was striking: the whole now presenting one red field of cultivation.

May 24th.—Again on the move at 9 a. m. The Khoord Cabul pass being now absolutely impassable from the stench of dead bodies, we took the direct road towards Cabul, having Alexander the Great's column in view nearly the whole day. The first three or four miles were over a barren plain, when the road entered among hills crossing a *ghat* of moderate height into a valley about three miles in width, in the middle of which we halted for half an hour at a deliciously cool and clear spring, which supplied a small tank or pond: just above this, crowning the hill to the left, stood a ruined Grecian *tope*. Resuming our way, we again entered some hills, the road making a continuous ascent for about a couple of miles to Alexander's pillar, one of the most ancient relics of antiquity in the East, and conspicuously situated on the crest of a mountain range which bounds the plain of Cabul on the southeast. It stands about seventy feet high; the shaft is of the Doric order, standing on a cubic pedestal, and surmounted by a sort of urn.

As we reached this classic spot, a view of almost unrivalled magnificence burst suddenly upon our sight. At the distance of some two thousand feet below, the whole picturesque and highly cultivated valley of Cabul was spread before us like a map: the towering mountain ranges of Kohistan and Hindoo Khoosh, clad in a pure vesture of snow, bounded the horizon, at the distance of nearly a hundred miles. The Bala Hissar was dimly discernible in the distance, from whose battlements the roar of cannon broke ever and anon upon the ear, betokening the prolongation of the strife between hostile tribes and ambitious chiefs. The descent was very long and tedious, and the road about midway very steep and bad.

On the way down another Grecian pillar was discernible among the hills on the left. The rocks were chiefly of micaceous schist, and a dark stone resembling basalt. The gum-*ammoniac* plant grew here; the young flower was clustered together not unlike a small cauliflower. It is an *umbelliferous* plant, growing to the height of six feet, and its general appearance and mode of growth resembling an *heracleum*. It has a strong disagreeable scent, which reminded me slightly of *assafoetida*. The gum exudes plentifully, and is at first milky, but afterwards turns to yellow, and has a bitter nauseous taste. The plant is called by the Affghans *gundele*, and the gum is sold in the Cabul *bazar* under the name of *feshook*.

At the foot of the hill we rested at a tank or pond supplied by a large spring which gushes from under the rock; another ruined Grecian *tope* crowned a small eminence at a few hundred yards' distance. The road now skirted the base of the hills to the left for about four miles, when we reached the fort of Ali Mahomed, Kuzzilbash, distant three miles from Cabul, and close to the Logur River, where we were accommodated for the night, having marched altogether about twenty miles.

May 25th.—The ladies of Ali Mahomed having removed to a neighbouring fort, we occupied their apartments, which lined two sides of an inclosed square, and were very commodious, and decidedly the best quarters we have yet enjoyed. The valley about here is thickly studded with forts, and very highly cultivated.

May 26th.—Captain Troup paid us a visit. He told us the *Sirdar* was living in the outskirts of the city about two miles from us, that Ameenoollah Khan joined him, but that Futty Jung still held out in the Bala Hissar, in hopes of being soon relieved by the arrival of our army. Mahomed Akber is desirous to obtain possession of the citadel principally on account of the treasure within it, as he never professed to dream of resisting our arms. He earnestly desired to be on friendly terms with the British government, and often said that he wished he had been so fortunate as to become acquainted with the English in early life, as he had been filled with prejudices against them which had greatly influenced his conduct, but which he now saw to be unfounded. It seems that Gen. Pollock offered on his own responsibility to release the ladies and children of his family from their confinement, but in his present precarious stale of life the *Sirdar* has declined the offer.

Hundreds of Hindostanees crowded the streets of Cabul begging for bread, which was daily served out to them by Nuwab Jubbar Khan and Zeman Khan. The civility of all classes to the European hostages and prisoners in and about Cabul was remarkable.

May 27th.—We all received permission to walk in the adjacent garden, and the gentlemen were allowed to bathe in a running canal near the fort, which, now that the weather had become sultry, were real luxuries.

May 29th.—Shuja Dowlah, the assassin of Shah Shoojah, paid us a visit. He was a handsome quiet-looking man, whom few would have guessed to be the perpetrator of such a deed. He tried hard to persuade us that the Shah had played us false, and that he had committed a praiseworthy action in getting rid of him. The murder was committed at the instigation of Dost Mahomed Khan, Giljye, by way of retribution for the attempt on Mahomed Akber's life at Charbagh by an agent of Shah Shoojah; but the act is much reprobated by all classes at Cabul, and by no one more than the Nuwab Zuman Khan, who has banished Shuja Dowlah from his house ever since.

May 30th.—Shah Dowla, another son of Nuwab Zuman Khan, paid us a visit, and inquired particularly if we were well treated by the *Sirdar*. We were informed that, in consequence of the *Sirdar* having demanded the persons of the Naib Shereef Mohun Loll and the late *wuzeer*, the Kuzzilbash had risen in a body against him, and declared their intention to hold their part of the city until the arrival of our troops. We heard a great deal of firing tonight, and the extreme vigilance of our guard led us to suppose that the *Sirdar's* affairs were not prospering. Dost Mahomed Khan arrived in the fort at night.

May 31st.—Guns were heard all night, and we were refused permission to leave the fort, as usual, today. Mahomed Rufeek, we were sorry to learn, had incurred suspicion, from his family having aided Gen. Nott at Candahar. He determined to throw up the *Sirdar's* service in consequence.

June 1st.—Dost Mahomed Khan departed for the city accompanied by Mahomed Rufeek. Permission was again given us to go into the garden, and to bathe in the canal as before.

June 2nd.—Intelligence was brought us that Gen. Nott had obtained a victory at Kelat-i-Giljye, in which 2000 of the enemy were killed.

June 3rd.—It was reported that Futty Jung had offered a large reward to anyone who would seize and escort us all to the Bala Hissar. The *Sirdar* made a fierce attack on the Bala Hissar in the evening, and a brisk cannonade was kept up on both sides for several hours, but without any decisive result.

June 4th.—Capt. Troup paid us a visit, bringing with him several necessaries, for which we had previously written to the *Sirdar*. It was believed in the city that one of the bastions of the Bala Hissar had been mined, but that the *Sirdar* was deferring its explosion in the hope that he might succeed without it, being unwilling to injure the defences of the place. But this report was probably set abroad for the purpose of intimidating the defenders, of whom only two men had been wounded during the whole siege up to this date.

A messenger arrived this morning from Jellalabad with letters for Futty Jung and Lady Sale. From the latter we learned that Gen. Pollock had written to Mahomed Akber, declaring it to be contrary to the laws of nations to make war against women and children, which it was hoped might shame him into the release of that portion of his prisoners, who came under the benefit of the rule.

Hopes began to be entertained of the safety of Dr. Grant of the Goorkha regiment, who was supposed to be concealed in Cabul. A shock of earthquake felt today.

June 6th.—About 5 p. m. a good deal of firing was heard, and our garrison was in a state of great excitement. Futty Jung said to have sallied from the Bala Hissar and carried off a quantity of Mahomed Akber's military stores and camels. At night we heard that the *Sirdar* had seized Ameenoolah Khan, whom he suspected of intriguing with Futty Jung, probably with good foundation. The *Khan* said to be worth 18 lacks of *rupees*, which it was the *Sirdar's* intention to make him disgorge. Ameenoolah Khan was originally the son of a camel-driver, but by dint of his talents, bravery, and cunning, rose to be one of the most powerful nobles in the country.

The late Ameer Dost Mahomed Khan feared and suspected him so much as to forbid him to enter Cabul. He possessed the whole of the Logur valley, and could bring 10,000 men into the field. The accession of such a man to his cause was of much importance to Mahomed Akber, and his seizure was a dangerous step, being likely to provoke the hostility of his son. Ameenoolah Khan was the chief instigator of the rebellion, and of the murder of Sir Alexander Burnes; after which he lent the weight of his influence to each party alternately, as it suited his purpose. Such a vacillating wretch was not long likely to escape retributive justice.

June 7th.—Contradictory reports were in circulation all day. Some affirm the Bala Hissar to have been taken; others that the *Sirdar* had sustained a ruinous defeat, and that he was engaged in plundering the city, prior to taking flight. That something extraordinary had occurred was evident from the mysterious deportment of the Affghans, and their anxiety to prevent our receiving any communication from without. A parcel of useful articles arrived for us from our good friends at Jellalabad, but everything was opened by the guard at the gate, who gave us only what they chose, and seized all the letters, to send to the *Sirdar*. There was no firing from the Bala Hissar today as usual. The climate in this part of the valley we found delightfully cool and pleasant, which may have arisen in part from the luxuriant cultivation round about.

The most common trees are the poplar, willow, mulberry, and oleaster, or *sinjut*, the bright silvery foliage of the latter contrasting strikingly with the deep green of the rest, and its flowers scattering a powerful and delicious perfume through the surrounding air. Purple *centaurias* adorned the corn fields, and a handsome species of *hedysarum*, with a lupin-like flower, enlivened the border of every field and water-course; whilst a delicate kind of tamarisk ornamented the banks of the neighbouring river. In the garden I found a very beautiful *orobanche* growing parasitically from the roots of the melon.

June 9th.—Capt. Mackenzie paid us a visit. From him we learned positively that the *Sirdar* sprung a mine under one of the towers of the Bala Hissar, near the Shah Bazar, on the 6th; that the storming party was driven back with a loss of sixty men killed, and that much damage was done in the adjacent part of the town by the explosion. On the following day, Futty Jung, finding his people disinclined to support him any longer, made terms with Mahomed Akber and the other chiefs, giving up a tower in the Balar Hissar to each, and himself retaining possession of the royal residence. Thus the citadel was now divided between the Dooranees, Barukzyes, Giljyes, and Kuzzilbashes, represented by Futty Jung, Mahomed Akber, Nuwab Zeman Khan, Mahomed Shah Khan, and Khan Shereen Khan. A curious arrangement, truly! and calculated to facilitate the union of parties already jealous of each other, and each of whom had, doubtless, an eye to the rich treasure of money and jewels still in Futty Jung's possession.

The story of Ameenoolah Khan's seizure turned out to be untrue. There was a violent quarrel a few days back between the two old Nuwabs, Zeman Khan and Jubbar Khan, when the former seized hold of the latter's beard exclaiming, "You are the fellow who first brought the *Feringhees* into the country, and to whom, therefore, all our troubles may be attributed." Abdool Glujas Khan, the son of Jubbar Khan, being present, drew a pistol and threatened to shoot Zeman Khan for the indignity offered to his father. Mahomed Akber sat by the whole time, laughing heartily at the scene.

June 10th.—A smart shock of earthquake during the night.

June 11th.—Capt. Mackenzie returned to the city. It was supposed he would start in a day or two on a fresh mission to Jellalabad; ,

June 20th.—Heard from Capt. Mackenzie that Mahomed Akber was waging war with Nuwab Zeman Khan; also that Gen. Nott had seized the person of Sufter Jung, the rebel son of Shah Shooja-ool-moolk. Ali Mahomed assured us that it was the *Sirdar's* intention shortly to march to Jellalabad, to pay his respects to Gen. Pollock! From other quarters we heard that he meditated carrying us all off to the banks of the Oxus.

June 21st.—We were told by Ali-Mahomed that the *Sirdar* had taken Nuwab Zeman Khan and his two sons prisoners, and, after seizing all his guns, treasure, and ammunition, had released them again.

June 25th.—Capts. Mackenzie and Troup paid us a visit. Mahomed Akber's late successful conflict with Nuwab Zeman Khan had rendered him, for the time being, supreme in Cabul. The Kuzzilbashes had tendered their unwilling submission, and had delivered up Mohun Loll, who was immediately put to the torture. Jan Fishan Khan, the laird of Purghman, a staunch friend of the British, had been obliged to fly for his life, his two sons having been slain in the fight. Khoda

Bux Khan, and Atta Mahomed Khan, Giljyes, fought against Mahomed Akber on this occasion. Both Capt. Troup and Capt. Mackenzie had since been allowed to visit the hostages, whom they found in the house of the Meer Wyze, the chief *moollah* of the city, to whose protection they had been committed by Zeman Khan, in consequence of the desperate efforts of the Ghazees to slay them. During their stay in the good *Nuwab's* house, their lives were in constant danger from those fanatics, who on one occasion actually forced their way into the building to accomplish their purpose, and were only hindered by the *Nuwab* falling on his knees, casting his turban on the ground, and entreating them not to dishonour his roof by committing violence to those under its protection.

Before sending them to the Meer Wyze, which was done at night, he took the precaution to line the streets with his own followers, with strict orders to fire upon everyone who should so much as poke his head out of a window; and he not only accompanied them himself, but sent his own family on ahead. Capt. Conolly had obtained convincing proof that Shah Shoojah originated the rebellion with a view to get rid of Burnes, whom he detested, and of several chiefs, whom he hoped to see fall a sacrifice to our vengeance; little anticipating the ruinous result to himself and to us. Poor Burnes had made but few friends among the chiefs, who now never mention his name but in terms of the bitterest hatred and scorn. He seems to have kept too much aloof from them; thus they had no opportunity of appreciating his many valuable qualities, and saw in him only the traveller, who had come to spy the nakedness of the land, in order that he might betray it to his countrymen. The King considered him as a personal enemy, and dreaded his probable succession to the post of Envoy on the departure of Sir W. Macnaghten.

Of Mahomed Akber Khan, I have been told from an authentic source that, on the morning of the departure of the army from Cabul on the 6th of January, he and Sultan Jan made their appearance booted and spurred before the assembly of chiefs, and being asked by Nuwab Zemaa Shah where they were going, Mahomed Akber replied, "I am going to slay all the *Feringhee* dogs, to be sure." Again: on the passage of our troops through the Khoord-Cabul pass on the 8th, he followed with some chiefs in the rear, and in the same breath called to the Giljyes in *Persian* to desist from, and in *Pushtoo* to continue, firing. This explains the whole mystery of the massacre, and clears up every doubt regarding Mahomed Akber's treachery.

June 27th.—To our surprise, the European soldiers whom we left in the fort at Buddeeabad, and whom we believed to have been ransomed, made their appearance. They all agreed in stating that they had been ill-treated and starved ever since our departure, which they mainly attributed to the evil influence of their own countrywoman, Mrs. Wade, who had disgraced her country and religion by turning Mahomedan, and, having forsaken her husband, had become the *concubine* of an Affghan in Mahomed Shah Khan's service, and had taken every occasion to excite prejudice and hostility against the English captives, who were plundered of the little money and the few clothes they possessed, and exposed to continual insults and savage threats. She actually was so base as to betray her own husband, in whose boot two pieces of gold had been sewn up with her own hands, of which he was deprived at her suggestion. On their arrival at Cabul, she had gone off to Mahomed Shah Khan's fort, taking with her a little orphan child named Staker, of which she had charge.

June 28th.—Capt. Mackenzie having been taken ill, Capt. Troup returned to the city without him. The *Sirdar*, we learned, had made preparation for a flight to Bameean, in anticipation of the advance of our troops; whither, of course, the prisoners would accompany him. His ultimate place of refuge, it was supposed, would be Herat.

June 29th.—A shock of earthquake. Capt. Troup came to see us again before starting to Jellalabad on a mission from the *Sirdar*. Futty Jung was this day proclaimed king by Mahomed Akber, who contented himself for the present with the title of *wuzeer*. Capt. Mackenzie still very ill.

✶✶✶✶✶✶

The Author's autograph manuscript breaks off here; but, as there remain still to be noted the events of three months, including those critical movements by which Mahomed Akber's captives were so nearly hurried beyond the hope of freedom, it is hoped that he will yet tell, in his own words, the remainder of the tale. In the meantime his private letters will make the conclusion less abrupt.

—Our real foe is Mahomed Shah Khan, but for whose baneful influence the *Sirdar* would have released the ladies long ago. The latter has many good points, and, but for one act, would be more worthy of clemency than the chiefs at whose instigation he did everything, and who would fain make him their scapegoat.

★★★★★★

July 29th.—We have had a good deal of sickness amongst us, and Mackenzie had a narrow escape of his life from a malignant fever. All the invalids are, however, recovering, thank God! I fear, however, that our prospects are blacker than ever. We had hopes, a few days ago, that a fair exchange would be agreed upon between Mahomed Akber and Gen. Pollock, of the *Ameer* and all the other Affghan prisoners for us poor wretches. But the General has since received instructions to advance on Cabul; and Mahomed Akber declared today to Troup, with an expression of savage determination in his countenance, that so surely as Pollock advances, he will take us all into Toorkistan, and make presents of us to the different chiefs. And depend upon it he will carry his threats into execution, for he is not a man to be trifled with.

★★★★★★

The public are aware how well Mahomed Akber would have kept this pleasant promise; but the next and last communication is from Cabul, announcing the happy deliverance of the whole party, whose varied fortunes have for the last twelve months excited such universal interest.

Camp, Cabul, 22nd Sept. 1842.

Cabul, Sept. 22nd.—Heaven be praised! we are once more free. Our deliverance was effected on the 20th, and we arrived safe in Gen. Pollock's camp yesterday evening. On the 25th of August we were hurried off towards *Toorkistan*, and reached *Bameean* on the 3rd of September, every indignity being heaped upon us by the way. There we awaited fresh orders from Mahomed Akber. Meanwhile Pollock's army advanced on Cabul, carrying all before them. About the 10th of September an order came to carry us off to *Koorloom*, and to butcher all the sick, and those for whom there was no conveyance. Fortunately discontent prevailed among the soldiers of our guard, and their commandant began to intrigue with Major Pottinger for our release. A large reward was held out to him, and he swallowed the bait. The Huzarah chiefs were gained over; and on the 16th we commenced our return towards Cabul, expecting to encounter the defeated and now furious Akber on the way. On the 17th we were reinforced by Sir R, Shakespeare who had ridden out from Cabul with 600 Kuzzilbash, horsemen to our assistance. His aid was most timely; for Sultan Mahomed Khan, with 1000: men, was hastening to intercept us. On the 20th, after forced marches, we met a brigade of our troops, and our deliverance was complete.

List of prisoners released on General Pollock's arrival at Cabul.

Major-Gen. Shelton, Her Majesty's 44th Foot.
Lieut.-Col. Palmer,*27th Bengal Native Infantry.
Major Griffiths, 37th Bengal Native Infantry.
Capt. Troup, Shah's service.
— Anderson,   ditto.
— Bygrave, paymaster.
— Boyd, commissariat.
— Johnson, ditto S. S. F., 26th Native Infantry.
— Burnett, 54th Native Infantry.
— Souter, Her Majesty's 44th foot.
— Waller, Bengal Horse Artillery.
— Alston,* 27th Native Infantry.
— Poett,*   ditto.
— Walsh, 52nd Madras Native Infantry.
— Drummond, 3rd Bengal Light Cavalry.
Lieut. Eyre, Bengal Artillery.
— Airey, Her Majesty's 3rd buffs.
— Warburton, Bengal Artillery, S. S. F.
— Webb, 38th Madras Native Infantry, S. S. F.
— Crawford, Bengal 3rd Native Infantry, S. S. F.
— Mein, Her Majesty's 13th Light Infantry.
— Harris,* 27th Bengal Native Infantry.
— Melville, 54th Bengal Native Infantry.
— Evans, Her Majesty's 44th Foot.
Ensign Haughton, 31st Bengal Native Infantry.
— Williams, 37th Bengal Native Infantry.
— Nicholson,   ditto.
Conductor Ryley, ordnance commissariat.
Doctor Campbell.
Surgeon Magrath.
Assistant-Surgeon Berwick, left in charge.
— Thomson.
N.B. Those marked thus * were of the Ghuznee garrison.

Ladies

Lady Macnaghten.
— Sale.
Mrs. Trevor, 8 children.
— Anderson, 3 *ditto*.

— Sturt and 1 child.
— Mainwaring, *ditto*.
— Boyd, 3 children.
— Eyre, 1 child.
— Waller, 2 children.
Conductor Ryley's wife,
Mrs. Ryley, 3 children.
Private Bourne's (13th Light Infantry) wife, Mrs. Bourne.
Mrs. Wade, wife of Sergeant Wade.

✶✶✶✶✶✶

Major Pottinger, Bombay Artillery.
Captain Lawrence, 11th Light Cavalry.
— Mackenzie, 48th Madras Native Infantry.
Mr. Fallon, clerk not in the service.
— Blewitt, *do.*   *ditto*

HER MAJESTY'S 44TH FOOT.

Sergeant Wedlock.	Drummer Branagan
— Weir.	Private Burns.
— Fair.	— Cresham.
Corporal Sumpter.	— Cronin.
— Bevan.	— Driscoll.
Drummer Higgins.	— Deroney.
— Lovell.	— Duffy.
Private Matthews.	Private Arch.
— M'Dade.	— Stott.
— Marron.	— Moore.
— M'Carthy.	— Miller.
— M'Cabe.	— Murphy.
— Nowlan.	— Marshall.
— Robson.	— Cox.
— Seyburne.	— Robinson.
— Shean.	— Brady
— Tongue.	—M'Glyn.
— Wilson.	Boys Grier
— Durant.	—Milwood

HER MAJESTY'S 13TH LIGHT INFANTRY.

Private Binding.	Private Maccullar.
— Murray.	—M'Connell.
— Magary.	—Cuff.

— Monks.

Bengal Horse Artillery.

Sergeant M'Nee.	Gunner Dalton.
— Cleland.	Sergeant Wade, baggage-sergeant
Gunner A. Hearn.	to the Cabul mission.
— Keane,	
(Signed)	G. Ponsonby, Captain,
	Assistant-Adjutant-General.
(True copy.)	(Signed) R. C. Shakespeare,
	Military Secretary.
(True copies.)	(Signed) T. H. Maddock,
	Secretary to the Government of India
	with the Governor-General.
(True Copies.)	J. P. Willoughby,
	Secretary to the Government,

Appendix

LIST OF CIVIL AND MILITARY OFFICERS KILLED DURING THE REBELLION, AT AND NEAR CABUL,
Between 12th October, 1841, and 6th January, 1842, the day of leaving Cabul.

Political.

Sir W. H. Macnaghten, Bart.	Murdered at a conference on	23d Dec.
Sir Alexander Burnes	Ditto in his own house in the city on	2d Nov.
Capt. Broadfoot, 1st Eng. Regt.	Ditto in Sir A. B.'s house in the city on	2d "
Lieut. Burnes, Bombay Infty.	Ditto in Sir A. B.'s house in the city on	2d "
Lieut. Rattray	Ditto at a conference at Lughmanee in Kohistan -	3d "

H. M. 44th.

Lieut. Col. Mackrell	Killed in action at Cabul		10th Nov.
Capt. Swayne	Ditto	Ditto	4th "
Capt. M'Crea	Ditto	Ditto	10th "
Capt. Robinson	Ditto	Ditto	4th "
Lieut. Raban	Ditto	Ditto	6th "

5th N. I.

Lieut. Col. Oliver	Ditto	Ditto	23d Nov.
Capt. Mackintosh	Ditto	Ditto	23rd "

37th N. I.

Capt. Westmacott	Ditto	Ditto	10th Nov
Ensign Gordon	Ditto	Ditto	4th "

35th N. I.

Lieut. Jenkins	Ditto at Khoord-Cabul	12th Oct.
Capt. Wyndham	Ditto at Jugdulluk	12th "

####### H. M. 13th Light Infantry.

Lieut. King - - -	Killed at Tezeen	- 12th Oct.
Local Horse.		
Capt. Walker, 1st N. I. -	Ditto at Cabul -	- 23d Nov.
27th N. I.		
Lieut. Laing - - -	Ditto Ditto	- 23d Nov.
Shah's Service.		
Capt. Woodburn, 44th N. I. -	Ditto Ditto	- 23d Nov.
Capt. Codrington, 49th N. I. -	Ditto at Chareeker	- 23d "
Ensign Salisbury, 1st V. Regt.	Ditto Ditto	- 23d "
Ensign Rose, 54th N. I. -	Ditto Ditto	- 23d "
Doctor Grant, Bombay Estab. -	Ditto Ditto	- 23d "
Lieut. Maule, Artillery -	Ditto in his camp at Kahdarrah	- 3d "
Capt. Trevor, 3d Light Cav. -	Ditto at a conference	- 23d Dec.
Local Lieut. Wheeler	Ditto in his camp at Kahdarrah -	- 3d Nov.

From 6th January up to the 12th January 1842 inclusive on the retreat.

Staff.

Dr. Duff, Superin.-Surgeon -	Killed between Tezeen and Seh Baba -	- 10th Jan.
Capt. Skinner, 61st N. I. -	Ditto at Jugdulluk	- 12th "
Capt. Paton*, 58th N. I. -	Ditto Khoord-Cabul pass 8th	"
Lieut. Sturt*, Engineers -	Ditto Ditto	- 8th "
Horse Artillery.		
Dr. Bryce - - -	Ditto on march to Tezeen	10th Jan.
5th Light Cavalry.		
Lieut. Hardyman - -	Ditto outside the cantonment -	- 6th Jan.
H. M. 44th.		
Major Scott - - -	Ditto on march to Tezeen	10th Jan.
Capt. Leighton - -	Ditto Ditto	- 10th "
Lieut. White - -	Ditto Junga Fareekee	- 10th "
Lieut. Fortye* - -	Ditto Jugdulluk	- 10th "

* These officers had been previously wounded at Cabul. Captain Paton's left arm had been amputated.

5th N. I.

Major Swayne *	- -	Killed at Junga Fareekee -	10th Jan.
Capt. Miles -	- -	Ditto Ditto	- 10th "
Lieut. Deas *	- -	Ditto Ditto	- 10th "
Lieut. Alexander	- -	Ditto Ditto	- 10th "
Lieut. Warren	- -	Ditto Ditto	- 10th "

54th N. I.

Major Ewert	- -	Ditto on march to Tezeen	10th Jan.
Capt. Shaw *	- -	Ditto Ditto	- 10th "
Lieut. Kirby	- -	Ditto Ditto	- 10th "

37th N. I.

Lieut. St. George	- -	Ditto Khoord-Cabul pass	8th Jan.

H. M. 44th.

Lieut. Wade	- -	Ditto Jugdulluk	- 12th Jan.

27th N. I.

Dr. Cardew *	- -	Ditto Tezeen -	- 10th Jan.

After leaving Jugdulluk on the 12th to the final massacre.

Staff.

Major Thain* H.M. 21st Ft. A.D.C.	Jugdulluk Pass -	- 12th Jan.
Capt. Bellew, 56th N. I.	- Futtehabad -	- 13th "
Capt. Grant, 27th N. I.	- Gundamuk -	- 13th "
Capt. Mackay, Assist. P. M. †	- Doubtful.	

Horse Artillery.

Capt. Nicholl -	- Jugdulluk Pass -	- 12th Jan.
Lieut. Stewart -	- Gundamuk -	- 13th "

5th Light Cavalry.

Lieut.-Col. Chambers -	- Jugdulluk Pass -	- 12th Jan.
Capt. Blair - -	- Ditto -	- 12th "
Capt. Bott - -	- Ditto -	- 12th "
Capt. Hamilton	- Gundamuk -	- 13th "
Capt. Collyer	- near Jellalabad -	- 14th "
Lieut. Bazett - -	- Jugdulluk Pass -	- 12th "
Dr. Harpur - -	- near Jellalabad -	- 14th "
Veterinary Surgeon Willis	- Doubtful.	

* These officers had been previously wounded at Cabul.

† Capt. Mackay, Assist. P. M. Shah's Staff, being mentioned in the text twice (pp. 216. 220.), I insert his name thus. It is not in the original list. — EDITOR.

H. M. 44th.

Capt. Dodgin	- Jugdulluk pass	- 12th Jan.
Capt. Collins	- Gundamuk	- 13th "
Lieut. Hogg	- Ditto	- 13th "
Lieut. Cumberland	- Ditto	- 13th "
Lieut. Cadett	- Soorkab	- 12th "
Lieut. Swinton	- Gundamuk	- 13th "
Ensign Gray	- Doubtful.	
Paymaster Bourke	- Jugdulluk	- 12th "
Qr.-Master Halaban*	- Jugdulluk pass	- 12th "
Surgeon Harcourt	- Ditto	- 12th "
Assist. Surgeon Balfour	- Doubtful.	
Assist. Surgeon Primrose	- Gundamuk	- 13th "

5th N. I.

Capt. Haig	- Doubtful.	
Lieut. Horsbrough	- Gundamuk	- 13th Jan.
Lieut. Tombs	- Doubtful.	
Ensign Potenger	- Ditto.	
Lieut. Burkinyoung	- Ditto.	
Dr. Metcalfe	- Gundamuk	- 13th Jan.

37th N. I.

Capt. Rind	- Gundamuk	- 13th Jan.
Lieut. Steer	- Jugdulluk pass	- 12th "
Lieut. Vanrenen	- near Soorkab	- 12th "
Lieut. Hawtrey	- Gundamuk	- 13th "
Lieut. Carlyon	- Doubtful.	

54th N. I.

Capt. Anstruther	- Doubtful.	
Capt. Corrie	- Ditto.	
Capt. Palmer	- Ditto.	
Lieut. Weaver	- Gundamuk	- 13th Jan.
Lieut. Cunningham	- Ditto	- 13th "
Lieut. Pottinger	- Neemla	- 13th "
Lieut. Morrison	- Gundamuk	- 13th "

H. M. 13th Lt. Inf.

Major Kershaw	- Doubtful.	
Lieut. Hobhouse	- Gundamuk	- 13th Jan.

Shah's Service.

Brigadier Anquetil	- Jugdulluk pass	- 12th Jan.
Capt. Hay, 35th N. I.	- Gundamuk	- 13th "
Capt. Hopkins, 27th N. I.	- near Jellalabad	- 13th "

Capt. Marshall, 61st N. I.	- Jugdulluk pass	-	- 12th Jan.
Lieut. Le Geyt, Bombay Cav.	Neemla -	-	- 13th "
Lieut. Green, Artillery	- Gundamuk	-	- 13th "
Lieut. Bird, Madras Estab.	Futtehabad	-	- 13th "
Lieut. Macartney -	- Gundamuk	-	- 13th "

LIST OF OFFICERS SAVED OF THE CABUL FORCE.

In imprisonment in Affghanistan.

Political.

Major Pottinger, C. B. Wounded at Charekar on - 6th Nov.
Capt. Lawrence.
Capt. Mackenzie, Madras Estab. Ditto in action at Cabul on 23d "

Staff.

Major-Gen. Elphinstone, C. B. Ditto on retreat at Jugdulluk 12th Jan.
(Died at Tezeen on April 23d.)

Brigadier Shelton.
Capt. Boyd, At. Cy. Gl.
Lieut. Eyre, Arty. D. C. O. Wounded in action at Cabul 22d Nov.

Horse Artillery.

Lieut. Waller Ditto Ditto - 4th "

H. M. 44th.

Capt. Souter - - - Ditto on retreat at Gundamuk 13th Jan.

H. M. 13th.

Lieut. Mein - - - Ditto in action under Gen.
Sale at Khoord-Cabul pass Oct.

37th N. I.

Major Griffiths - - Ditto on retreat in Khoord-
Cabul pass - - 8th Jan.

Dr. Magrath.

Shah's Service.

Capt. Troup - • - Ditto on retreat in Khoord-
Cabul pass - - 8th "

Capt. Johnson.
Capt. Anderson.

Paymaster.

Capt. Bygrave - - The toes of one foot nipped off by frost on retreat.

Mr. Ryley, conductor of Ordnance.

54th N. I.

Lieut. Melville - - Ditto on retreat near Huft Kotul - - - 10th Jan.

Shah's Service.

Dr. Brydon - - - Escaped to Jellalabad.

ALSO FROM LEONAUR
AVAILABLE IN SOFTCOVER OR HARDCOVER WITH DUST JACKET

ESCAPE FROM THE FRENCH *by Edward Boys*—A Young Royal Navy Midshipman's Adventures During the Napoleonic War.

THE VOYAGE OF H.M.S. PANDORA *by Edward Edwards R. N. & George Hamilton, edited by Basil Thomson*—In Pursuit of the Mutineers of the Bounty in the South Seas—1790-1791.

MEDUSA *by J. B. Henry Savigny and Alexander Correard and Charlotte-Adélaïde Dard* —Narrative of a Voyage to Senegal in 1816 & The Sufferings of the Picard Family After the Shipwreck of the Medusa.

THE SEA WAR OF 1812 VOLUME 1 *by A. T. Mahan*—A History of the Maritime Conflict.

THE SEA WAR OF 1812 VOLUME 2 *by A. T. Mahan*—A History of the Maritime Conflict.

WETHERELL OF H. M. S. HUSSAR *by John Wetherell*—The Recollections of an Ordinary Seaman of the Royal Navy During the Napoleonic Wars.

THE NAVAL BRIGADE IN NATAL *by C. R. N. Burne*—With the Guns of H. M. S. Terrible & H. M. S. Tartar during the Boer War 1899-1900.

THE VOYAGE OF H. M. S. BOUNTY *by William Bligh*—The True Story of an 18th Century Voyage of Exploration and Mutiny.

SHIPWRECK! *by William Gilly*—The Royal Navy's Disasters at Sea 1793-1849.

KING'S CUTTERS AND SMUGGLERS: 1700-1855 *by E. Keble Chatterton*—A unique period of maritime history-from the beginning of the eighteenth to the middle of the nineteenth century when British seamen risked all to smuggle valuable goods from wool to tea and spirits from and to the Continent.

CONFEDERATE BLOCKADE RUNNER *by John Wilkinson*—The Personal Recollections of an Officer of the Confederate Navy.

NAVAL BATTLES OF THE NAPOLEONIC WARS *by W. H. Fitchett*—Cape St. Vincent, the Nile, Cadiz, Copenhagen, Trafalgar & Others.

PRISONERS OF THE RED DESERT *by R. S. Gwatkin-Williams*—The Adventures of the Crew of the Tara During the First World War.

U-BOAT WAR 1914-1918 *by James B. Connolly/Karl von Schenk*—Two Contrasting Accounts from Both Sides of the Conflict at Sea D uring the Great War.

AVAILABLE ONLINE AT **www.leonaur.com**
AND FROM ALL GOOD BOOK STORES

ALSO FROM LEONAUR
AVAILABLE IN SOFTCOVER OR HARDCOVER WITH DUST JACKET

IRON TIMES WITH THE GUARDS *by An O. E. (G. P. A. Fildes)*—The Experiences of an Officer of the Coldstream Guards on the Western Front During the First World War.

THE GREAT WAR IN THE MIDDLE EAST: 1 *by W. T. Massey*—The Desert Campaigns & How Jerusalem Was Won---two classic accounts in one volume.

THE GREAT WAR IN THE MIDDLE EAST: 2 *by W. T. Massey*—Allenby's Final Triumph.

SMITH-DORRIEN *by Horace Smith-Dorrien*—Isandlwhana to the Great War.

1914 *by Sir John French*—The Early Campaigns of the Great War by the British Commander.

GRENADIER *by E. R. M. Fryer*—The Recollections of an Officer of the Grenadier Guards throughout the Great War on the Western Front.

BATTLE, CAPTURE & ESCAPE *by George Pearson*—The Experiences of a Canadian Light Infantryman During the Great War.

DIGGERS AT WAR *by R. Hugh Knyvett & G. P. Cuttriss*—"Over There" With the Australians by R. Hugh Knyvett and Over the Top With the Third Australian Division by G. P. Cuttriss. Accounts of Australians During the Great War in the Middle East, at Gallipoli and on the Western Front.

HEAVY FIGHTING BEFORE US *by George Brenton Laurie*—The Letters of an Officer of the Royal Irish Rifles on the Western Front During the Great War.

THE CAMELIERS *by Oliver Hogue*—A Classic Account of the Australians of the Imperial Camel Corps During the First World War in the Middle East.

RED DUST *by Donald Black*—A Classic Account of Australian Light Horsemen in Palestine During the First World War.

THE LEAN, BROWN MEN *by Angus Buchanan*—Experiences in East Africa During the Great War with the 25th Royal Fusiliers—the Legion of Frontiersmen.

THE NIGERIAN REGIMENT IN EAST AFRICA *by W. D. Downes*—On Campaign During the Great War 1916-1918.

THE 'DIE-HARDS' IN SIBERIA *by John Ward*—With the Middlesex Regiment Against the Bolsheviks 1918-19.

AVAILABLE ONLINE AT **www.leonaur.com**
AND FROM ALL GOOD BOOK STORES

ALSO FROM LEONAUR
AVAILABLE IN SOFTCOVER OR HARDCOVER WITH DUST JACKET

FARAWAY CAMPAIGN *by F. James*—Experiences of an Indian Army Cavalry Officer in Persia & Russia During the Great War.

REVOLT IN THE DESERT *by T. E. Lawrence*—An account of the experiences of one remarkable British officer's war from his own perspective.

MACHINE-GUN SQUADRON *by A. M. G.*—The 20th Machine Gunners from British Yeomanry Regiments in the Middle East Campaign of the First World War.

A GUNNER'S CRUSADE *by Antony Bluett*—The Campaign in the Desert, Palestine & Syria as Experienced by the Honourable Artillery Company During the Great War.

DESPATCH RIDER *by W. H. L. Watson*—The Experiences of a British Army Motorcycle Despatch Rider During the Opening Battles of the Great War in Europe.

TIGERS ALONG THE TIGRIS *by E. J. Thompson*—The Leicestershire Regiment in Mesopotamia During the First World War.

HEARTS & DRAGONS *by Charles R. M. F. Crutwell*—The 4th Royal Berkshire Regiment in France and Italy During the Great War, 1914-1918.

INFANTRY BRIGADE: 1914 *by John Ward*—The Diary of a Commander of the 15th Infantry Brigade, 5th Division, British Army, During the Retreat from Mons.

DOING OUR 'BIT' *by Ian Hay*—Two Classic Accounts of the Men of Kitchener's 'New Army' During the Great War including *The First 100,000* & *All In It*.

AN EYE IN THE STORM *by Arthur Ruhl*—An American War Correspondent's Experiences of the First World War from the Western Front to Gallipoli-and Beyond.

STAND & FALL *by Joe Cassells*—With the Middlesex Regiment Against the Bolsheviks 1918-19.

RIFLEMAN MACGILL'S WAR *by Patrick MacGill*—A Soldier of the London Irish During the Great War in Europe including *The Amateur Army*, *The Red Horizon* & *The Great Push*.

WITH THE GUNS *by C. A. Rose & Hugh Dalton*—Two First Hand Accounts of British Gunners at War in Europe During World War 1- Three Years in France with the Guns and With the British Guns in Italy.

THE BUSH WAR DOCTOR *by Robert V. Dolbey*—The Experiences of a British Army Doctor During the East African Campaign of the First World War.

AVAILABLE ONLINE AT **www.leonaur.com**
AND FROM ALL GOOD BOOK STORES

ALSO FROM LEONAUR
AVAILABLE IN SOFTCOVER OR HARDCOVER WITH DUST JACKET

THE 9TH—THE KING'S (LIVERPOOL REGIMENT) IN THE GREAT WAR 1914 - 1918 *by Enos H. G. Roberts*—Mersey to mud—war and Liverpool men.

THE GAMBARDIER *by Mark Severn*—The experiences of a battery of Heavy artillery on the Western Front during the First World War.

FROM MESSINES TO THIRD YPRES *by Thomas Floyd*—A personal account of the First World War on the Western front by a 2/5th Lancashire Fusilier.

THE IRISH GUARDS IN THE GREAT WAR - VOLUME 1 *by Rudyard Kipling*—Edited and Compiled from Their Diaries and Papers—The First Battalion.

THE IRISH GUARDS IN THE GREAT WAR - VOLUME 1 *by Rudyard Kipling*—Edited and Compiled from Their Diaries and Papers—The Second Battalion.

ARMOURED CARS IN EDEN *by K. Roosevelt*—An American President's son serving in Rolls Royce armoured cars with the British in Mesopatamia & with the American Artillery in France during the First World War.

CHASSEUR OF 1914 *by Marcel Dupont*—Experiences of the twilight of the French Light Cavalry by a young officer during the early battles of the great war in Europe.

TROOP HORSE & TRENCH *by R.A. Lloyd*—The experiences of a British Lifeguardsman of the household cavalry fighting on the western front during the First World War 1914-18.

THE EAST AFRICAN MOUNTED RIFLES *by C.J. Wilson*—Experiences of the campaign in the East African bush during the First World War.

THE LONG PATROL *by George Berrie*—A Novel of Light Horsemen from Gallipoli to the Palestine campaign of the First World War.

THE FIGHTING CAMELIERS *by Frank Reid*—The exploits of the Imperial Camel Corps in the desert and Palestine campaigns of the First World War.

STEEL CHARIOTS IN THE DESERT *by S. C. Rolls*—The first world war experiences of a Rolls Royce armoured car driver with the Duke of Westminster in Libya and in Arabia with T.E. Lawrence.

WITH THE IMPERIAL CAMEL CORPS IN THE GREAT WAR *by Geoffrey Inchbald*—The story of a serving officer with the British 2nd battalion against the Senussi and during the Palestine campaign.

AVAILABLE ONLINE AT **www.leonaur.com**
AND FROM ALL GOOD BOOK STORES